THE
COUNTERFEIT
COSSACK

Eda and me on our wedding day, January 1, 1945.

ARTHUR FEDER
AS TOLD TO
JEFF BEAL

THE
COUNTERFEIT
COSSACK

THE LIFE OF ARTHUR FEDER

Outskirts Press, Inc.
Denver, Colorado

Outskirts Press, Inc.
http://www.outskirtspress.com

ISBN: 978-1-4327-5235-4

Library of Congress Control Number: 2009942816

Outskirts Press and the "OP" logo are trademarks belonging to Outskirts Press, Inc.

PRINTED IN THE UNITED STATES OF AMERICA

To my loving and lovely wife Esther,
who has unfailingly provided me with
emotional, intellectual and spiritual nourishment.
To my beautiful children Irving, Larry and
Hedy who are my pride and joy.

PREFACE

You have to be tough. You have to be. If you're not, you can get squashed. And don't think there aren't a million agents of mayhem out there glad to do the squashing. If I didn't think this way I wouldn't even be here to write this. You have to be tough, and you have to be quick, because sometimes you only got about a second to get tough. I'm not saying you have to be mean. That's not the same. But you've got to be able deal with this world as it is, and that usually requires some tenacity.

This is a story mostly about World War Two. That madness claimed countless millions of lives, and I have to admit that, although a lot of them were plenty tough, misfortune overcame their grit. But it's dangerous just to leave things to chance. You've got to grab every opportunity that comes along, because you can't hang around to find out if it's your lucky day or not. And the only way to find out is to choose life. It's precious, so you have to put up with it at any cost. You never know when it'll get better. When our tranquil little village was invaded nobody knew what was going to happen, and I certainly had no idea that I would be its only surviving citizen. A lot of people over the years have asked me why I think

I made it. I was lucky to be sure. But I'd also have to add that, when any opportunity for survival came my way, I seized it with both hands and held on tight. And, as I didn't have to hurt anyone, except armed enemies, or betray my faith, I feel no shame for having survived that awful conflict. In me my family endures, and my kids and grandkids justify my struggle. God gave us life and free will, so ultimately it really is up to us. I hope you make all the right choices. Here's the story of how a lot of choices affected my existence. You decide if I made the right ones.

Arthur Feder
Sunny Isles, Florida

TABLE OF CONTENTS

SIENIAWA

My father was a fish monger. If you trust in clichés about entire nations, as some sadly do, such an occupation as this does not sound like a very prosperous one for a person of Jewish culture. According to the popular lore of that era and in that area, all Jews were supposed to be uniformly rich and powerful, plus somehow corrupt. But for a thousand years Poland, where we lived, had been home to millions of members of the tribe of Abraham who could barely afford to rub two *zlotys* together. There were some wealthy Hebrews to be sure, as well as some who managed to achieve positions of status and authority, but for most protagonists of the Diaspora, from the dark ages to the present, a meager existence seemed predestined. All over Eastern Europe the Jewish people were so accustomed to poverty they accepted it as if they were the western counterparts of Hindus calmly enduring their karma. Economic hardship seemed like a foregone conclusion, so most of them did not even endeavor to aspire to wealth. They were not examples of suffering humanity however, because for them wealth manifested itself in an entirely different way. They possessed richness of the spirit. Undistracted by glimmering mounds of gold they sought refuge within religion.

They fervently studied the ancient scriptures and entered into communion with God by submitting to His every mandate. For example, my father, Yisroel Ben Yehuda Feder, often traveled to neighboring towns to sell his fish. If the Friday night sun began to set while he was en route back home he stopped wherever he was and did not resume his trip until the sun of Saturday afternoon began its descent. He simply would not travel on the Sabbath, not even if he could see his own house in the distance. His trips were for business and one does not conduct business on that holy day. The sojourn there and back was part of that transaction, and he would not cheat, not even by a meter. He knew it was *shabbos* and so did The Lord, and being righteous gave him a fulfillment nothing else could. That was his wealth, as it was for millions of others on that continent. He prayed, worked, dressed, ate, fasted and lived his entire life as a pious Jew. He wore a beard and *payis*, attended services twice a day, and observed all religious celebrations with an eye to detail. And on those rare occasions when fortune cast a glance his way, and enabled him to save up a little extra money, he spent it on Sabbath essentials such as an elegant table cloth, seat covers, wine goblets, silverware, plates, or a candelabra. This finery had nothing to do middle class ostentation, but rather to honor God on His day. Yisroel had no pretensions about being clever in a worldly way, preferring to live simply according to Torah. He took every word literally, and held the Ten Commandments as sacred. He rose in the morning with a prayer on his lips, and when he closed his eyes at night he did so without any shame or regret for anything he had done that day.

My father was not alone in his ethos, nor was he considered an oddball or a religious fanatic in Sieniawa, our village. There were several hundred men there who behaved just as he did. They were the Orthodox of our *shtetl*, and proudly attended the smaller of our two Jewish houses of worship. The grander one, simply referred to as the *shul*, was brick and housed the Reform congregation.

Its congregants cut their hair, were clean shaven and wore modern dress. They believed that by their so-called normal appearance they'd assimilate into Polish society and curtail anti-Semitism once and for all. Yisroel, on the other hand, had no intention of disguising himself or blending into Gentile Polish society. You could spot him a kilometer away, driving his horse drawn cart, laden with fish. His broad chest and beard could not camouflage his cherubic countenance, and for all his robust physique he looked gentle and serene. His calm demeanor and beatific smile made you feel well protected to be in his presence. He dressed precisely like what he was, a religious Jew, serving with blind faith a God he could not see. He and all the other orthodox men attended the humbler wooden synagogue, swaying back and forth, *dovitting* in rapt meditation. At prayer their arms were bound with the leather thongs of *tiffilin*, the phylacteries that end in a box on the forehead. Their shoulders were completely wrapped with *taluses*, traditional Jewish prayer shawls. It was all done to comply with what they were sure were God's instructions on how to worship. Whichever building claimed your affiliation, the Polish powers in place counted you as a lice ridden, lying Commie Yid. The gentiles, brainwashed by their clergy since time immemorial to mistrust us, were always two drinks away from some mischief. But most of Sieniawa's two thousand inhabitants were Jewish, so there was a general mood of security among the citizenry. Our whole world consisted of about three hundred families living in a collection of small houses. A quarter of the twentieth century had already transpired and the present was not an epoch of great historical significance, neither for Poland nor for Europe in general. Most of the world was at peace, and nobody seemed to be starving. And we were utterly unaware of any political seeds of destruction that were being sown elsewhere, such as in neighboring Germany. So, for the moment, we had no need to worry. Despite all that, Father was a bundle of nerves. His wife who had already borne him four daughters was more than eight months pregnant. He adored his little girls, as he did his wife, but like men everywhere, in every culture and society, he needed to produce an heir. Some men in town were starting to doubt his virility, and he felt he could not bear the shame of topping Tevye's dubious feat. He desperately wanted a son, and was eager that his wife deliver herself of one. He felt that the odds were in his favor, so his nerves were tinged with confidence. The due date, though not so reliably divined in those rustic times, was pending, and with only a few radios in Sieniawa, and no newspapers at all, gossip was the number one source of local news and entertainment. And the hottest topic in the rural grapevine was my mother's pregnancy. One reason why we had so few radios was due to the lack of electricity. There was one thin line that supplied us with this modern convenience, but it wasn't potent enough to reach everywhere. Basically, just the main street with its few stores got electronically blessed, when it worked at all. All this confirmed my mother's star status on the gossip grid. Father chose to escape the speculation and wagering over the pending birth through total immersion in his work. After all, if he was going to have another child, regardless of gender, he was going to need more money. Of course, costs would probably be minimal. The child would be born at home, as the others were, and so far no doctor had yet been required. Midwives tended to such things back then, and there was rarely ever a need for medication. Actually no doctor had ever come to our house. And who had money for fancy medications? We cured ourselves as best we could with tried and true cures, like leeches. In many respects our lives were absolutely medieval and ruled by superstition. Regardless, Yisroel preferred to play it safe, and go out and earn. His business was straightforward, and practically took care of itself, so he could continue to fret without much threat of losing any precious work time.

Basically, what my father did was to pick up fish from one place and deliver it to another. But he didn't have to cast a net, or race to an early morning fish market, or be a great salesman, in order to make a living. He bought his catch of the day from a fish farm that bred carp. It was the thriving enterprise of some forward thinking landtsmen who formed ponds from a dammed tributary of the San and stocked it with the popular fresh water fish, letting nature take its course. The texture and taste was greatly appreciated by my father's loyal customers who either boiled it to make gefilte fish or fried it for a main course. The preference though was to cure them in smoke houses. The fresh water carp were easy to sell, and provided my father with a reliable source of income. Our little southern town was four hundred miles from the Baltic Sea, and it was four hundred in the opposite direction to the Black Sea, so salt water fish were out of the question. The river San was about a two mile walk west, half through trees and the rest over open fields, but fishing there was a hit or miss occupation. You might pull up a sturgeon or other bottom feeder, and never make a kosher catch. Plus, you'd have to associate with a lot of local gentiles who might throw you in the river for a laugh, if they let you fish there at all. All things considered, the carp farm was the only alternative for the observant orthodox of Sieniawa and surrounding region, and my father could rely on a modest living from it as long as the small earthen dam held.

Adding to my father's income was the commercial activities of my mother, Hadassah. She was as pious as my father, but that orthodoxy did not prevent her from entering into commerce. She ran a small grocery store, selling the fruit, vegetables, grains, and dairy products of the local farmers, as well as a little tea and coffee, and of course that carp. She often hitched our horse and wagon herself to trade in a nearby village. Though her clientele were mostly Jewish she did cater to occasional gentiles, availing themselves of her carp for Catholic fish Fridays. Besides matching my father in income she was his feminine counterpart in religion. She wore a *sheitel*, a wig to hide the beauty of her hair from all but her husband, and she was a Jewish matriarch -a real *Yiddishe mama*- in every sense of the word. She kept a clean Kosher home, and passed the prayers and customs of our people along to her daughters. She lived for her husband and kids, and treated us with tenderness and affection, patiently teaching us life's lessons. And like her husband, she hoped this pregnancy would result in her long awaited son. From their joint income they had long since saved up enough for the services of a *moyle*, just in case.

One detail of daily life that made the fish and grocery trades sufficient for our needs was the fact that we owned our own home and didn't have to pay rent. We had inherited it from my grandfather, but that was the only detail about previous generations that any of us ever discussed. Of course, the where and the why of their immigration to this area were not difficult to surmise. Anti-Semitism constantly drove the Jews of Europe from one place to another, either due to the issuance of edicts or violent pogroms. Whichever was the case he inherited this single story house and didn't need to concern himself with any further lodging issues until his eldest daughter married. When that happened he helped his son-in-law build an identical house not ten feet in front of his own, filling up the remaining space on his little plot of land. Each house had three small bedrooms off of a kitchen which was the hub of constant activity and a de facto living room. Thus, in this extreme southeastern corner of Poland, in Jaroslaw County, most Jews lived out their lives under similar circumstances, pious and poor in differing degrees, and surviving at the whim of governments indifferent to their welfare. And if not for the coming war I probably would have ended up as deeply committed to faith and fish as my father.

Our house bore evidence that a generation of Feders existed prior to our own in Sieniawa, but there were no other relatives on my father's side around. Mother, on the other hand, was a native of our little shtetl, and she had a brother nearby who was married with children. As far as we knew our two families constituted the whole of our clan in that part of the world.

Besides establishments like my mother's there was a weekly market where traveling merchants offered unique items for sale Also, farmers and herdsmen brought their vegetables, grains, eggs, and cheese to sell. The event was hardly more than a flea market, but had things not usually found in the bins at my mother's store. There were pots and pans made in factories in far away Krakow or Kiev, colorful machine loomed cloth and thread, tobacco, clocks, and an occasional used newspaper or magazine to get a glimpse into the outside world. Sieniawa was practically in a time warp, so the market was not to be missed. In the seven years since the end of the Great War our town had seen no industrialization at all. Our only expansion was in humanity. Each family had between three and ten children, and as the death rate could not overcome the birth rate, even with omnipresent infant mortality and microbes as yet unfamiliar with penicillin, the town naturally grew in population. Of course, most of its citizens were children, and a stroll through our town made you feel as if you had stumbled upon a large kindergarten at recess. But this was typical for Eastern Europe, especially for Jews. The descendents of Abraham and Moses were usually denied permission to live in big cities except in ghettos, so country life was far more desirable than surviving in such confined, unsanitary neighborhoods as those. All across eastern Poland, and over the border into the Ukraine, Russia, Lithuania and Estonia, were countless miserable hamlets, inhabited with impoverished Jews clawing a hardscrabble existence off the land, praying for the Messiah to come. And who knows, maybe the next boy to be born could be him.

My mother went into labor on February fifteenth, 1925.

Speculation and last minute wagers intensified. Only the clocks persisted in their normal routine as my father, sisters and neighbors put their lives on hold, totally preoccupied with the event at hand. Each of my mother's contractions was cause for discussion, and in between her breathing was monitored and analyzed. Only world class boxing matches received such detailed coverage. Outside, among the patient and concerned men, a shot of schnapps accompanied each subsequent contraction. Finally, with sweat poring off of my mother and father in equal portions I, a healthy male child, came into the world. A mid-wife raced to the window and cried out, "It's a boy!"

History tells us that King Henry the Eighth of England was, for all his power and wealth, an unfulfilled man, because he did not have a son. It took the establishment of a new church and the lives of three wives to help him realize his desire, and they say his jubilation was unbounded and legendary. Whatever joy felt by that monarch I am told that he had nothing on my father. My emergence from my exhausted mother into that dingy little bedroom was as if eternal heaven, glowing and ethereal, manifested itself on Earth. Father, generally a trusting soul, rushed to my mother's side to confirm and behold the miracle. Peeking between my legs even before he beheld my face, he echoed the mid-wife's pronouncement, "It's a boy!" He repeated it a dozen more times in different pitches, meters, and at varying decibels.

As for my part, I had done nothing at all, yet I was hoisted up as if I had just slid into home and won the World Series for the Chicago Cubs. Despite the bitter winter father displayed me, naked and legs akimbo, to the waiting throng of bearded well-wishers.

"Mazel tov! Mazel tov!" Over and over the Hebrew words collided in the frigid air, creating a cacophony of congratulations.

"La chaim! La chaim!" Schnapps flowed like the San and even the rarely uncorked slivovitz made its cautious appearance to further embolden the festivities. A fiddler arrived and music completed the festive atmosphere. The women were no less joyous, though limiting their celebratory libations to a less intoxicating Shabbos wine. Everybody hugged, though gender specific in their pairing, and smiles were seen all around, even if I was grimacing and crying most of the time. Every wail of mine was met with a huzzah of exultation.

"What lungs! You've got a cantor there, Yisroel."

"I didn't think ya had in ya!"

"Izzy, you betrayed me! I lost five zlotys!"

Each exclamation produced gales of laughter and the men laughed until their tears flowed and their jaws ached. Toasts, songs, and all manner of celebration was ultimately mitigated by the common sense of the women, herding their men back home, allowing the new Feder to suckle in peace with his mother. My father, fatigued from dancing and merry making, and no less fulfilled than Merry Old England's liege, lay down next to his queen and sighed.

"Hadassah, you done good. You done very good!"

He drifted off to sleep with a hirsute smile of contentment spread from ear to ear. He had a son. Now it didn't matter if he had more daughters, which he would. He had a son.

The following morning my father made an exception and missed work. He just could not pull himself away from home. Besides, he wanted to make absolutely certain nothing was wrong. The town's sole physician, an old country doctor, came by. He counted my fingers and toes, weighed me, poked and prodded me to see if my parts were in the right place and in proper working condition. Then he pronounced that everything was in order, allowed my father to foist a modicum of liquor upon him, and filled out some routine paperwork. Six days after my birth, as Jewish law decrees, my parents celebrated my bris, the ritual circumcision which is the mark of the covenant between our people and the Lord who has mysteriously chosen us. Jews have been observing this rite of passage since Abraham performed the first one on Isaac, but in all that time I'm sure no such festive mood as mine has been surpassed. The party that followed made the night of my birth seem like a wake. It went on from early in the morning until sundown, and practically the whole town, orthodox and reform, came by to see me, and wish, "Mazel Tov!" For months my ecstatic parents were the celebrities of Sieniawa. Every facial expression of mine was catalogued and discussed. How much I ate, how long I slept, whose eyes, hair and nose I possessed, and how often I crapped, were all serious topics of conversation.

It was no surprise that my birth caused such a stir. From one year to the next not much ever happened in Sieniawa. Except for some apparatus of the Industrial Revolution, like a sewing machine, there was scant evidence that it wasn't a century earlier. My home town was like a Jewish Brigadoon. The closest railway station was twelve miles away, reachable only by a wagon drawn by a team of clip-clopping horses, blithely unaware of any particular schedule to uphold. A single motorized bus came through our dirt roads weekly, ultimately bound for the metropolises of Krakow, two hundred miles to the west or to Lvov, about the same distance in the opposite direction. The wonders of modern civilization eluded us, but we were blessed with clean air and water, plentiful timber, fertile earth, blue skies, and the regard and affection of our family and neighbors. Most of our citizens felt that their cups were half full and then some.

I was named Avrom Yisroel Feder and from the moment of my birth until my early teens I led a charmed childhood. I was doted upon by my parents and my four older sisters. My parents had another girl before I was born, but she died in infancy, so now I was not only a boy, but the baby of the family as well. I was practically royalty, and my every caprice was catered to. Of course, I was unaware of any real opulence or ostentation to covet, so my demands were relatively easy to meet. And while we were certainly among the lower economic classes I do not recall want. I always had plenty to eat, clothes on my back, shoes on my feet, and no end of love and attention. I was hugged and kissed by my parents and sisters so continually it was almost annoying, and it is conceivable that they came dangerously close to spoiling me. I was also the non-stop recipient of the affectionate attention of Marisha, our maid. Marisha was a Christian woman who had been with us as long as I was aware, and she was the sole vestige of middle class comfort we enjoyed. In order for my mother to be able to run her store she had to have help at home, and my parents' double income allowed that luxury. Of course, paying a domestic servant in 1930 Poland was hardly the hefty sum it would be in other places and times. Marisha was so destitute when she came to work for us she considered her job, which offered pennies for pay plus room and board, to be absolutely resplendent. Mother taught her to cook like a Jewess, and she was delighted to do everything she was bid. All smiles and warmth she bathed me and dressed me and was in every way like a second mother to me. When you add to this the regard of my sisters, all of whom considered my appearance to be just one notch short of the Messiah's, you could not say that I was lacking in love or attention. And when I wasn't luxuriating in that ocean of love I was playing. With so many kids in Sieniawa it was easy to organize soccer matches. There was an open lot right next to my house and if it wasn't raining or too cold we played soccer like fanatics. Soccer is the poor kid's friend. All you need is a ball and a patch of dirt. We played every spare moment we could squeeze between school, *cheider* and chores. Actually, it's amazing we were able to play as much as we did. At times it was just among members of the tribe. Other times we challenged the gentile kids. And sometimes we played mixed teams. Our goal posts were motley, and we lacked a regulation ball, but we loved that game more than any other form of play.

There is one cliché about Jews that I proudly admit is true: Education is king. So when I came of age I attended two separate schools. I went to public school in the day and *cheider* in the evening. *Cheider* was the traditional religious school for Jewish boys found all over Europe at that time, and my father dutifully brought me there by the hand every single day. I don't think he ever passed up the chance to demonstrate to the world that he had son. Our teacher was a stern Rabbi with a long beard and he taught us to read from the Torah and the Talmud and also imparted our history to us. And none of this was ever subject for debate. We doubted nothing, accepted everything, and obeyed our parents and elders without question. Public school was different in that it was not exclusively for Jewish children. My sisters attended another school just for Jewish girls and, apart from seeing its yearly group photo, no male had the privilege of access to anything to do with it. Boys attended the two room public school house with both Jewish and Christian kids. The older kids helped the younger ones, and the teachers saw that we were all occupied with reading, writing, math, and social studies. It was there that I experienced my first taste of anti-Semitism.

Though not a daily occurrence some of the Christian boys made occasional derogatory remarks about their lice ridden Yid classmates and their lying ways. Sometimes they threw stones, and once in a while they even went beyond the verbal assaults and beat us up after school. It wasn't life threatening, but I got an occasional black eye or bloody nose. I had to take it because I was too small to properly fight back, and I was the target of bullies, specialists in assaulting the defenseless. To defend ourselves we often walked home in groups. The insane part about this badgering was that our attackers were our former playmates. They would apologize a few days after an incident and we'd be playing soccer together again as if it never happened. At least that's what they thought. After the first attack we never saw them in the same light again. Perhaps their parents or peers had baited them into attacking the Christ killers and they had to do it just to prove their manhood. For whatever reason we learned young to be wary of the *goyim*, or strangers, in our midst. When I got older I usually made a better showing of myself. After all, if I was going to have to endure random attacks I thought it best to make my assailants pay for it a little themselves. The public school teachers, all Gentiles, were generally fair, and I never saw or heard any of them exhibit any blatantly bigoted behavior toward us. Of course, our so-called impartial teachers never did anything to stop the attacks either. The most painful part of all of this was that our own parents, to whom we looked to for protection, were powerless to amend the situation. Thus, I got the message that we were different, and our lives were fragile.

I had to learn about the Jew haters on my own, because my father always seemed to be too busy to address the issue when I wanted to. Whenever I went to see him for some clarification on the matter either my mother or older sisters would stop me, explaining that he was still in prayers. I probably should have pressed the issue, but respect for my elders meant never invading their private moments. If they were working or praying then that meant they were in the busy adult mode, not the parent mode, and usually my patience wore out before they were free. But kids talk among themselves, so we had it pretty well figured out. It was obvious that we Jews had to be careful. We were never going to be one hundred percent safe. No wonder my father and the others were religious. This world, as it was, was clearly not our home. The next one might be better, and the Messiah would fix things when he came. Help and comfort were in his hands and God's. But all succor seemed to emanate from a transcendental realm. I never heard evidence of any political solution being discussed. Despite the iniquities of Polish society, even when lurking in the shadows, the practical mundane solutions of Zionism had not yet spread to our town. For the time being, the remedy for our redemption lay in the rigors of daily adherence to Jewish law, and the prospect of the Messiah. Until such time as his physical appearance in our midst we would continue to pray to God in His kingdom not to forget us down here. While growing up I often slept in the same bed as my parents where my father would tell me his beliefs and what it meant to be a man.

"Ovram. God expects a lot from us, and it's our responsibility to live as He decrees. He gave us life, and we must be worthy of that life, grateful and humble before Him. He is greater than we can imagine, so whatever we do is not enough. We must praise his name. *Baruch hashem.* Blessed be the name."

He spoke so much about this holy name that, with an innocent child's curiosity, I couldn't help but wonder why we didn't actually say it.

"But father, what is God's name? Does anyone know it?"

"It doesn't matter if we know it. We are so unworthy that we dare not pronounce it. But don't worry. He knows when we address Him. Just have faith. Always have faith."

The reality that my father imparted to me was one of minimal material sense gratification and maximum spiritual surrender. It sounds stern, but seemed joyful as lived by him and his whole generation. Besides taking delight in incessant prayer our celebrations were endless. Major holidays like Pesach, Rosh Hashanah and Yom Kippur were events. Simchas Torah, Shavuous, Purim, Chanukah, and their varying degrees of gravity and gaiety, consumed our time, attention, and imagination. And when there was no particular holiday there was the weekly promise of Shabbat. From the setting of the sun on Friday to its counterpart on Saturday it was the Lord's Day, and all Jews were duty bound to keep it holy. Every Friday morning the preparations began for the sacred sundown. The women, mothers and daughters, cleaned their houses and cooked a feast for the families to enjoy that evening. They scrimped during the week, but always saved up enough to have at least one chicken for shabbos dinner. In addition to that they baked fresh challah and a noodle dish called *lukcheon kugel*. There were vegetable and potato casseroles, and for the more well to do families there were meat dishes, such as *kedempe fleisch*. With carp in such abundance, there was never any lack of gefilte fish, crowned with boiled carrots, and garnished with fresh ground horse radish, whose aroma permeated the air all day and made our eyes water. The aromas were marvelous, and the tastes and textures even better. During the week we had enough to eat, but the fare was usually simple. The Sabbath was a much more opulent culinary experience, and I savored them then, as well as in my memory. Everything was juicy, luscious and plentiful, and it all melted in your mouth. I can't imagine that even a king ate better than we did on Friday night. The colors, smells, and flavors are more than mere nostalgic exaggerations. Those meals, made with love, were delicious and satisfying for man and boy alike. For the adults there was wine. First was a sweet red one for the shabbos blessing, afterwards the more refined varieties were uncorked for the main meal. For the kids there were sweet desserts. But there was not an atom of dairy in sight. There was no butter spread on the challah, or cream sauces of any kind. That would have broken the strict dietary law of *kashrut*. Our homes were kosher which meant that meat and dairy never went together in the same meal. They never even went on the same plates. Every Jewish family in Sieniawa owned two complete sets of dishes. This was not because they were rich, but because kosher laws dictated that a plate that had meat on it would contaminate any dish used for dairy. It didn't matter if the plate was washed in soap and boiling water, dried with a sterile towel and stored in a sealed cabinet for a year. Once meat was served on a particular plate it could never be used for cheese or butter or anything baked with dairy in it. Human stomachs were similarly governed. Only after a prescribed amount of time had elapsed after eating meat could a person then consume something prepared with dairy. And when that time came the other dishes, re-served for dairy, were set on the table. Then, and only then, the cake was cut, and coffee with milk was served. And every course of every Sabbath meal was served on a beautiful white table cloth on fine china, and eaten with the best flatware a Jew could afford, even if he had to save up for a year to buy it. Everybody bathed and dressed in their finest, but none of it was done to impress the Schwartzes. One gave one's best to honor the Lord on His day. And everything, the cleaning, the setting of the table by the children, the cooking, all had to finished before the Friday sun began to set. Once the first rays of that sun ducked behind the western horizon no more labor was allowed. Working on the Sabbath was anathema. My mother would no sooner cook on the Sabbath than my father would travel. The ovens were turned off as soon as the sun began to set, but the food warming within remained. Cooking was work, but the ovens stayed hot for while, and Talmudic scholars had long since deter-mined that the inanimate piece of metal was incapable of moral transgression. Our parents and a thousand generations before them had lived this way, and had no plans other than to continue do-ing so until God dictated otherwise. After the meal my father read from scripture. We also sang traditional Jewish songs and often re-ceived guests with special musical talent or mastery of Jewish lore and theology. Before the shabbos meal was Shabbat services in the little synagogue. And when that was concluded I observed another weekly ritual. As poor as most Jews were there were some who were so destitute they could not afford a shabbos meal. These men were virtually beggars, or *schnorers*. The ridiculous cliché that all Jews are rich was especially inadequate to explain the existence of those wretched landtsmen. They were often lazy, but just as often, unemployed or unemployable due to some psychological condition or mental disease that prevented them from confronting the world with any confidence or competence. And sometimes they were just *schlimazels*, men who perpetually suffered from bad luck. Whatever the reason was that led to their state we simply accepted them without judgment. And it was traditional for those who could afford to, even barely so, to invite one or more of them home to share their shabbos bounty. More than mere tradition, Jewish law held that charity was central to a righteous life. It was a *mitzvah,* or good deed, and men like my father took such things seriously. The pathetic men sat on a special bench in the synagogue, waiting to be invited, and my father always took two or three of them home with us to celebrate the Sabbath, sit at the table with us, honor the meal, and spend the night as well. After all, they couldn't travel on the Sabbath either. Only when Saturday's sun started to descend could they depart. I observed this weekly ritual and thought nothing of it. It was normal life in Sieniawa, and it felt good.

In addition to the weekly wonder of Shabbos there were weddings, Bar Mitzvahs and brises. Marvelous touring Klezmer bands happily performed at them, either for meager pay or just room and board. And Rebbes, our Hebrew sages, made periodic visits to wretched towns like Sieniawa to impart some Talmudic wisdom and inspire everyone. A rich Jewish life flourished in our little corner of paradise, and it fulfilled and sustained us beyond any material consideration. Most of our population was Jewish so when we greeted people on the muddy roads it was usually in Yiddish. Absolutely everyone kept kosher, and there hadn't been a pogrom or any kind of trouble for a long time. Across our nearest border the wicked Tsar had been deposed, bringing an end to the officially sanctioned anti-Jewish demonstrations that had characterized Russian life for so long. And the Polish government hadn't bothered us for a good while either. We lived in a peaceful Jewish world and were content. Of course, we lived in a bubble, oblivious to the storm that was slowing brewing beyond the borders of Jaroslaw County.

From day to day, year to year, our lives, cemented in routine, continued in its cocoon. Now and then travelers would tell us of the troubles in the outside world, and by the time I had turned five the world had become mired in a grave economic morass. Sieniawa was not seriously affected though, because it was basically an agricultural society. The dirt still produced things to eat, and the carp, oblivious to world economic trends, continued to mate. And if money was short we just relied a little more on the barter system which had never really become obsolete in our lives.

By the time I reached six years of age I was allowed to accompany my father on his carp treks. A little boy's first best friend is his dad, and I was thrilled to tag along as often as I could. And whenever he let me take some responsibility, like feeding our horse or knocking on a customer's door, pride swelled my little chest. On those rounds he gave me no end of education about scripture and a thousand and one practical details about surviving in the woods of southeastern Poland. And when my little legs grew weary I gleefully mounted our old mare, Babe. It was the only time in my life up to then that I had gotten from one place to another by any means other than walking on my own legs.

By the time I reached Bar Mitzvah age though news about Germany and their ranting bellicose *fuehrer* was a daily reality. The sparse electric current that reached us was now eagerly awaited, and each radio broadcast was well attended. Of course this barrage of current events was probably more vexing to my parents for its distracting nature than for the negativity of its contents. But for me the radio had a different effect. It opened my eyes to the outside world. I also got glimpses of it when the buses came through depositing traveling salesmen eager to share their stories with impressionable little boys. Of course, we were not completely ignorant of life beyond the town limits of Sieniawa either. We had text books in public school, and I had seen pictures of the world's landmarks. I knew that Africa had people with dark skin, India had snake charmers and the guards at Buckingham Palace wore tall furry hats. With little more than pictures in a book however the outside world seemed like a fairy tale, wondrous but ultimately incredible. The radio however was more immediate. A voice told you what happened not just back during some historical epoch, but that very week, and sometimes that very day. Being a typical precocious kid I was attracted to that world. I had already seen Sieniawa. I had seen it every day for my entire life. I knew every person in it personally and longed to meet someone new. My father was content to commune with God, who was past, present and future for him, but I was itching for something else. Plus, I was approaching manhood and was eager to sow my wild oats.

When I was thirteen we celebrated my Bar Mitzvah. Back then it was not the grand affair that it was to become for later generations. I just read my *haftorah* piece and it was done. Whatever party might have followed was so modest that I cannot even recall it. And the idea of gifts for a poor Polish boy was so unheard of as to be laughable. By that time in my life I had never even touched money. In any case, according to Jewish law I was still a man. I was short and in no need of a shave any time soon, making me a pretty poor specimen of one, but my parents, as always, were immeasurably proud of me.

Father was especially thrilled over having a male heir when Passover came. Before my birth he had celebrated our release from Egyptian bondage countless times, but bereft of a son to ask the traditional four questions that Moses' son had originally posed so long ago. But now he beamed down on me as I recited, "Ma nish ta nah…" And as I had only sisters it was my role year after year.

Despite the repeat performances my father's ecstasy never waned. Of course, my father's affection for his daughters was not dimmed by my entry into this world. He loved us all equally. There was Sarah, Zelda, Sonia, and Rachel, all older than me. And after me came one last girl, Bella. A sixth girl was born who died in her infancy, and it is a source of great sadness for me not to be able to recall her name. Besides me only God is left to remember her. In any case, regardless of my preferential treatment as the male heir, the girls got their own special treatment.

In addition to the few radios within the limits of Sieniawa a few families possessed Victrolas. One of our neighbors was a girl who was just a little bit older than me, and she invited me to listen to her records on her family's elaborate invention. I don't think she especially liked me or cared for my company, but she knew that my mother's store sold candy, and if I was willing to get her some on a regular basis, she'd let me listen to her wonderful, modern music machine. I agreed to the arrangement, but I felt terribly guilty. Be that as it may, there was no resisting the dual temptations of being alone with a girl and listening to forbidden music. The combination was too compelling to deny, so I stooped to rob from own mother. I embezzled some candy from the store and took it as payment to the girl's house. It was a rare treat for both of us.

The device was lovely, made from a deep red burnished wood that gleamed. It was crowned with a large bell from which the sound magically emanated. There was a handle on the side that she cranked round and around, and the disc on the surface than rotated without any further effort on her part. The records themselves seemed quite mystical to me. They were thick black lacquer, hard and brittle, and so costly, hard to come by, and fragile, that I was not permitted to handle them. The girl delicately removed one from its cardboard sleeve and ceremoniously placed it on the rotating platter, lowering the mechanical arm to its rim. When the needle came into contact with the surface of the record there was a hiss and then sound. It was muted and scratchy, but hypnotic. Actually, my first encounter with a Victrola was almost frightening, and ultimately embarrassing. How did such small musicians fit inside that box? Once I could repeat back the real explanation of how it supposedly worked, it was no less thrilling. Of course, I really didn't understand its scientific principles at all, but I became more relaxed. The girl was playing some kind of music from far away that was like nothing I had ever heard. This is not surprising. After a life lived exclusively in Sieniawa she could have played almost any piece of music in any style and I would have been equally awed. My musical experience was limited to liturgical and Klezmer. Our cantor sang regularly, and once in a while someone traveling through town might squeeze an accordion, but the Victrola's music was completely foreign to my ears. She told me it was called a tango and was meant for dancing. I had seen plenty of dancing, but never with a man holding woman. She gave me tango lessons often enough for me to remember the steps, but I'm sure no notion of becoming a dancer crept into my head. The music and the girl were the principal attractions, and it was on my mind plenty while waiting for and anticipating our next session. Guilt invaded my consciousness for the first time in my life, owing to my confiscating candy from my own beloved mother. Such a thing had never crossed my mind before, and now the sin was compounded by my utter lack of shame. Fear was all I felt when considering the prospect of capture. My teenaged hormones held precedence over the issue of morality, and even my buddies were vexed over my frequent absences from soccer. As slight defense I will offer in evidence that the tango lessons were not exclusively about subtle sex. I did enjoy the music. As a matter of fact, I appreciated the cultural uplifting so much I considered plotting to get my parents to invest in one, recruiting my sisters as accomplices. I could tell my folks that our lives would benefit from the presence of such an edifying contraption. Of course, I never got the *chutzpah*. I knew I'd get a lecture from my father citing dozens of Talmudic references and quotes from Maimonides and Hillel. My time would continue to be filled with shul, school, cheider, soccer and chores.

In 1939 every kid in the world did chores, and in Sieniawa we had our share. As a matter of fact, between all of us kids, along with Marisha, we manned the home front, leaving my parents to dedicate themselves almost exclusively to commerce and religion. One chore I especially remember was helping roll out the Seder matzo. This was no simple task, because it was a yearly job for my parents to supply half of the town with the traditional unleavened bread at Passover. My sisters prepared the dough, and we all rolled it together. We had to get it as thin as possible, and it was my grave responsibility to make the lines. I tried my best to keep them straight, but compared with the mechanized matzo of today I'm sure it must have looked crooked and comical. On the other hand nobody examined it so closely either. My father felt proud that everyone who ate the matzo, and beheld those imperfect lines, was reminded of who had made it. Likewise, I was proud to be entrusted with such a responsibility. At that time of year my father also made borscht. He collected beets for weeks before the holiday and enjoyed this rare trip into the kitchen, cooking up that hearty soup. While my mother purified the house of *chamitz* my father chopped and spiced and stirred. We all relished that borscht, sitting on our Seder cushions, sharing the deep red soup, and it gave him *nachis* that all his neighbors ate his Seder borscht too. It was a real mitzvah, and it made the whole town feel like one big happy family. Another thing my sisters and I did together was dress up on Purim. We invented colorful costumes with funny hats and gleefully traipsed around the village begging candy door to door. It was the highlight of our simple lives, as it must have been for millions of other poor Jewish children across Eastern Europe on the eve of World War Two. This simple life was about to disappear with barely a trace to remind us that it was real. But it was indeed real. We all dwelt in quaint villages, living according to ancient scripture, enjoying naïve pastimes. We were born in our homes, obeyed our elders, married other unsophisticated people like ourselves, worked at practical trades, honored the Sabbath, sang and had children. We were satisfied, minded our own business and never harmed a soul. But there were others, unsatisfied with their lives, covetous and irresponsible. And their brief but loud time in the sun was coming. Meanwhile, we blithely persisted in our quiet lives, unaware of their wicked plans.

Since the time of my birth Sieniawa had modernized to the degree allowed by the presence of a couple of radios. We didn't listen regularly, and my father, along with many of the orthodox, considered it a dangerous waste of time. But the knowledge of the outside world that rode the radio airwaves was undeniable and disturbing. By now everyone knew about Adolph Hitler and the Nazis. But Germany was all the way over on the other side of Poland. Four hundred miles seemed like a galaxy away, leaving our remote corner safe. We enjoyed a sense of security so blissfully false it was sad, and we were about to learn just how uncomfortably close such a distance could really be.

My parents and the four sisters born before me.
Sieniawa, approximately 1920-1923.

L-R My sister Rachel, Zenig (husband of cousin Sara), sisters Kayla &
Zelda. Cousin Sara sits in front. The other man and the old woman
are unknown. Sieniawa, approximately 1938-1939.

The Apthekar family before Esther was born.
Approximately 1923.

Boys and girls were educated separately in Sieniawa.
This is the school for girls. My sisters are among them.
Approximately 1925.

INVASIONS

||

I turned fourteen in 1939, the year the world changed forever. In the seven months between my birthday and the bloody onset of the unfathomable horror of war, the youth of Sieniawa was starting to awaken to new ideas, and the concept of Jewish self determination was finally manifesting itself in our remote village. One day a man got off the weekly bus and made his way down to the synagogues. He spoke to the elders about Palestine, our homeland, and it sounded wonderful. If the Messiah didn't personally appear among us we could do just as well living in the land where his appearance was first foretold. With the blessings of our parents he organized a meeting at the public school. I do not know what charm he must have possessed to convince our *goyishecup* schoolmasters to let us use that facility, but he did. The meeting was a real rarity for us. Nothing out of the ordinary ever happened in Sieniawa. We lived scheduled lives. We knew when the seasons were going to change and when the religious holidays were coming. There was hardly ever a surprise. If a woman gave birth prematurely we talked about it for months. So it was quite extraordinary to host this Zionist meeting, and it was very well attended. Our passionate guest spoke about a man from Hungary named Theodor Herzel and his dream of establishing a homeland for Jews in Palestine. Palestine was where Jerusalem was, a city holy to Jews. King Solomon had his temple there. Of course, it had been under the control of the Ottoman Empire for centuries, and now under the British, but Jews had been living there almost continually since Biblical times. It was where we were originally from, said the charismatic young man, and where we belonged. Poland was not our home. Nowhere in Europe was safe. We could suffer a pogrom at any moment. We lived at the mercy of anti-Semites, and we'd never be safe until we had our own country.

The meeting got a lot of us excited. In Poland we couldn't even own land, much less a nation of our own. Before he left he found someone to take up the cause and organize the youth. Soon I was part of Beth Al, which was kind of a Jewish Boy Scouts, complete with uniforms. We were Zionist youths with the dream of a Jewish homeland planted firmly in our heads and our hearts. Our zealous though charming recruiter was so well spoken that he not only convinced the school teachers to host the original meeting, but to continue to allow the Zionist Boy Scouts to meet there on a regular basis after he left.

I had never ventured more than a few miles away from Sieniawa, and only when accompanying my father on his fish delivery routes, so I found the notion of going all the way to the Middle East inconceivable. I had seen pictures in my school books of far away places, but they were just pictures. Actually going to one of those destinations never crossed my mind. Whoever considered such a thing? Krakow seemed like Oz to me, so Jerusalem sounded like an out and out fairy tale. My friends and I had never considered such a thing, but now we thought it might actually be possible. Maybe people like us really could leave Sieniawa and go to romantic sounding far off places like Palestine. And once we became aware of the world outside Poland we even entertained the idea of doing something besides being fish mongers, tailors, merchants or Rabbis. All we had ever done was live day to day, with no thoughts of distinguished careers, like doctors or lawyers. None of us had ever nurtured aspirations that lay beyond our town. I lived fourteen years without a thought for the future, but now the future had my mind in its grip. My pals and I talked incessantly about Palestine and all the other places that lie along the route. Prior to the Zionist's visit we had never even met anyone from another country, but now we were becoming worldlier and more sophisticated by the moment. We discussed the route to Lvov, and how we might then get to Kiev, and then on to Odessa, and sail all the way to the Holy Land. But these conversations were strictly among the Beth Al gang. Our parents were so provincial it gave them culture shock to think about going to the county seat in Jaroslaw. They had no concept of visiting Embassies or Consuls, or getting passports or visas. Palestine for them was no nearer than the moon. Of course, the reality was that, even with a heart full of desire to go to the Holy Land, our grandiose plans could never graduate beyond the talking stage. We were too poor to plan a trip even to Krakow, much less plan an international itinerary. Our financial state would have put a damper on the most enthusiastic Zionist spirit. While me and my friends, the recently Bar Mitzvah'd, were considering all this, war broke out.

As the youth of Sieniawa dreamt of a land that did not yet exist, our fate was being plotted by countries that were all too real. We envisioned our tiny illusory nation, but neighboring states, dissatisfied with the contours of their borders, aspired after empire. The Germans and Russians, bitter antagonists, were beating their plowshares into swords and Poland lay in between. To buy time before they attacked each other, they agreed to divvy up this land as mutual spoils. We were at a Beth Al meeting, discussing how to irrigate the desert, while the Germans and Soviets were signing the nonaggression pact that was the overture to the bloodiest, most destructive and sorrowful conflagration man would ever know. A bomb had already been released from so high up we couldn't see it, but it was plummeting down at us at lightning speed. Sieniawa was in the cross hairs, but none of us suspected a thing. The Germans were fueling their tanks and I was wondering if my sisters had saved me any of that strudel from last night. Soon though, the war would be impossible to ignore.

We had heard about Germany's leader, Adolph Hitler, and his insistence that certain territories belonged to Germany. And lately we had heard he wanted a piece of Poland. The adults discussed this, insisting it would lead to nothing.

"What do we care if one group of *goyim* grabs some land from another group?"

"What does that have to do with us?"

"Let him! He'll be satisfied then."

"Yes. Then there'll be no war."

"What war? Are you a *mishugina*?"

"You think after the last one anyone wants another war? Nobody's that *mushuga*!"

The superior intellect of the adults convinced the younger citizens of Sieniawa that there was nothing to fear. It was all a lot of noise, and it would all blow over. So when the radio told us that the Germans invaded Poland we were shocked. Still some of the older citizens with longer beards held fast to their view of things.

"So, the Germans grab a piece of Poland. Think that's the first time? You ever hear of Bialystok? First it's Poland. Then it's Russia. Then it's Poland again. This kind of *mishigas* has been going on forever, and will always be like that. What can we do?"

It seemed to make sense. Besides, the German invasion took place all the way over on the other side of Poland. We'd never see them this far east. And the news we heard from the radio was unreliable. When the Germans crossed our border we heard that the heroic Polish troops were activated to intercept and repel the foul invaders. Then, after a frighteningly short time, we heard that the fighting had ceased and the Germans were now in control of Poland's national radio system. So, our fellow Poles exaggerated their competence and our conquerors exaggerated everything else. We were totally in the dark. We didn't know that this new kind of army traveled so fast. We never heard such phrases as *blitzkrieg* or *wermachte*. We had never seen a tiger tank, not even in a picture. And in my whole life I had only seen airplanes twice, both times high overhead. Once I heard the buzz of a far off motor while I was a little boy, riding on our mare, and I looked up. My father explained it, and the metal bird captured my imagination for days. But not seeing another one, and my father having already exhausted his scant knowledge on the subject, I soon forgot about it. The second time was while my friends and I were playing soccer. All the boys looked up at once, and one boy took advantage of it and scored a goal past the distracted goal keeper. We fell to arguing over the legitimacy of the score and when we looked up again it was gone. With such meager experience with aircraft we would never comprehend what a Stuka dive bomber could do. We were sitting ducks.

We all thought we were far away from the fighting, so mother and father continued on their usual routes, he delivering fish, she buying produce from farmers on both sides of the San. As my mother steered her horse and cart through the last few houses on the approach to the crude bridge that spanned the eastern and western banks of the river, a man hailed my mother. She recognized him. His name was Stanislaw Zowistowski.

"Mrs. Feder. Stop. You cannot cross the river any more."

My mother was incredulous.

"Is the bridge out?"

Now it was the man's turn to express his disbelief.

"Don't you know? The German are on the other side of the river."

My mother was not even sure of its implication.

"But I'm a civilian. A woman. What would they want with me?"

"Look, Mrs. Feder, do you remember Nikola Kwalushka, the cobbler?"

My mother nodded, now listening very intently.

"He went across the bridge three days ago to deliver a pair of boots he made for someone. Nobody's seen him since."

"That's not proof of any funny business. Maybe he'll be back soon. I have to go across the river and buy from the farmers I always buy from. I got a business to run!"

The man looked very grimly at my mother.

"Go across that river Mrs. Feder, and I'm certain the Germans will arrest or kill you."

My mother's mouth dropped open.

"But how could such a thing be?"

The man was insistent and grabbed the bridle of our mare, frightening my mother.

"I didn't want to scare you, but I'm telling you that nothing on the other side of that bridge is worth going after. That's the truth. Believe it if you want or not."

Mother had often spoken with this man and he always seemed like a reasonable and reliable fellow. Now though, his mood was far more urgent and insistent than ever. He seemed gripped by fear, and meant for his condition to be contagious. He stared deeply and coldly into my mother's eyes like death personified. She had never looked into a human face so foreboding and it made her blood run cold. With no further discussion on the matter she knew she must turn around and go back. For now anyway, the western bank of the River San did not exist. The edge of her universe was here. To go beyond it was to sail off the edge of the world. The same went for everyone else in Sieniawa, and its repercussions were quick in spreading. My father could no longer visit customers there either, and slowly his business dried up. My mother continued to drive her horse and cart around, buying vegetables and dairy from the few farmers still producing. Fall was heavy in the air and most of the crops were already gathered. But not many farmers were able to sell their usual output. It was war, and the government had claimed most of it to feed its troops. We tried to carry on as if the world wasn't at war, but it was increasingly harder to ignore. The store was losing money and bad news was the only kind we ever heard any more. Besides that, some people were packing up and going east. Then the inevitable happened. The war came to our town.

I was on my way to school when I heard the grinding gears of a truck. It wasn't Thursday, the day the cross country bus always visited, so I was curious. I looked toward the sound and was stunned to see a large group of uniformed men carrying rifles. They weren't marching in formation, yet seemed purposeful. The trucks and the men all had red star insignia and some men without rifles were shouting in heavily accented Polish.

"Not to panic! No harm will befall you! We are Russian soldiers from glorious Union of Soviet Socialist Republics, and we have come to liberate you from your evil capitalist taskmasters! Even now fascist Germany invades your western frontier. But we will protect you from their imperialist aggression! Do not fear!"

They wore grey uniforms with a five pointed red star on their caps. Their pants were tucked into their boots, and bloused out like riding pants. Some rode motorcycles, and others stood on the running boards of large vehicles, the likes of which I had never seen. I recognized the weekly bus, but if it weren't for the pictures I had seen in school textbooks I wouldn't have had any idea of what I was looking at now. Besides the vehicles there men of a different kind. It was my first sight of soldiers.

Sieniawa was peaceful and had no need for armed lawmen to patrol our dirt roads. Occasionally a marshal from Jaroslaw County came by to see if we were all still here and in one piece. He carried a pistol, sheathed in a leather pouch on his hip, but he never took it out, not even to show it to anyone. We didn't have a cinema so I never saw men at arms in action, not even in make believe. There were hunters around, and I had heard and observed their guns fire, but an army was something new to my friends and me. Guns and uniforms seem to hold an undeniable attraction to boys, and as long as they weren't shooting anyone, we couldn't help but satisfy our curiosity and stay. Our parents on the other hand were far more wary, and insisted we get inside. But even as they were herding us inside, a uniformed man strived to assure everyone that we were safe.

"Please, Polish and Jewish friends, hear us. We are not your enemies. We will make your lives better. Our wonderful leader, Josef Stalin, sends you greetings. We bring the balance of communism to you. No fear please. We follow the teachings of Karl Marx, a Jew, just like you. We request all family leaders to proceed to your school house, assuming you have one, where we will explain the wonderful changes coming to your poor exploited village."

We kids were overwhelmed. Whatever it was it was certainly adventurous. And the man said they followed a Jew. Maybe he was like Theodore Herzel? Maybe our dream country was at hand? The adults however were reticent. They understood that the presence of arms, even though shouldered, was a threat, and indicated a change that was anything but for the best. Furthermore they could not ignore this veiled threat. If armed men politely suggested you go somewhere then the best course of action, especially if you are unarmed, is to comply. This was the most outrageous thing that had ever befallen our village. Absolutely nothing exciting had ever happened here, and now we seemed to be catching up in a great big hurry. For the adults of course it was catching up much too quickly. Regardless, cooperation was our only defense. Besides, these particular Russians behaved better than any of our previous encounters with their lot. Too many adults in Sieniawa could remember Tsarist pogroms, and many of the older women of our village had been raped by Cossacks. So far though, this group seemed better behaved. Perhaps their new political philosophy had a civilizing affect on them. In any case, one of the townsfolk guided this Russian to the school house, followed by several dozen curious men. When the officer was satisfied with the attendance he stood where the teacher usually did and made another speech.

"People of Sieniawa. I am Commissar Glentz of the Soviet Politboro. As you may know from radio reports Germany has invaded your country. They follow a man named Adolph Hitler whose government, the Third Reich, has the worst possible intentions for your people."

At this our fathers turned toward each other and gravely nodded.

"But we have made a pact with them. They cannot cross the San River. If they do then they'll be attacking the mighty Soviet Union and we will crush them like a bear crushes a honeycomb."

Commissar Glentz seemed proud and happy to be able to crush his enemies, but the whole prospect of such a situation had everyone panic stricken. Just a month before our biggest problem was an early cold front. Now we had to contend with a war, as well as hosting a foreign army. A bearded man raised his hand.

"Why are you here, in Sieniawa? Are you on your way to fight this Hitler?"

"My dear sir, we are not at war with Germany. I am just reassuring you that if such a need arises we will come to your defense."

This seemed to have a salutary affect on some, though most voiced their concerns.

"We heard some things on the radio. And newspapers make their way to our remote town. This Hitler hates Jews. What is our situation now? Please be truthful."

Commissar Glentz reflected for a moment, and then spoke to us with words and tone that calmed our worst fears.

"Lenin, the brilliant revolutionary founder of the Union of Soviet Socialist Republics, tells us that to persecute Jews is to commit counter revolutionary activities. Hating Jews, or any other segment of the Russian population, was what the Czar and his corrupt and outdated regime did. That was the old way, and we're here to introduce you to the new. Yes my friends, it's a new world, and the Serfs, Jews, Mongolians, and even the Uzbeks, have a part in it. So, you have nothing to fear from us. Actually, we want to help you. We want to help the whole world. Communism offers every man, woman and child a chance to participate in their own destiny. You just need to be properly educated. Soon we will begin that process. A better way of life awaits you. All of you."

A friend of my father asked, "We hear that communism is atheist. We are Jews and we worship the Almighty. What then will happen to our religion?"

"For now, all I can tell you is that Marshal Stalin is not your enemy. We have come to offer you a better way of life than Poland ever did. Now, let me address the youth of your town for a moment."

This got my attention and I focused more intently on his speech.

"Young comrades in the glorious Soviet Union offer you advanced education in many fields. Think about what you might like to do with your lives. The future belongs to you, and to everyone, I say this. We have to come to help you, not enslave you. Do not fear. You will stay in your homes and with your families. Together, we will build a new world. A brighter future is dawning for us all. Good night, comrades!"

All smiles, the jolly commissar left, but he did not leave us in a tranquil state. We understood none of his political rhetoric which was composed of new words, all long and foreign sounding. He seemed to speak in slogans, and we didn't even know what he meant by commissar. Mostly, we were confused and had more questions than answers. Had we known what heinous crimes were being committed by their totalitarian counterparts on the western side of the San we would have kissed the boots of the gleeful Red, but we were completely naïve. In my life I had never seen more than one man in uniform at a time, and he was just a policeman. Now we had to contend with a hundred of them. And they all carried large guns, though I didn't think they came to hunt in our woods. For as long as I knew Sieniawa had known only peace and tranquility. A few fights with gentile kids and a couple of harsh winters were the sum and substance of our travail. But now the word war was on everyone's lips. The commissar, or whatever he called himself, was right about that. Our old lives definitely looked like they were over. The reliable rhythms of small town life were broken forever. Worse yet, nobody could even guess what was going to happen tomorrow.

The next day did not bring the war any closer, and that was a relief. We went about our business, trying to pretend that there weren't a hundred armed uniformed men standing around speaking a foreign tongue. Considering that we had been conquered it was thus far bloodless. Nobody got raped or killed, and there was no looting or pillaging. The invading forces were unconcerned with us, and they occupied themselves with chatting amongst themselves and smoking. Whenever we made eye contact they nodded with a ready grin and went back to their loitering. A few times they even offered to help. One old man dropped a bundle he was carrying and a young Red Army private immediately bent down and retrieved it. The elderly man nervously accepted the courtesy and nodded before beating a hasty retreat, leaving the soldier tipping his military cap in mid-gesture. One of the kids kicked the soccer ball far out of bounds and a soldier, probably an avid sports fan himself, kicked it back with aplomb. The shuls were left alone, there were no repressive measures implemented, and the *goyim* behaved as they always did. The status quo seemed to prevail. All in all, it was a refreshingly unique kind of invasion. Regardless, some residents opted for a status quo further east, and we observed several refugee families dragging their weighted down carts in that direction.

Despite the proximity of the Nazis the war was not the subject at hand for Commissar Glentz. He wanted to educate us and make us all happy comrades. And I must confess that one of his bold new plans sounded especially attractive to me. He said that the glorious communist system of education would gladly train a bright young fellow like me to be an engineer and commission me to run a train. I had never dreamed of anything as ambitious as that. Becoming a carpenter's apprentice might have been the loftiest position to which I aspired. Compared to cleaning carp, carpentry seemed intellectually rewarding, but being a bona fide engineer was like a dream. The image of me standing in the cab of a locomotive, hand on the throttle, the other tooting the whistle, practically made me swoon. They were even going to give me a uniform, as well as unlimited free train travel. Having never even ridden on a train I imagined I'd be like Aladdin on his flying carpet. It was too good to be true. First though my parents would have to put their stamp of approval on this. If I was going to do this I'd have to convince them, and doing so meant presenting a point of view that differed from theirs. This practically amounted to defying them, something I had never done. The greatest test of wills between us heretofore had been two Seders before when I went against my mother's ad-

vice and ate a second helping of kugel. The belly ache convinced
me to thereafter accept their sage counsel. This time though I was
determined to prevail. My father was just as adamant.

"No Ovram, you'd have to live among *goyim*. They'd give you
tref to eat and you'd have no choice. It's a sinful existence out there!
Besides I'm not getting any younger and you're the man of the family after me. You have no brothers and neither do I. What will your
mother and sisters do without you?"

He had strong arguments, first warning me about an impious
life and then using guilt. I had anticipated the second part, and was
ready with a decent comeback.

"Dad, they pay engineers! I've thought the whole thing out.
When I finally become an engineer I'll send all of my pay home to
the family. It's probably more than the fish business makes now.
And I could give free train rides to all of you. Anyway, the school's
only thirty miles away, which is close by train. I could come back
all the time."

My salary argument overshadowed the impiety problem for the
moment, and all he could do was shake his head slowly and say, "I
don't know. I just don't like it."

After I mentioned the failing fish trade I was worried I might
have offended him. After all, when a man loses his ability to provide
for his family he feels emasculated. But father was not offended,
because he never saw himself primarily as a business man in the first
place. *Gescheft* was not his thing. It was just a necessity for buying
a few things. His real avocation was religion. He knew that everything emanated from God and it was in our best interest to glorify
Him. *Baruch Hashem*. He used to always say that worshipping God
was as basic as watering the roots of a tree. If you do that then all
the parts of the tree will thrive. Absolute pronouncements about the
almighty dropped from his lips on a daily basis. He might be reading and then look up and say, "If God wants to kill you nobody can

protect you, and if God wants to protect you nobody can kill you!"
And when the Nazi presence on the west bank of the San hurt his
business it merely meant that he had more time for praying.

Arguing with my mother was less direct than confronting my
father. My main position with mother was to convince her to help
me convince father I really didn't have any logic to sway her, so I
just whined. I was also handicapped in my negotiations with her by
my fear that she might mention the candy filching. I'd always suffered grievous guilt over those sweet thefts though she had never
said a word. Like Poe's Telltale Heart I was sure she really knew.
Ultimately though, it all boiled down to whining. I prevailed upon
their common sense to accept that it was time for me to leave the
nest, contribute to the family's welfare, and align myself with a
nation committed to fighting anti-Semitism. But it was all just nagging, the modus operendi of the spoiled. I had been told many times
by my friends that I was too used to getting my way. Of course, it
was probably the result of preferred treatment by my parents. The
exuberance felt at my birth had never really subsided. I was still
the long awaited boy, the son every father and mother wants. They
might suggest I already ate enough *kugel,* but they never actually
denied me a third helping. This however was the biggest test so far.
Of course, even if I was victorious I knew there would be sacrifice
on my part. First of all, I would be away from my family for the first
time, though I couldn't even imagine what that would be like. I'd
be leaving the love and warmth of my sisters and the camaraderie
of my friends. Then, there were the specific deficits, like missing
Marisha's cooking. And there'd be no more shabbos feasts. Even
though I was only thirty miles away, less than an hour by train I was
told, the distance from Sieniawa to the station was twelve miles by a
very slow horse drawn cart, and could take hours, condemning me
to travel on Shabbat, a sin my father would not allow.

The ultimate detail of my plan was a clincher provided to me by the Soviet Authorities. The Reds, our so-called friends and saviors, had announced their plans to shut down our local school. Stalin did not approve of capitalistic Polish public education, and wasted no time in closing its doors. As Jews revered formal education, and our only access to it was now terminated, the engineering school offered the sole alternative. That point, plus a great deal of nagging, finally weakened my father's position and he relented. Both my parents were heartsick over it, and after informing me of his acquiescence he walked me outside to talk to me in the waning moments of twilight.

"Ovram. You're becoming a man, so you have to be aware of so many things. All your life I've been teaching you how be a *mensch* and live with dignity in this world. I've taught you to honor God above all. We all see that the world is changing before our eyes. I don't like it, I'll tell you that. However, there's no denying it. But Ovram, that doesn't change a fundamental thing. God is still to be honored. Do not be deluded by the modern world. Who knows what things you will see once you leave here? I am afraid for you. I must tell you that I am afraid for all of us. I pray that the lessons you have learned in Sieniawa will protect you out in the world. I love you, so I trust you. You go with the blessings of your mother and me. Write to us, and come back and see us as soon as you can. You know how much your mother and sisters are going to miss you. Above all, Ovram, keep Hashem within your heart."

I was elated over getting my fathers' permission and blessing, but having it I was forced to contemplate its significance. I was nonchalantly discussing the thirty mile distance to the school without confronting the fact that my own father had probably never traveled a greater distance in his life. He had moved to Sieniawa from Belz, just thirty miles away to the north east. But those thirty miles brought him to Sieniawa and total contentment. The subject of why he made that move was never discussed or even broached.

He never mentioned it, and it would have been unseemly for us children to bring it up. In spite of his limited travels he spoke of the world as if he knew it in its most fundamental sense. What motivated people here, in Belz or in Constantinople was universal, and wherever you died ultimately mattered not. You would be judged for your character whether you were from a castle on the Danube or a shtetl near the San. He married a local maiden and never considered if the grass was any greener anywhere else. But for me, thirty miles seemed like it would be just the beginning. I had only seen the world in photos, but I wanted the real thing. And if the Soviet engineering school brought it to me, then I would embrace it.

One political thing I learned quickly was that totalitarians don't mince words or waste time. No sooner did I sign up for engineer school than I was scheduled to begin. I would have to leave home and study in the first railway station to the east in another small town called Lubaczow. In reality it was not very far, but having never left home it seemed like the other side of the world. Marisha made me a farewell dinner which I greedily over-ate. I could barely sleep from excitement, and in the early hours of the following morning I hugged all my sisters and my mother, climbed aboard our old wagon and let Babe and my father personally escort me to the train station. Actually it was not a proper station at all, but some wooden planks posing as a platform next to a bend in the tracks. The local population hardly warranted a real depot, so several area villages shared the crude collection of boards, collecting and depositing passengers there just as we did. On the way there my father repeated the advice he had given me the night before, though he spoke in a less assured tone. A great sadness enveloped him, and words, even words about God, failed him. His son, the light of his life, was going away, and he felt powerless and miserable. I perceived his melancholy but it could not dim my own elation over the coming adventure. To him the clip clop of the horse counted out the last precious remaining moments of my childhood. For me it was a countdown to the start of my new life. Our mare went too fast for my father, yet too slow for me. When we finally got to the tracks we made some small talk about the train and the rails and the specific instructions that Commissar Lentz had given us. Now that the Germans were just across the river this pile of lumber was the end of the line. The railway came here just for the benefit of a few miserable hamlets, but no longer dared to venture further westward.

We weren't there twenty minutes when we heard the chugging. There was no dramatic steam whistle to herald its coming, but its noise could hardly be mistaken for anything else. It was as if the executioners were coming for my father, but I was so excited I almost wet myself. The most elaborate machine I had heretofore seen was the weekly bus. Pictures of locomotives graced our text books however, and I knew that the continuous puff of smoke approaching over the trees signified an iron monster that dwarfed all other motorized land transportation. The sound got louder, and my father started praying for my protection. It finally emerged from the trees in all its deafening clanging glory, and my father's voice rose in competition, shouting his thanks to the Lord of Hosts for protecting me. It screeched to a tumultuous stop and released a torrent of steam, enveloping everything within fifty feet in an unearthly cloud. My first train did not disappoint. I was awestruck though Babe was scared out of her wits. Her whinny of condemnation of such cacophonous modernity could not go unnoted. As for my poor father he was already paralyzed from grief.

I retrieved my two bundles and readied to climb aboard. We possessed no such thing as actual luggage. Who in our family traveled? So, my mother had wrapped up my clothes in a blanket and tied it with cord, wiping her eyes every few seconds as she did. If my father was depressed my mother was desolate. Her baby boy was leaving home. The other smaller bundle was full of leftovers from Marisha's farewell banquet.

As soon as the train came to a complete stop a conductor climbed down with some papers in his hand. He glanced at them and then at me.

"Feder, Ovram?"

I was amazed by such efficiency. If I had been a big city boy from someplace like Warsaw I might've likened the experience to comic book encounters with space ships and aliens. But I was an unsophisticated rube from a tiny town with dirt roads, and there was no point of reference for my introduction to the twentieth century.

My father was too heavyhearted to be impressed by the industrial revolution. Still floundering in his emotional trance he nodded an abrupt greeting to the conductor and handed up the bundles. Then he turned to me gravely and said, "May God be with you."

He hugged me longer than he ever had in my life and put his hand on my head, murmuring, *"Shma Yisroel adenoi elohenu adenoi echad."*

I confirmed that I was indeed Ovram Feder, and then climbed aboard the stairs of the coach. At once, the industrial revolution lurched. The ever efficient totalitarians were not going to waste any more time than absolutely necessary on this pile of boards in the middle of the forest. Perhaps it even resented having to run in reverse. There was no siding to turn around, and it seemed mildly anticlimactic to start my first journey by going backwards. On the other hand, it provided my first lesson in the operation of modern mechanized transportation. They could go in either direction, besting Babe, though she took no notice of it.

"Goodbye papa. I'll come back soon. Goodbye"

My father waved until the backwards train rounded the turn

from whence it had emerged just four minutes previously. He had a lonely ride back to Sieniawa, and though I was forlorn to leave my family I was elated by my virgin excursion on the iron horse into the great world beyond our little village.

LEAVING HOME

|||

I deposited myself upon a leather bound sofa that looked far more comfortable than it actually was, and looked around. Besides me and the conductor the only other passenger was a soldier who was such a veteran of train travel he was sound asleep and snoring, providing fierce competition for the thundering engine.

The fastest I had ever moved in my life was in a foot race. Now I was absolutely flying. The conductor informed me that we were moving at thirty miles an hour, which only gave me a foggy notion of our rate of movement, but the forest moving past my field of sight let me know that I was breaking my own personal land record. After a few minutes the dizzying speed and constant vibration made me nauseous, and I had to sit still and close my eyes. Soon thereafter the train slowed and we came to a turn around where I got my second lesson in modern railroad procedure. There was a short stretch of parallel tracks with another engine on it. The cars were detached from its locomotive, and the other waiting engine, facing east, was backed up and attached to the short line of cars. Now the very same train took off, but in a direction that appeared forward as opposed to backward. The conductor bragged that we could move faster forward than backwards, and that we would soon reach fifty. He laughed when he did, because his novice passenger was wide-eyed with terror and shaking. I had to sit as quietly as possible with my eyes squeezed shut, and think about something soothing from Sieniawa, my only point of reference. I thought of the houses, the trees, the people, and little by little I was able to sneak occasional peeks. After what seemed like a long time I was comfortable enough to open my eyes and take a good look around. The conductor took pity on me and sat down to comfort me.

"Don't look to the side. It'll make you uncomfortable. If you sit facing backwards and watch the forest going by in reverse it's more calming."

Relaxed by his prescription I asked him some questions about the engineer school, but he pled utter ignorance about it. Although he had been a conductor on the Polish railway system for twenty years he didn't understand what the Russians were doing here. We chatted for a few more minutes, and then the juggernaut stopped by another pile of boards in the middle of nowhere. A farmer with a bundle of produce climbed aboard like he'd done it a hundred times before, and we were soon back to cruising speed. We stopped just one more time, and by then even I was used to it. We swept in an arc, southwest to northwest, until we ended up at our destination, a town called Lubaczow, twenty five miles west of Sieniawa, as the crow flies, though nearly double that in our semi-circular route. It was a bona fide railroad station, so I got my horizons broadened yet again. The signs were in Polish, but I saw the same hammer and sickle emblem that they had hung in the old school house in my village. Looking back I can imagine what culture shock the residents of that place must have been going through. Of course, hailing from the virtual time warp of Sieniawa as I did it was hard to discern any difference between one political symbol and another, so the coat of arms of Poland and the Soviet hammer and sickle were equally foreign to me. Everyone here was probably gripped with anguish over the presence of these imperialist heathen invaders, but it was all so overwhelming to me I suffered no disillusion. My grand adventure was on track and on schedule. Everything I saw, smelled, heard and felt was new and exciting.

The conductor did not have to direct me anywhere, because the engineer school was right in the station. As instructed by Commissar Glentz I reported, and they received me with pomp befitting the circumstances. The man who appeared to be the teacher shook my hand in almost comical manner and said, "Welcome comrade Feder. I am your instructor, Comrade Chalik. Address me as Comrade Teacher. Then, the students stood up and repeated the greeting in unison. There were about forty students, wearing what appeared to be uniforms identical to the one worn by the conductor. They were seated along long tables, fiddling with some contraptions I didn't recognize. There were a few pictures of men on the wall. One had a big bristling moustache and full head of thick hair slicked back. He also seemed to be wearing some kind of tunic with big buttons. The other looked older and wore a regular suit and tie like the businessmen I had always seen getting off the weekly bus back home. He was bald, and had an odd kind of beard, trimmed around his mouth but with clean shaven cheeks. The teacher himself was young and also looked like a businessman. He had no facial hair, and wore wire rimmed spectacles. He called on one of the students to give me a guided tour and get me settled. As there was little to show the entire tour lasted all of five minutes. My guide's name was Dimitri, but he indicated that I should call him Comrade Dimitri. He showed me the other classroom, identical to the one I had already seen, including the portraits on the wall, but it was empty. Then he showed me the dining hall, equal in size to the sum of both classrooms. While I was there I invited Dimitri to share some of the lunch I had packed. He accepted, but had to correct me for neglecting to call him comrade. I opened the oversized cloth napkin and we dug in. Comrade Dimitri ate rapidly, nervously looking around, and indicated I should do the same as we were expected back in class quite soon. Apparently he had never tasted any of these Jewish delicacies before and ended his culinary experimentation abruptly. He then led me outside to the end of the platform to several cattle cars which had been converted to student dormitories with wooden bunk beds and boxes for our belongings. It was not what a typical college student might expect of a dorm room, but it was an impressive example of Soviet recycling ingenuity, and it looked fine to me. My own room back home was hardly less Spartan. Dimitri showed me the unclaimed bunks out of the ten that were there, and I staked my claim, leaving my bundles on top of it. My guide immediately corrected me, pointing to the box at the foot of the bed. Between his nervous eating and this knee jerk reprobation concerning my luggage I should have perceived that the atmosphere at school was strict. Of course, submission to authority was nothing new to me. Besides honoring my parents and public school teachers I had been brought up in Orthodox Judaism which in and of itself is rife with rules. And *cheider* was as strict and exacting as any institution. I was so accustomed to obeying orders and respecting regulations I didn't take any special notice of the severity of Soviet totalitarianism until it was too late.

Upon returning to class they presented me with my own uniform. It was impossible for me to hide my excitement, and comrade teacher wholeheartedly approved my request to put it on at once, simultaneously commending my eagerness to become a glorious cog in the great Soviet machinery of progress. Of course, such rhetoric was utterly lost on me. My head was already swimming from the trip, and this new way of talking just confused me. Instead of plainly speaking these people were always making speeches, spouting platitudes about their government's excellent agenda. Thus far my father had been my main influence in life, and the only entity he ever glorified was God. Regardless, the whole experience, from bullet train to unique apparel, was extraordinary. With no mirrors in the cattle car to admire my bold countenance I paused before a window in the station to behold the new Ovram Feder, glorious Soviet cog, and took a moment to tilt my cap rakishly. What an inconceivable day. Just hours before I had met my first master of the iron horse, and now I was arrayed as finely as him. What next?

I returned to class with my chest puffed out like a rooster expecting further praise. Comrade teacher though was all business, and just wanted me to take my seat along side my comrades and join the revolution, devoid of self indulgent, petty bourgeoisie, false pride. It was just a brief moment of disappointment, but it was an omen that the days of special treatment were at an official end. For fourteen years my whole family had indulged every caprice of the male scion, and I had grown happily accustomed to my role as sun of the Feder solar system. Now I was expected to sacrifice my individual happiness to the greater good of their cultural revolution. Clearly, I had a lot to learn, and they wasted no time in showing me the socialist ropes. When addressing me pity imbued their every tone and gesture. They seemed to feel truly sorry for anyone so one hundred percent ignorant. When they realized I had no idea who the mustached man in the picture was, they stared at me, mouths agape, for so long they looked like a still life painting. Adoring the man as they clearly did, their attempts to objectively describe him failed, and I was left to my own devices to piece together what his role was.

"You mean he's like the king?"

Such an archaic term produced gales of laughter from my comrades, so I was forced to take another stab at it. Obviously king was too puny a term to define this person's role, so I went for broke.

"You mean he's like the Messiah?"

The room fell deadly silent, and the students turned as one to Comrade Teacher.

"Comrade Ovram, this is your first day, so I will be tolerant of your benighted circumstances. So, listen well. Religion is the opiate of the masses, and concepts like God and the Messiah are fictitious fairy tales for little children."

Nobody had ever said such a thing to me and I wasn't sure I understood. I recognized some of the words, but the overall meaning eluded me. As I was about to reassert my intellectual independence a classmate coughed. It sounded a little phony, and the boy apologized for the disturbance. Glancing his way when it happened, along with everyone else, it seemed as if he were looking back only at me and imperceptivity shaking his head. Comrade teacher took advantage of what he erroneously interpreted as my deference, and continued.

"In any case Comrade, Marshal Stalin is our beloved leader, a shining example of revolutionary manhood. His courage, strength of will, keen intelligence, and benevolent character, qualify him to rule, and he need not rely on such invention as holy piety to affirm his right to govern. Through his personal sacrifice, empathy for the common man, and visionary determination, he has proven himself to be greater that any make believe God up in the sky."

As Comrade Teacher carried on my coughing comrade looked at me askance and subtly signaled to me to stifle any further protest. While I was every bit as ignorant as the teacher implied I was not stupid. The coughing boy's message was clear and I knew that we'd discuss this later, away from prying ears and eyes.

When the teacher's biography of Papa Joe drew to a close several students wiped tears from their eyes. And seeing as how catching one boy up on revolutionary history was distracting the others from the matters at hand it was decided to continue my education later and resume the class that my arrival had interrupted.

The class I had momentarily stopped involved fixing a small apparatus about which I was as equally ignorant as everything else. Being engineers meant understanding the functions of a huge machine, but we had to start small. If we could learn to take apart and reassemble a relatively uncomplicated device, such as a loom or sewing machine, then one day maybe we'd understand a locomotive.

After my first day of class, and my first serving of Soviet institutional cuisine, which did not compare favorably with Marisha's, I got to know the other students. They were mostly Polish gentiles from the surrounding area, but there were a few other Jews. One of them was comrade cough, and he brought me up to speed on Karl Marx and atheism.

"Ovram, they don't believe in God or religion. Not Catholic or Lutheran or Eastern Orthodox or Jewish. They just say that God doesn't exist, and you gotta go along with it and keep your trap shut. Nobody prays or goes to church or celebrates holidays. That's the way it is. But at least they don't act like anti-Semites. Not so far anyways."

As they didn't go to church we got most of the weekend off. And as I now qualified for a one hundred percent discount on the train, I took advantage of the free time and went home. As long as I was back in class on Monday morning it was alright. My second train trip was even better than the first, because I experienced less travel sickness. And the horse ride to Sieniawa crept at such a snail's pace I almost jumped off and ran.

My family was so elated with my surprise visit there was no mention made of my traveling on the Sabbath. Half the town came to see me and admire my uniform. My sisters doted on me, and parents couldn't hide their pride in Sieniawa's most urbane citizen. The tiny bit of traveling I had done this past week qualified me as a raconteur in comparison with most everyone else, and there was no end of questions about the great big wonderful world out there. Mostly though I wanted to be with my family and gorge myself on shabbos left-overs. Best of all, my brief return raised my father's spirits. When he had seen me off the week before he felt as if he might not see his son for a long time, if ever again, but now he realized I wasn't so far away after all. For the rest of my visit he had a smile stuck on his face, and when he drove me to the tracks he was chatty instead of dour. Of course, he still warned me to be wary about the ways of the goyim. After all, whatever else the communists were they were certainly goyim. I shared with him what the other Jewish engineer students had told me about Marx and Trotsky and other Jews involved in the communist movement, but this did little to assuage his concern. He was still content to be with me, and when I boarded the train, taking a moment to introduce him to the conductor, who was now practically my buddy, he waved a joyous farewell. "See you next week!"

Back in class I was getting more in tune with the rhythm of totalitarian life. They spent nearly as much time teaching me Marxist Doctrine as they did science, necessary for future engineers. I even had to join the Soviet version of the Boy Scouts. It was like a juvenile introduction into joining the communist party, without which I would never be allowed to become a real engineer. One thing though took precedence over my indoctrination into socialism, and that was the war. Technically, the Russians weren't in it, which everyone was now calling World War Two, but they had their own small one going on against Finland. Back in public school I had been pretty good at geography and knew where the fighting was going on, but what wasn't as clear was why. My teacher tried to tell us that Finland was the aggressor, but it was hard to believe that such a tiny country would pick a fight with gigantic Russia. Apart from that we heard that the Germans had also attacked France, Belgium, England, the Netherlands and other countries, besides continuing their occupation of Poland. I didn't believe it, but I kept my mouth shut about it. I kept my mouth shut about most everything. I did what I was told, followed the rules and became a good student. And on weekends I continued to go home. For my family my weekly visits were still a thrill, but I felt guilty that they now anticipated the Sabbath as that time when junior came home. It had become my day instead of the Lord's. They even cooked special main courses for me, like chicken with prunes. Of course, father was as observant as ever, and it was a pleasant surprise that the atheist communists had not shut down the shuls yet, or impeded Jewish life in any way. As far as World War Two and Sieniawa were concerned, so far so good. Business was dreadful, but they still had enough to eat. Poland was always fertile, and even if you didn't become rich you could always fill your belly.

Several months passed and I was feeling very confident. I had no problems at school or home, and the war seemed far away. As per custom I went home for a weekend of eating and relaxing. My sisters showed me the dance steps they had learned from the Victrola girl, and we all had a great time. Sunday afternoon rolled around and I put on my clean uniform. Marisha had taken up the custom of washing it whenever I visited. I pulled on my heavy winter coat over my uniform and picked up my little bundle of food which I now shared with the other Jewish students at the engineer school, and walked out to our cart. Father was standing with our mare, examining its eyes.

"Ovram, the mare's a little under the weather and I'd rather not tax her anymore today. So, just take Nikolai's wagon."

Nikolai was the owner of a wagon and brace of draught horses that went daily to the pile of boards that was our train station. I often got a ride from him one or both ways, so it was nothing for me to take it now. I hugged everyone in my family and walked over to Nikolai's place. It was quite cold and starting to snow. Nikolai was all set to go and we were away in seconds. With two horses

Nikolai's wagon was faster than our one horse power cart, and I anticipated a trip of a little less than an hour. The train wouldn't be there for me for another two hours so we had plenty of time.

I tightened my coat collar because the snow was starting to fall much harder. The larger animals were snorting and smoke was pouring out of their large nostrils with each breath, not unlike the train. They knew the way so well Nikolai could just as well sleep, and he often did. He was so bundled up his girth made him appear like a third horse up there on the wagon with me. The other two horses continued to maneuver by rote, each step becoming more of a trudge due to the mounting flurries. After twenty minutes the snow was up to their knees. After half an hour their legs were no longer visible, nor was our progress. The horses were strong, but the white powder was so thick and dense even those brutes could hardly walk. Each step was a challenge and they snorted and neighed in protest with Nikolai's uncharacteristic urging. What I thought would be a typical leisurely trot to the tracks was now an anxiety ridden race. And it became unbearably tense when I heard the locomotive. Among the quiet leafless stands of winter trees, and out in the open stretches between them, the chugging sound of the motor was growing more insistent by the moment, and I realized we might miss the train. And as hard as Nikolai tried he could neither cajole nor oblige his great equine beasts to negotiate the road any longer. We crept along and I heard the train around the next bend, releasing steam. My friends on the train were probably delaying their departure for my benefit, and had they been able to hear me, as I could them, they might have procrastinated five more minutes. But they could not hear a horse snort a half mile away, no matter the animal's girth, and they begrudgingly began their return journey without me. I heard the now familiar sounds of the locomotive accelerate, and within a minute the thick carpet of white absorbed all sound. We were left standing in a snowfall, testing the theory of whether or not a locomotive makes noise in the woods if nobody is there to hear it. I missed the train back to school, but thought that even the rule fixated communists would understand an act of nature and forgive one of their best students his first tardy.

Nikolai was kind enough not to abandon me to an icy fate. We collected some brush and built a nice fire along the tracks. Even the horses drew near. And with my bundle of shabbos leftovers we were able to pass the rest of the day there, and spend the night as well. It stopped snowing shortly after the train departed, so conditions, while bad, did not worsen. We had heat, food and company. In the morning Nikolai left, and I sat, tending the fire, waiting for the next train. After only a few hours it came and I eagerly jumped on board. My friend the conductor greeted me, but with a chagrin.

"You weren't in class this morning, and they're a little upset with you."

"The snow slowed the cart."

"Don't tell me. Tell them."

I heard what he was saying, but I thought little of it. After all, I was popular with the students and I was practically Comrade Teacher's favorite. It'll be okay.

When I walked into class I flippantly tossed off a quick, "Sorry, I was snowed in," and sat down. Comrade Teacher did not seem glad to see me, and the students were staring at their own feet. In a tone I had rarely heard before a cold voice called me to my feet.

"Comrade Ovram, are you aware that the people's engineering class begins punctually at eight in the morning?"

It was such an obvious and rhetorical question I hardly knew how to respond. Thus far, in the four months I had been here, I had never had any problems. The friends I made early on had guided me, and told me to strictly obey the rules if I wanted to stay out of serious trouble.

"I am sorry Comrade Teacher. But the snow was so heavy the horses couldn't...."

"Be still Comrade Student!"

I was stunned by how shrill he had become. He directed me to follow him, and he led me into the dining hall. At the dining room tables were seated a committee of men and women, convened, I soon learned, for the sole purpose of reprimanding me.

'Thank you, Comrade Teacher," said one of the women. I was directed to stand before them, and after reading some paperwork one of the men looked up and leveled a malevolent gaze at me. It was not so much mean-spirited as it was cold and impersonal.

"Comrade Student. It has been brought to our attention that you routinely go home on weekends, yet you have never once requested permission to do so. In so doing you have exploited the people's trains for your petty bourgeoisie holidays. And now you take advantage of the people's generous dining hall. They cooked breakfast for you and you did not have the decency to eat it. Valiant Soviet soldiers are dying in their attempts to repel the Finnish invaders. They could use that food. Yet we deny them to give it to you, and you lack the spirit of cooperation to come and honor it. You have beguiled us, lied to us, robbed from us, and you are nothing more than a parasite, sucking at the teat of Mother Russian, and you are bereft of the impulse to contribute to its noble cause. Furthermore, you feel no shame for what you've done. All you feel is fear for the retribution you deserve. This is the appreciation you show to Marshal Stalin for extending a helping hand to the people of Poland."

It seemed like so much to take in, but I felt compelled to defend myself.

"I am lonely for my family. I meant no harm, and certainly harmed no one. I had no mischief in mind. The horses...."

Again I was cut off. From then on I was denied the right to defend myself. They wanted to make an example of me lest other impertinent Polish kids defy the authority of the Soviet Union. For the crimes of exploiting the Soviet Union and shirking my duties I was sentenced to a year in jail. They put handcuffs on me and led me outside where I was instructed to sit on the bench and keep my mouth shut. I was desolate, and more than a little afraid. Previously one of the most popular students I was now friendless. Everybody knew from past experience to shun me lest they get included in my dilemma. Practically speaking, I no longer existed.

They were going to take me Lvov, an actual city, bigger than any I'd ever seen, fifty miles due east, and temporarily incarcerate me there for two weeks. Then they were going to send me three hundred miles further east to the grand city of Kiev to serve out my sentence. All this for being a little late to school. It seemed like a bad dream. I'd awake any second, shake the snow flakes off me and ask Nikolai for the time. I hadn't injured anyone or stolen anything, or even tried. There must be some mistake. Sitting there I reflected on my first day and Dimitri's terror over the possibility of being caught eating with me. And my coughing Jewish friend had made it clear from day one to always follow the rules. Now I saw what happened to transgressors. The Soviet system did not tolerate dissent. No matter how slight or unintentional, this swift justice was one way of maintaining order. If you were an enemy, such as a Finn, they might shoot you, hang you, or torture you, but a civilian citizen of the Soviet Union, guilty of a political crime, as opposed to a violent one, such as me, was always locked up. That way the government appeared benevolent. Of course their jails were so awful they prompted more suicide than anywhere else on Earth.

Having never been in any jail there was no way of knowing what was in store for me. But what I was most afraid of was losing contact with my family. They must be told. Next week I wouldn't show up, and they'd think something went wrong. They would go and speak with Nikolai and he'd tell them about our delay, if he hadn't already. My absence would confirm a suspicion that I was being punished. My father would get Nikolai to take him to the tracks and wait for the train. When it came he would speak to the conductor and inquire about me. Then he would take his first train trip and come and visit me. But how? If he didn't hurry I'd be three hundred miles away. Such a distance for our family was unimaginable. They might as well be off to France or Peru or Palestine. But at least they would know about me, and that I'd be back in a year. Knowing nothing at all would be unbearable. If I could just get some word to them my ordeal would be less by half. But I could hardly send a message with any of my classmates, because nobody would get close to me. They were petrified, but not stupid. Surely, they would realize how vital it was to get word to my poor family. They must know that I'd do the same for them. Yes, my parents would find out, if from no other source than the conductor. They'd surely learn my fate, and deal with a year of separation. They wouldn't have to come this far after all. They'd miss me at first, and stare at my empty chair at the shabbos table. Finally, my father would command that it be removed and placed in a corner. Occasionally my mother or sisters or Marisha would cry when serving one of my favorite dishes, but those tears would dry up after a month or two. Then, after ten months or so they'd get excited, anticipating my return. And finally, they would prepare the biggest feast they ever made to celebrate my release and return. It would be bad, but not unbearable.

When it was lunchtime the other students went into the dining room, reconverted back from a courtroom, and I prayed they'd remember to bring me something. My prayers went unanswered however, because they were afraid to get within fifty feet of me. I hadn't eaten since the afternoon before when Nikolai and I enjoyed our snowbound picnic of shabbos leftovers. Remembering that made me even hungrier, and I felt that forced starvation was far too harsh a punishment for someone as young as me. What a relief it was when Comrade Teacher showed up with a plate for me. The other authorities had departed, leaving just a fat policeman to accompany me to Lvov. With his bosses gone Comrade Teacher reverted back to his usual self, and convinced my guard to allow me one last meal before commencement of my year long diet of prison food. Eating with relish I became more convinced than ever that the conductor would somehow get word to my parents. I just had to endure a year.

TO LIVE OR TO DIE

IV

The train that I took back and forth between Sieniawa and Lubaczow was never more than six cars long, including locomotive and tender, but the train that carried me to Lvov was at least ten times that length. I had met hundreds of bus passengers from Krakow, stopping off in Sieniawa on their way to Lvov, but I never thought I'd actually go there myself. Of course, my circumstances hardly qualified me as a tourist or traveling drummer, and I just sat on the train like a lamb on its way to slaughter. My police escort stayed glued to me and he suffered from gas so bad nobody else would sit near us. Of course, I had no choice myself. He squirmed to release it and had no shame over it. The poor slob had probably been that way his whole life and had grown quite used to it. Beyond that he was not such a bad sort. He was old enough to remember life before the glorious revolution and had not yet been transformed into a socialist robot. But he also knew how the game was played, and that he had to protect himself by behaving like an obedient comrade whenever confronting the system. That's basically how everyone behaved. After a few minutes into the trip the fat guard fell asleep, though his flatulence did not. In a way it was worse. Awake he could adjust himself to issue silent reports, but asleep he farted as noisily as a cow. It had one salutary affect in that I lost my appetite. And after five hours of that nonstop gastric distress the train, making less noise than my traveling companion, pulled into Lvov.

From the station I could see more electric light than I imagined existed. Before I could get a good look however, the guard dragged me off to my temporary cell. It was now night, the worst possible time to arrive at such a dreary, depressing place. The guard signed some papers and I was remanded into the custody of some political authority with a high number. And like everything else its name indicated that it belonged to the people. The communist doctrine assigned ownership of everything to some vague entity called the people. I never actually met that mysterious person or committee, but I do know that there were authorities present everywhere to make you feel as if you were anything but an owner. And this place was the worst example of that impersonal proprietorship. The atmosphere, which was dirty, cold and damp, was horribly oppressive. There were faint hints of conversation growing louder by the second as I approached my new home, and as the sound grew in intensity I became terrified. As soon as I got my first look at the cell I felt that I was not meant to be there. There must be some mistake. This must be where they send the most violent anti-social criminals in Europe, but not kids like me. Why are they sending me here? Alright, I learned my lesson! I'll ask for permission before visiting home next time! I promise! And I'll never be late again, I swear. You convinced me. I'll be a good little comrade from now on! Now take me back, please. I want to be an engineer. I want my momma! With every step my panic intensified. There was a knot in my stomach as big as a turnip, and I was almost paralyzed with fear. My legs were numb and my vision was blurry and growing dark. Then a rusty iron door squealed opened and I was pushed into a large cell filled with dozens of boys jeering and cackling at my fate. When the door clanged shut they also hooted and yelled at the guard who just ignored them. I retreated at once to a back corner and stood there, leaning against the wall with my arms folded across my abdomen hugging my own arms. I stared at the ground trying to ignore everything else, and my breath came in short gasps. My vision was still blurred, and I had to blink back a few tears that had escaped to betray me. As the newest thing in the cell I was the center of interest and curiosity, and so far I had not made a good impression. Furthermore, my senses were overwhelmed with the aggression that was coming my way. The old veterans had formed a reception committee for me, as they probably did whenever that monolithic door admitted a fresh victim.

"We got a little lost boy here!"

"Lost for sure!"

"Yeah, he's too good to be here with the likes of us!"

"Yeah. Too good to be with idiots like us!"

With every bellicose syllable they got closer. And just as they stepped into punching range a large form appeared between us. This kid, bigger than the others, looked older and more mature as well.

"I'm just gonna have myself a word with the new meat. That is, if you don't mind. You don't, do you?"

This guy talked even tougher than the others, and my sense of danger soared as I anticipated getting a sound thrashing from him. He grabbed me by the collar and practically lifted me off my feet which made the welcoming committee snigger in appreciation. He backed me up against a wall, and I felt absolutely doomed. This galoot was going to slaughter me. I had nothing to anticipate but his fist in my face. The next three seconds might even alter my looks permanently. Instead of hitting me though he leaned in close, his nose practically touching mine, and whispered in a threatening tone.

"Now listen up. You got exactly one second to get your shit together before these punks eat you alive. If you're not hard as nails in here you'll break apart."

To further dissuade the others from getting a piece of me, he yelled, "Got that?!"

As soon as his voice echoed off the cell walls he returned to his whispered tutorial.

"Now tell me to fuck off and push me hard."

I was still gripped by panic, but what he said next shook me to my soul.

"Do you want to live or do you want to die?"

There was no time to consider anything. In that instant, less than a heartbeat, I went through prison college. This person was obviously a veteran, yet for no apparent reason he took mercy on me. This was a crash course and I had to participate in my commencement exercise at once. So, I pushed him as hard as I could and delivered my graduation speech.

"Fuck off!"

My professor fell back or at least pretended to. He recovered, stood tall and glared at me. He turned around to face the others who were by now duly impressed with the new meat, and then he retreated back to his own corner. Flushed with fake victory and newly acquired bravado, I glared at the ad hoc reception committee and successfully bluffed them. Everyone fell silent, the subject was changed, and they went and sat back down. To keep my new associates at bay I assumed a scowl on my face that was half Benito Mussolini and half mountain gorilla. Inside my head though I was trying to comprehend what had just taken place. It all happened so fast. One thing for sure, that big guy saved me from a bad beating. But another thing became clear to me. As benevolent as this guy was in trying to help me he would have wasted his time had I not caught on so quickly. From deep within me there awoke a dormant trait that had been ingrained in my genetic makeup, waiting to be revealed. For centuries my people had been faced with disaster which could only be averted by the quickest of responses. No matter how comfortably settled we were in Eastern Europe we might be confronted by doom at any moment. All it took was a drunken gentile to start chanting the words Christ Killer and fifteen minutes later a mob would be crashing down the door of some Jew who was tranquilly reading a book in his favorite easy chair. As soon as he heard them he'd have to take action or perish. No more book or easy chair. No more house. The alternative was no more life. He had to recognize the situation and immediately react with the proper response. There were no multiple choices. It was flee or die. And there were other less dire circumstances where he still had to perceive subtle anti-Semitic words or attitudes and adjust his behavior to escape someone's mad wrath. Though my brush with potential violence had nothing to do with anti-Semitism, a well honed instinct to recognize danger was alive within me, and now saved me.

The mood of these teenaged beings was familiar. They were just like the gentile bullies who used to attack me in Sieniawa. I wouldn't take it from them, and I knew that I couldn't take it here either. Even though I had never been in such a situation it was clear from what the big guy said, along with my experiences back home, that standing up for myself was now more essential than ever. Of course, I was still miserable about being there. Who wouldn't be? But the physical interplay of pushing that big guy and bluffing the others had the effect of convincing not only them, but myself as well, that I could probably endure this. After all, if these guys could, why not me? And to further convince myself I thought of Sieniawa and my father.

"Ovram. You might not meet another Jew there at this engineer school. You might have to take some beatings and some abuse.

Listen to me, it won't kill you. Fight back, of course, just like you do here. But, you'll be okay. I know it. We Jews are tough people. We've taken abuse for two thousand years, and another two thousand before that, doing battle with a hundred tribes that all wanted to annihilate us. But we're still here. So, take care of yourself. They can't kill you, because our Lord wants to protect you. I know it!"

I fell asleep on the floor with the words of my father whispering in my ears. I was comforted. It was if he had wrapped his big bear like arms around me and hugged me. I was warm and safe, at least in my head. He was right. We were tough. We had to be.

In the morning I was awaken by all the other boys jostling for a position to get their breakfast. As I groggily opened my eyes I saw my mentor clearly for the first time. I hadn't really seen him the night before in the dark cell, and now I was glad to finally meet him.

"Thank you," I said.

He slapped me. Not that hard, and it was more emotional shock that physical pain. I was wide eyed and he almost did it again.

"Only babies thank people in here! Are you a baby?"

"No," was all I could dutifully reply.

He looked at me as if he were analyzing me, the way someone does when they're considering buying a horse.

"And lose that wide-eyed shocked expression. Lose it for good!"

I narrowed my eyes and made a furtive pledge never to look like a lost deer again.

"Do you want to live or do you want to die?"

I grimly looked back and sneered, "Live."

"Let's grab some bread while there is some," was all he said in response.

I followed my tutor's example and pushed my way through the crowd to where they were just starting to distribute breakfast, a bowl of cabbage soup and piece of dark bread. Soon I discovered that it was easy to confuse breakfast with dinner as they always gave us the same thing. After getting my dented metal bowl of soup and scrap of bread I followed my teacher over to his corner. Soon I learned that this was his domain, hard earned through many scrapes. The soup tasted more like salt than cabbage, and the bread made its engineer school counterpart seem like challah, but it staved off the hunger. While we ate my professor grilled me.

"What was your big crime? Why are you here?"

"I missed a half day of school."

"That's really pathetic. It might even be the single most mama's boy crime I've heard here yet. Anyone gets wind of that and you're washed up."

"So, what do I tell people?"

"Anything but the truth. Tell 'em you and a friend killed your mother's lover."

"Will they believe me?"

"Well, you can't tell anyone you're here because your teacher was cross with you. They gotta think you're dangerous. They gotta respect you. In here fear equals respect."

"Tha..."

I started to thank him and then remembered not to. So, I changed gears and spat out, "You're damn right!"

This made him grin in spite of himself, and he congratulated me with, "Yeah. You'll make it alright!" Next he dug deeper.

"This isn't another trick question. Just tell me the truth, now. What's your name?"

I felt nervous for a second. Maybe this guy was like the goyim in Sieniawa, and would like to bully a Jew. He certainly could play the role if he wanted to, because he was so much bigger than me. But I decided he sounded reasonable enough to trust.

"Ovram Feder."

"Oh Jesus! Why don't you just carry a sign around your neck that says, punch me!"

Now I started to feel uneasy. My professor continued.

"Me personally, I don't care if you're a Yid or whatever, but you're probably gonna be the only one in here, so you better do something about it. Look, most of the kids here aren't really bad. They're just victims of too many petty rules, like you. But they're also a bunch of ignorant morons. Plus, they're gonna send you to Kiev which makes Lvov look like one of your shuls. There they'll toss you in with who-knows-how-many other rule breakers. But you can be sure none of them answers to names like Ovram."

He thought for a moment and then his face lit up with self satisfaction.

"Ovram Feder, you are now Arturo. Arturo Arkadivonovitch. It fits you to a tee."

I dutifully repeated it several times, each time wrapping my mouth around it more comfortably. It was definitely a clever idea to give me a Russian sounding name. I was going to be their guest for a good while and I had to fit in. They had taken over Poland, and back in Mother Russia they were the established rulers. As I continued to refine my pronunciation my guru came up with a suggestion.

"Tell everyone they can just call you Arkadi, like a nickname! That'll go over big!"

"Damn straight," was what fell from my lips, and Pygmalion couldn't hide his glee.

"Yeah, you learned real good. Here's your diploma."

He hauled off and hit me in the face. I was so stunned my eyes automatically popped wide open in dismay. In a heartbeat I slammed my lids shut, and realized that he had done it with my best interest at heart. In truth, if he really wanted to hurt me he was big enough to have done some significant damage. Of course, everything he said made sense. I was going to have to transform myself in order to survive this year long ordeal. For most of my life I had slept in a soft bed, ate my fill, and was the object of unlimited affection. Now, I looked around and saw how harshly different my life was going to be. We slept on a cold cement floor without blankets, crapped in sight of everyone else into a barrel, and ate barely enough to keep body and soul together. And I was surrounded by kids far dumber and dirtier than me. The lack of privacy could drive a person insane, but somehow I was going to have to bear it. If it weren't for the kindness and concern of my mysterious teacher I probably wouldn't have lasted one day. I dared not express my gratitude to him, but I owed it to him. As it turned out I had learned just in time, because a new group of kids came in a few hours later. I was leaning against a wall like I owned it and one of the new lambs, every bit as green as I had been just the day before, approached me with that deadly wide-eyed expression, curious to know all about me.

"What are you in here for?"

I leveled my iciest stare at him and said, "You don't even wanna know junior!"

From then on I had a fighting chance, although that kid kept following me around like a puppy, hoping to learn jail house survival skills at the feet of the seasoned veteran. He was such a willing disciple I could have slapped him silly and he would have interpreted it as advanced Zen therapy.

The truth is, after a day anyone could pick up on the routine. Life in jail revolved around three events. The first was eating. This required a keen sense of smell to anticipate its arrival and allow you time to muscle your way to the door to be there while it was still hot and plentiful. You grabbed your portion and made a bee line for your private patch of floor. Eating led to the second event, elimination. This did not require the same spirit of competition as eating, but you had to be assertive. The public facility was an old wooden barrel in a corner of the cell furthest from the door. You stood by it to piss and, grasping the corner bars, leaned in backwards to defecate. There was a lid, of course. Between you and that barrel was a solid mass of humanity with nothing to do but make life hard on every other fellow human in the room. The golden rule did not exist in Soviet prisons in 1941. Every living soul in that mass could tell when someone needed to answer nature's call, but nobody courteously stepped aside to let you through. Few though were actually willing to fall to blows over it. After all, preventing anyone from using the barrel would have just produced an even worse smell in the room.

The barrel itself was the focus of a right of passage for the more gullible newcomers. They usually told a new arrival that everyone had to spend his first night's rest sitting on the barrel's lid. If you were too weak to duke it out right then and there then you sat on the lid and tried to fall asleep despite the nauseating stench. At some point in the night physics took over and the lid became upset by the uneven distribution of your weight, and your butt invariably plunged at least a few inches into the vile morass. The deeper you slid the greater the laughter from the mob. And if you got stuck and couldn't climb out on your own it was a catastrophe. While gales of hysteria swept through the cell you bargained away half your food for a month to get someone to pull you out. That barrel was our sole convenience. Running water was nowhere in sight.

The third daily event of life behind Soviet bars was sleeping. Although there was nothing to tire us our interior clocks obliged us to take rest when the sun did. There were no beds or chairs and the most desirable places to lie down were those furthest from the door, the barrel, or either of their paths, and only a combination of grit and tenure determined your place in the pecking order. You usually started in the worst zones and slowly worked your way to the better ones. I was only going to be here for two weeks so I had to endure a bad spot with precious little hope for progress. The room was so dense with bodies that everybody had to roll over together. There were no blankets, but the sum of our body heat assured the population that nobody died from frostbite. But the same crowd that provided warmth in the winter did the same in the summer, making June to August a sweat soaked bog. Regardless of season it was an overcrowded, filthy mess.

I tried often to associate with my guru, not so much for protection as for intelligent company. I was in total agreement with his appraisal of the intellectual capacity of most of our cell mates, and I just naturally gravitated to him. But he'd have to stay there a while longer, so he couldn't risk harming his reputation as a menace, or lose its accompanying privileges, just to pal around with Ovram Feder.

One night I was sitting on my patch of cement and was overtaken by an odd and rare mood. I recalled the Victrola and my tango lessons, and it dawned on me that I hadn't listened to any music in a long time. Though I always enjoyed the klezmers that traveled through town and played at weddings, I was not a music maven myself. But now, for some inexplicable reason, I wanted to hear music so badly I was even willing to make it myself. The one artifact of refined living that was left to me when they tossed me that cell, a comb, was still in my pocket. I remember seeing an old beggar in Sieniawa wrap a comb in a piece of paper and hum into it. It wasn't as lovely as a violin, but it had a kind of funny musical tone all its own. I already had the comb so I looked around for a piece of paper. Such a commodity was as rare as anything else in jail, so I went to my friend.

"You got a piece of paper?"

"Are you kidding me?"

I thought for a moment and tried to make him an offer.

"I'll give you my soup tomorrow morning for one sheet of paper."

He thought for a moment, and came back with, "A week."

I didn't think I could live for a week without soup, and came back with, "Two days."

"Three," was all he said, and I nodded. As long as I had the bread I could make it.

He got up and paid a visit over on the other side of the cell with another tough guy. In five minutes he came back and handed me the paper.

"Remember, three days of soup. And don't make me come looking for you."

Later I learned that he had bartered one day's worth of soup for the paper. This meant he would have two extra soups and gave up nothing. I sat back down on my little space and inspected the components of my musical instrument. The comb was about four inches long, and the paper was more than sufficient to wrap totally around it. I combined the two and stared at it. I must have been crazy. What would these jail house punks do to me when I started playing? Maybe I should forget the whole thing. But I remembered what my mentor told me. These were just school age idiots like me, and they'll probably like it. After my self inflicted pep talk I made an exploratory hum. It was just a note, but every head in the cell turned toward me. The forbidden wide eyed look made a rare appearance and then everyone pretended to be tough and impassive again. But nobody stopped me. I thought and thought but couldn't come up with a tune. What frustration! I was all set to play, but had no repertoire. Mostly, all I knew were Hebrew melodies from shul. At first I thought it would be suicide to play that in such a place, but then I realized that none of these kids had ever listened to Jewish liturgical music. None of them had even heard it once, let alone were versed in it. Finally, an old wedding song came to me. Closing my eyes to remember the tune I took a deep breath and launched into it. Every eye and ear was on me, and I actually got through it without any heckling. When I was done I opened my eyes to find everyone staring at me. It was incumbent upon me to return the stare, and I calmly put my instrument away. Before I could another prisoner spoke up.

"You know the Children's Waltz?"

I did not, and I probably wouldn't know any of the songs these guys knew. They were big city kids from Lvov, and listened to the radio all the time. They knew songs from other countries.

"Sorry, I just play what I play."

I'm not even sure what that meant, but it sounded tough. All I could do was hum another *frailoch* and hope not to get beat up. My audience granted me total artistic freedom and I was a hit. The best advice to a musician is to always leave your audience hungry, and that's just what I did. If they wanted more they'd have to tune in tomorrow. For the rest of my brief stay In Lvov I regaled my cell mates with a couple more concerts, and it helped the time pass.

With no prior warning they came to take me to Kiev. As I has nothing to pack there was not much ceremony, and I barely had a moment to turn and shoot a meaningful look back at my teacher. He understood it, and for an instant we made a nonviolent, civilized connection. Who knows what an interesting person he would have turned out to be and what friends we might have become? His brief tutelage made a big difference in my life, and it has never left me. A day does not go by when I don't reflect on it.

The train that took me to Kiev dwarfed anything that I had previously seen. Polish trains were garter snakes, and this was an anaconda. It must have had a hundred cars. Our destination was a little over three hundreds miles to the east, but the need to pass through some major cities on the way added another hundred miles to the trip. It was an almost completely flat journey, allowing the train to get up great heads of steam and reach velocities of seventy miles an hour. I had never seen another river besides the San, but now I rode on trestles over such waterways as the Bug, Styr', Ikva, Stubla, Sluc', Teterev, and Kamenka. We even crossed some more than once, because both the rivers and the tracks snaked back and forth through the same territory. We left Lvov and swept up north to Dubno and Zdolbunov, then dipped down even further south to Sepetovka, Berdicev and Kazatin. Finally we veered back north for Fastov, Bojarka, and the end of the line, Kiev, capital of the Ukraine region. I relished every mile of the journey, because my ultimate destination was an overcrowded, filthy cell with awful food. Every mile and minute was some measure of reprieve.

As every hour went by I couldn't help but wonder if that old conductor had gotten word to my parents. I even broke another commie rule and prayed that he did. Looking out the window gave me no further education after my first hour, because the panorama never varied. There were wide open spaces interspersed with small forests. Whenever I fell asleep and opened my eyes again I saw exactly the same vista. If I was lucky I caught sight of a herd of elk, and once or twice I heard a howling wolf. Many times we passed through collections of houses that reminded me of Sieniawa and it shattered my tough guy persona. I saw smoke wafting up from crude chimneys and imagined the peasant delicacies they were cooking. Maybe I had even passed a shtetl or two where impoverished shabboses were being celebrated. Even a humble Friday night dinner was far better than any I had known in a while or was likely to know for a long time to come. When would I again see a woman light candles and bring its warmth and light to her head? How many more days behind bars before my next chorus of *hamotzi lechem min ha'eretz* or *b'ray parie hagofen*? My little socialist faux pas had changed my life for good. But I took heart in what my father told me. He said we had been doing battle with tribes that wanted to annihilate us for thousands of years, but we're still here. He urged me to take care of myself, and he begged God to protect me. I hoped he was right, because it was now going to be put to the test. All too soon my reminiscing and sight seeing came to an end. We rumbled to a stop, and brutes in woolen coats came on board and dragged me off to my home of the next twelve months.

The prison was not far from the railway yard which was the most complex maze of iron rails one could possibly imagine. The whole city, though surrounded by nature, was industrial, dreary and foreboding. Bleak stretches of concrete were the norm for Kiev, and the memory of the millions of trees I saw from the window of my coach would have to suffice for quite some time.

They checked me into prison and searched me. The only thing to find was found and they took it away.

"You think this a spa? You'll have no need of a comb here you little hoodlum!"

To prove that he was right they marched me into a room and shaved off my hair. Then they threw me in a cell, my residence for the next year. There was no orientation or list of rules to observe. In Lvov I had already learned everything I needed to know. We were not here for indoctrination, education, or rehabilitation. We were shunned, plain and simple. Lock away the misfits and society will benefit. If you don't follow the rules you get punished, and that's what this was all about. Our punishment was to be penned up like cattle and ignored. A hundred kids like me were crammed into a massive room, and as soon as I walked in I asked myself if I wanted to live or die. This ultimatum from my old mentor was now my permanent barometer. Whatever I faced, no matter what they threw at me, it all boiled down to that one basic choice

There was nothing to do to pass the time, but wait for food. And if you weren't fast you fasted. Only the stealthy got fed here on a regular basis, and nobody got released from any Soviet jail fatter than when he went in, that's for sure! Every new day was exactly the same as its predecessor, and the diet suffered from the identical sameness. Monotony was our constant companion, and only by attributing some degree of importance to the trivial goings on within our microcosmic society could you endure another day. If someone had a toothache or a nocturnal omission it was topic for discussion for hours. Days blended into nights and back into days until you couldn't even determine what day of the week it was. There was no schedule, such as laundry day or exercise day. The atmosphere was bleak, and there was nothing to look forward to. At first, I tried to keep count of when it was shabbos, but it became impossible. And if you asked a guard what day it was, or anything else for that matter, you got labeled a suck-up, and targeted for abuse. Even with all that, there was something we needed to know that did not classify us as babies, and that was the war. Without being asked the guards usually had periodic updates. Mostly the news had more to do with what the Germans were up to than our part in it. The names I had learned in geography class all seemed to be getting conquered by Hitler. When I was ten I was memorizing the capitals of Scandinavian and other western European countries, and now they all seemed to be occupied by the Axis. Then we heard some eastern European countries had fallen in line with Hitler as well. Albania and Romania made pacts, and it got to the point that we were able to tie in the expansion of the Third Reich with the principle diversion in jail, gambling. Day and night home made decks of cards were dealt out to little cliques of bored juvenile convicts. Any meager remnant of individuality, such as a pair of sox, was valid stakes, and kids were constantly acquiring and then losing, and then reacquiring the same artifacts over and over. And if you had nothing you lived dangerously by wagering your next bowl of soup or piece of bread. On rare occasions some coveted *mahorka* found its way into the juvenile side of prison. *Mahorka* is a Russian ersatz tobacco, made out of God knows what. Over on the adult side of jail it was the main currency and preoccupation, but it seldom made an appearance among us children. Whatever else we were, the authorities still considered us minors, ill prepared to deal with the adult vices of cigarettes and vodka. But in the eyes of our concerned caretakers playing cards, and any other kind of gambling, seemed harmless enough to our delicate sensitivities. So, in addition to full houses and inside straights, we were betting which country the Germans would conquer next. Having almost nothing tangible to wager over, we bet on the intangible, the outcome of German aggression. But it got complicated. For instance, fights broke out over the determination of vague political status, such as neutrality.

"Yeah, well the Turks sided with 'em in the last war, and if they're not fighting 'em now then they still must be on the same side. So I win!"

"Nah, that ain't the same thing, you stupid serf. The fat guard even said so!"

Such in depth political analyses would go on for hours or days. The League of Nations was long dissolved, but such topics as fueled those long since silenced debates were still honored in our cell. Anything to stave off the tedium.

Besides adapting to Soviet rules and regulations I also had to learn to live among gentiles. Back in engineer school there were a few other Jews, and my mysterious Kiev mentor knew my secret. Here though, I was just another *goykuppe*, and had to tolerate no end of jokes and barbs about Jews. Naturally, they never said the word Jew, what to mention such urbane terms as member of the Jewish faith or Hebrew Nation. Jews were Yids, and always dirty devils. Although Marx and Lenin taught forbearance of my people, most Russians were peasants, short on formal education, and long since brain washed by the Eastern Orthodox Church and their equally ignorant parents, to see Jews as sub humans. They told jokes about how dirty and dishonest we were. And with so much time on their hands they analyzed their problematic lives and determined that it was the work of dirty dishonest Yids. Everything was their fault, from the lousy food to the incompetent bureaucracy, and I had to take it. To keep me from suspicion I made an occasional grunt of approval or nodded my head with chagrin. And if they asked me if I had any similar tales to tell I just shrugged and told them that I never even met a dirty Yid, and was glad for it. They didn't exclusively obsess over Jews though. They had a long list of others to berate. A popular target was the Uzbek. They lived far away to the southeast and it was no fib to say that I had never met one of them. Actually, until jail I hadn't even heard of them. But, if my erudite cellmates were to be believed, the Uzbeks were the stupidest people in the vast Union of Soviet Socialist Republics. Whenever they made jokes about the poor dumb Uzbeks I wondered if an Uzbeki kid was hiding among us keeping secret the true nature of his birth, just as I did. Sometimes I even found their jokes funny, though I was able to appreciate the humor even more by redirecting their mockery right back at them, a bunch of bull headed retards if I ever knew any. As I was far less gregarious than most of the other kids, but had demonstrated my reluctance to suffer fools, I slowly earned a reputation as a smart fellow, worthy of respect. Mostly they admired brute force, but the mystery of a sharp mind beguiled them and they held a begrudging regard for the strong silent types, like me.

The minutia of our humdrum lives often took the worst turns, with thievery occupying the consciousness of many. When that occurred the guards responded with the harshest possible retribution. This was a Soviet jail after all, so it was as rife with civic regulation as any other tier of the communist system. You were meant to stay in the cell and keep quiet. You didn't steal, speak unpatriotically or commit homosexual acts. Nobody actually said so, but I assumed homicide was also frowned upon. Anyway, as tempted as many of my cohorts probably were, very little theft took place. But if you did possess something it became a major concern to keep it.

Although getting robbed was a risk time itself is a heartless thief. I was still growing and my feet no longer fit inside my shoes. Of course, they were extremely worn, but one boy's trash is another's treasure, so I hid the fact that they were of no practical use to me and bartered them for a weeks' worth of another kid's bread, plus his hat. I really had no need of the hat, and it was probably a bourgeoisie affectation to wear it in the first place, but acquiring it in the bargain allowed me some jail house status, and that was important. Of course, I was now bare foot, but I would have been anyway. Meanwhile I ate slightly better for a week and got better established among the hierarchy of our little pecking order. For me, it was a win win situation. And the other kid felt good about it too. Of course, it wasn't long before he also outgrew them and did as I had done, bartering and benefiting as well. Never has a pair of shoes prompted such commerce.

Days dragged by without change, and the only welcome event was the occasional shower. Every four weeks or so they took us to a room with shower faucets and let us bathe. We stripped off our stinking clothes and rubbed ourselves under the stream of cold water. There was no soap, but it still felt wonderful. If we were fast we could even wash our clothes. We held them up to the shower head and squeezed them. The water that came out of our shirts and pants was black from the grime. After two or three rinses they started to get clear, and it was a welcome relief. Back in the cells we had to be careful not to be robbed of our clothing, and it gave us something to do, turning our shirts and pants over and over until they were dry. When we finally put our slightly cleaner clothes back on over our slightly cleaner bodies it felt great. And the day after our showers we could anticipate a trip to the barber. One by one we were led into a room where an adult prison trustee with shears relieved us of our flea infested hair right down to the scalp. Such was Soviet Prison hygiene for juvenile delinquents. Our nails were black, and we had no toothbrushes, but that rare unpredictable bath was a blessing.

Obviously, the totality of this experience must be seen of the negative side of life's ledger. But I was always a half-full-cup kind of guy and I couldn't ignore the one very positive result of my wretched period of incarceration. After about six months I spoke fluent Ukrainian. It was similar to Russian and would give me a good base to learn that tongue should the need arise. By eight months I spoke Ukrainian without a trace of Polish accent. Besides the language I was getting socially acclimated. By the time ten months had elapsed in that rotten prison I had heard so much about Russia and Stalin from the other kids I could pass for a native of the Soviet Union. The fact is I hadn't spoken a syllable of Polish or Yiddish since crossing into the Ukraine, and I was actually in danger of forgetting my native tongues. I talked like any other fifteen year old Soviet boy with all the slang, and I knew all the details of communist life. In less than a year I had been transformed into a totally different person. I was taller, spoke a different dialect, and automatically answered to the name of Arturo Arkadivonovitch. I wondered if my parents would even recognize me. And with my freedom imminent I thought about them a lot. My sisters would probably giggle over my being able to speak Ukrainian, though I'd probably get back into speaking Polish quickly enough. Hopefully, they'd let me back into engineering school, appreciative of my new found linguistic ability. My mind was abuzz with such things, even though I knew it would only make me bitter to open my eyes and see those dank prison walls. But I had calculated that I was due for release in a couple of months, and I couldn't keep my mind from getting out ahead of my body. At night it was an irresistible urge to mentally travel to Sieniawa and imagine my reception. Hugs and kisses, and a great banquet. I was right in the middle of my second helping of imaginary kugel when the loudest clap of thunder I ever heard in my life shook me from my dreams and the entire building as well.

What a deafening sound! It was like a terrible storm, but there was no rain. I had read about earthquakes back in geography class, but I never dreamed I'd actually be in one. Everyone in the cell broke the unwritten rule and we all looked at each with eyes as wide open as they could go. We were absolutely gripped by panic. What in the world was going on? With no concern for our jail house image we all yelled for the guards who came running at once. That alone let us know that something was up. Their explanation however did nothing to put us at ease. On the contrary, it was the most disturbing news I ever heard. We were being bombed. Hitler broke his pact with Stalin and was attacking Russia with tanks, artillery, airplanes, and the full brunt of his wermachte, the same war machine that had conquered most of Europe. The air assault was the first step to their invasion, and the explosions were terrifying.

No wagers were paid on this German aggression. We were at war, and all bets were literally off. The guards announced that we were all going to be released as soon as possible. At once they opened our cell and led us into the interior courtyard. Mercifully, the prison authorities thought we had a better chance of riding out this air raid with no roof over our head to cave in and crush us. Once out there we mingled with the other prisoners, including the adults who were at least as well informed as the guards. They seemed to think that we'd all get set free, on the condition that we go straight into the army. Mother Russia needed every able bodied man to protect her from the German aggressors, including criminals, political undesirables and juvenile rule breakers. Patriotism was sweeping through the jail as it was everywhere else in the world.

In fifteen minutes I learned more about the war from the adult prisoners than I had learned in the previous six months from the guards. Austria and Italy fought alongside Hitler, the Germans had overrun France, Belgium, Poland, Holland and Norway, and courageous England fought alone against the Nazis. I grew up without ever considering any place further away than the next village, and now I was aware of events across the whole continent. Catching up on war news changed my whole perspective. I had to think not only of the conflict, but my relation to it. All this time I had been thinking that I was deep in the heart of Russia. My train journey had crossed so many bridges I had always assumed that I was on the other side of the world. Now I became frightfully aware that I was actually on the western extreme of Russia, and extremely vulnerable to German aggression. Previously, the Nazis had been just two miles from Sieniawa, across the San. Now they were literally overhead. One of the adults explained to us ignorant kids that a German airplane could take off near Lvov, bomb us here and return to its base. I was getting a military education, and it was terrifying. I had no prior knowledge or experience of war whatsoever, and this crash course was totally upsetting. My body quaked, and I feared for my life. The worst part of this awakening was thinking about my family. If this was happening to me here how much worse was it in Sieniawa? Just as I was thinking about that the bombing stopped. I was relieved and didn't even ask what was happening. The fact that the explosions had ceased was good enough for me. In any case, the adults were quick with explanations.

"They're returning to base to refuel and reload. They'll be back for sure!"

"Why are they bombing an old prison?"

"They don't care about a jail. It's the rail yards they're after. We're just caught in the crossfire!"

All in all it was the scariest day of my life. Far worse than getting thumped by goyim. Even scarier than jail itself. It was something you just couldn't deal with. I could punch a gentile bully in the nose and afford myself some protection and satisfaction. I could bluff and swagger in jail to improve my status. But this was arcane and insurmountable. We were powerless to defend ourselves. Then a prison official came out to address us.

"Comrades. Yes, I say comrades. Because at this moment we must stand united. We have been invaded by the German army in a treacherous sneak attack in violation of Hitler's promise of nonaggression toward the Soviet Union. He seeks to enslave us, as he has the rest of Europe. But he will soon find that we are not as soft as the decadent French. Under our glorious leader, Joseph Stalin, we will repel the invader and push him all the way back to Berlin where he came from. We will crush him and his whole army of sauerkraut sucking bastards. Starting at once we will be reviewing all prisoners here for fitness for military service. In most cases I believe you will qualify. Of course, juveniles are too young to be drafted into the army, so they'll be released with the hope that they'll make their way home and volunteer for the civic home guard. Comrades, never fear. Under our Iron ruler we will repel the barbaric Hun. Long live Mother Russia!"

The entire yard resounded with huzzahs and patriotic slogans. Two hours before they had been demoralized shadows. Now, their manhood restored to them, they were all gallant defenders of their homeland. For me freedom meant going back to my family.

One adult seemed particularly sympathetic to my plight, but told me with no sentimentality what my best plan of action should be.

"Lvov? Are you crazy, son?! West lies the German army. You go east, young man, and you keep going east until you can't go anymore. There's nothing you can do for your family now. Pray for them if you want, but save yourself."

His words sounded like a death sentence for my family, and I felt sick to my stomach. It sounded inconceivable. How could they be dead? They're civilians. Maybe the Germans just marched past Sieniawa. It's so small and inconsequential, barely more than a clearing in the woods. Why would they even bother with it? Did they want the carp to feed their troops? But surely they wouldn't hurt my family. What threat would an old fish monger and his five daughters pose for a mighty country like Germany?

All night I asked myself these questions and sought opinions from the adults. But the situation at hand took precedence. We were all fearful that the planes would return, so we dedicated most of our cognitive powers to that risk.

Ironically this day, which had introduced me to terrors never before imagined, now brought me unanticipated creature comforts the likes of which I hadn't known for almost a year. First of all, just being outside was in and of itself a treat. It was a balmy June night and the warm breezes felt heavenly. Also, the courtyard had spigots which afforded me a chance for a good scrubbing. On our infrequent visits to the showers the time had been limited, but now I was able to douse myself to my heart's content. The grime behind my ears, on the nape of my neck and my tuchis was deeply ingrained, and though soap was still nowhere to be found, a good rubbing left me clean, even if a bit raw. My shirt was next, and after leaving it out in the breeze to dry, an exploratory stroll around the large yard rewarded me with a most unexpected bounty. I stumbled upon a lonely looking pair of shoes, and without waiting to see if their owner was missing them, they found their way onto my feet, albeit without the luxurious comfort of socks. After my investigative tour I retrieved my dry clean shirt, and for the first time since my incarceration I felt half civilized. All in all, except for the terror of the bombing, Hitler's treachery had thus far provided me with a pleasant evening, some exercise, a bath, cleaner clothes, shoes, and the promise of freedom. I was almost grateful to him.

Russians were always talking politics, though I couldn't understand any of it, and Der Fuhrer's incursion sparked especially sharp political discourse among the adults. A year earlier Commissar Glentz' discourses in Sieniawa left me totally in the dark. Now, after a year of listening to political tinged conversations in our cell, I was able to comprehend a bit more of these intensely intellectual exchanges.

"You see? It's coming true. The class struggle that Marx predicted. The Germans claim themselves to be of a higher class than everyone else. It's got a fancy new name, but it's still the same old thing, class war."

As the night wore on the guards came and went, updating us with conditions in the area. They even told us the hour, and by what time we'd be free in the morning. In nearly a year we hadn't known what time it was, and now we were all counting the minutes until our release. Finally, the first feint glow of the sun made its appearance, accompanied by some very official looking men toting typewriters and stacks of paper. Tables were set up and we were formed into several lines before them, with the juveniles getting our very own. Soon the click clack of typewriters resounded off the prison yard walls like pecking birds, and one by one we were ordered to step forward. They asked us our names, and our answers were typed onto official identity cards, graced with authentic red ink stamps. This was the luckiest break of all. Not only was liberty bestowed upon me, but I'd be able to move around freely without any fear of being badgered over being a Jew. I went into jail as Ovram Feder, a name that clearly marked me as a member of Abraham's tribe, but now I was getting out under any name I said. Such trust was remarkably uncharacteristic of the Soviet system, but the situation forced them to relax their usual intense level of scrutiny. The order was more like an invitation.

"Next!"

I stepped forward in my new shoes.

"Name?"

"Arturo Arkadivonovitch."

I'd been pronouncing this name for over eight months so now it gracefully rolled off my tongue and sounded completely natural and believable to this clerk. He typed it onto a creased cardboard rectangle, removed it from the roller, had me sign it, moistened his rubber stamp in red ink and slammed it down over my signature. Then he folded it and handed it over, yelling, "Next!" He never looked me in the eye or hesitated. It was a rare opportunity to get one over on the Soviet Union, and I'm sure I was not alone in taking full advantage of it. Scores of prisoners probably rebaptized themselves that morning. Criminal, school, army and marital records went up in smoke as men got a new lease on life with imaginative new identities. Next, we were herded over to a second table where we had our first opportunity to display our virgin ID card. Pleased to see my shiny new paperwork, as well as my healthy respect for rules and regulations, they rewarded me with twenty rubles cash and a loaf of bread. Having already exhibited sincere thanks for my identity card I now focused all that remained of the gratitude within my soul on that lovely loaf of crusty rye. I took a good bite of it at once, and while merrily masticating they ushered me to the large iron gate, opened it and wished me luck. I was free.

In my position one could not help but feel elation. Freedom and a full belly were mine. On top of that, I had shoes, felt relatively clean, and for the first time in my life I had an estate. Never had financial matters insinuated itself into my personal life. My parents had always seen to such things, and since then I had only known the engineer school and jail. So having money was foreign to me, though intriguing. With all the boons of this amazing day the best thing, apart from not being bombed, was the sun. I had not felt the direct rays of that fiery orb on my body in over eight months, and it was a summer day so lovely even World War Two couldn't dim its magnificence. I turned toward it, squinting and grinning in innocent delight. Not since Sieniawa had such a naïve pleasure been mine, and I couldn't help but wonder what was happening there. Were they enjoying the sun as I was? Was it shining there at all? Was it bringing bounty to the vegetable gardens? Did the robins sing this morning when it rose? Were things still the same there? I hoped so. The alternative scenario suggested by the adult prisoners was unthinkable and I prayed it was untrue. So what if the German flag flew over what was once Poland? We had lived under many banners and it never made any difference. Wars made immigration redundant. Sometimes we didn't have to move to another country, because the country moved to us. The eastern border constantly fluctuated and both Jewish and gentile allegiances were affirmed first by one vow and then another. Sometimes we didn't even switch languages. We just continued to speak Yiddish, the lingua franca of Ashkenazi Jews. So, if the Germans wanted their flag to fly over this land where so many others had already flown, what of it? If anyone asks us where we live we'll respond by saying Deutschland. Besides, we always thought the Poles were far more anti-Semitic than the Germans. Jews had good jobs as lawyers and doctors and teachers in Germany. Sure, this Hitler made vile speeches about us, but he's just one man. Perhaps things won't be so bad after all, and this German invasion was a good thing. Maybe my parents and sisters were enjoying this warm June day as I was.

FREEDOM

V

I luxuriated in the golden glow of the sun without even considering how long. After all, I was free, and there was no limit to sun bathing or anything else. So, I took another big bite of bread and continued confronting the sun's rays with a silly uncontrollable grin, chewing all the while. The heat, the brightness, so long denied to me, felt too good to pull myself away. Finally, familiar voices caught my attention.

"Arkadi, where ya gonna go? Whacha gonna do? What happens now?"

It was a trio of my old cell mates. As much as anyone can be a friend in that jail these three kids had been mine. They thought I was one of those odd smart guys and had grown to trust me. Anyway, now that we were on our own, we felt more secure in a group. We were a band of little comrades. As my friends looked to me for a decision I suggested the train station. Reality had not seeped in, and I actually thought I might grab a train home and see my family. I was as dense as an Uzbek.

Speaking fluent Ukrainian, as I now did, I inquired of the first adult we passed for directions to the railway station. Although I had lived in Kiev for the better part of a year I had never seen anything beyond my cell walls. It was my first experience in a big city and it was fascinating. In the span of a single minute I saw more buildings and people than I ever had in my life and more was coming by the second. All the innocence I had suppressed in jail now blossomed and I gawked, wide eyed and slack jawed, at the cosmopolitan immensity before me. It was utterly unique. Back in Sieniawa if I passed someone in the street we always regarded each other. But here people seemed to run by one another without so much as a nod. And running did indeed seem to be the gait of preference. If I would have seen anyone running back home I would have followed them to see what all the excitement was about. Here everyone seemed excited, and everything was exciting. It was the most dramatic spectacle I had ever beheld. The variety and pace of Kiev was so distracting I couldn't pay attention to our route, so my pals had to ask people on the street how to get back on track. Fortunately, we had not strayed too far and they just had to point. Based on how I would've behaved back home I should have been running in the same direction as all these other people, but it slowly dawned on me that half of Kiev was scurrying in the same direction as we were. Within minutes I found myself standing before the train station, though blocked a sea of people, jostling and shouting, making an awesome din. Everyone carried bundles and valises and were full of anxious talk about the need to keep moving east. Many were refugees from the west, and Kiev was just the first step of their ever eastward trajectory. That's what we overheard. The tumult had me at its mercy, and my buddies were no less intimidated. I had never really known where they came from, but observing their timidity before this throng made it clear to me that they were like me, inexperienced yokels. In jail they had exhibited the perquisite measure of jailhouse bravado. However, bluffing a room full of kids and a throng of adults requires different degrees of chutzpah, and my little comrades clearly shrunk from the task at hand. We were all in over our heads, but as in jail, we had to go with the flow or perish.

Perhaps I truly was cut out to lead the three musketeers of Kiev's juvenile hall, because it was I who first took control of my senses, and thus our merry band. I was the D'Artagnan to their Athos, Porthos and Aramis, so I made a decisive declaration for all of us. All for one, and one for all.

"We have to find out what time the trains leave."

My voice, focused and full of purpose, snapped my friends awake, and they eagerly obeyed me. For the moment I was their de facto commander, and we were of one mind. So, I told them to stay put while I make my way through the crowd, just as I had a thousand times before, going to the cells' corner barrel, all the while explaining my mission to whoever would listen.

"Where are the trains to Lvov? I have to go west. To Lvov please."

Without exception everyone told me to forget that part of the world.

"Are you crazy kid, the Germans are there, and they're killing everyone and destroying everything in their path. Poland is already lost to those bastards, and we're being invaded too! East is salvation. You have to go east. East!"

Those words stabbed me through the heart. My family was west. Even further west than Lvov. If grand Lvov was overrun by Nazis what then of tiny Sieniawa? The confirmation of what that adult prisoner told me was such bitter disappointment I shuddered. My whole body spasmed and I became woozy. I had dreamed of nothing else but going home for almost a year, and now I was told that it was not only impossible, but that I might not even have any more home at all. Chaos engulfed my senses, and I actually staggered. They're killing everyone? How could this be? Why would they do that? What's the point? Don't they want someone left to rule over? Isn't that what power is all about, to Lord it over the losers? Political discussions, overheard in darkened cells, put forward such ideas. Late at night Marxist doctrine had permeated the air of our cell, critical of capitalists out to control the masses. Control them, not kill them! There was never any talk of wiping anyone out. It's not possible or practical. They must be exaggerating. Of course! I mean, all the Russians I met so far were notorious bullshit artists. They love to stretch the truth. I could not accept that my parents stood in harm's way. How could I live without them? Every day for the last year has been filled with thoughts of them, and now I am to be denied them?

I stumbled around like a drunken madman until I recalled my father telling me how tough we Jews are, and that we always manage to survive. Yes, it is possible that they're okay. And I knew what my father would want more than anything in this world for his one son to carry on. If anything happens to the father then it is the son's duty to continue the struggle. As long as I lived so did the family. And just as this realization settled into my consciousness my three cohorts found me.

"So Arkadi, what are we gonna do?"

"Yeah, everyone says we gotta get outa here."

"Catch a train or something."

I got my second wind and declared, "That's exactly right. We gotta catch a train as soon as possible. The Nazis are on their way here now. Those airplanes were just their calling card. Let's grab a train to Char'kov. It's two hundred miles east. Come on!"

I had never heard of that city, but I overheard some people talking about it, and how far away it was, so it sounded like a good place to start. Well experienced at pushing ourselves through crowds, we jostled our way up to the ticket window.

"How much is a ticket to Char'kov?"

There were a hundred other people yelling different city names, yet the woman in the ticket boot remained calm. She had authority and was not about to surrender it to any person or mood of panic. She methodically attended to every inquiry, and when she got to mine her passive face parted its thin lips and said, "You cannot go that far. The glorious Red army has commandeered the rail lines past Poltava. Want to go there?"

One town sounded as good to us as another, so we agreed. But when she announced the fare my friends and I gaped at each other with those wide eyed expressions which we had denied ourselves for so long, and retreated from the mobbed ticket booth. We regrouped beyond the crowd and made alternative plans.

"Arkadi, that's ten times what we have!"

"What are we gonna do, Arkadi?"

"Yeah Arkadi, what are we gonna do?"

When I received my twenty rubles I had no idea what its value was. Had I received twenty zlotys, dollars or pounds sterling I would've been equally in the dark, such was my perfect ignorance regarding monetary systems. Besides, my entire life within the Soviet Union had thus far been as a guest of the penal system, and no opportunity had arisen to expand my knowledge on the subject. Plus, only negative things about capitalism had come to my attention, so it was natural to surmise that the worker's paradise was free of this contaminating paper. Now, I found out that folks here paid for things just as we did in Poland. But I had no idea what anything cost. Not train tickets, soap or bread. I was loose in the largest country in the world, and I had a lot to learn.

My pals were even more pathetic than me. My illiteracy sprang from being a foreigner, while they were raised here. What was their excuse? Interestingly, they were unaware of my roots. My perfect accent was my armor, and I felt confident I'd not be found out. Of course, being discovered by my Russian comrades would never be the same complication as being found out by our invaders, but I decided it best to bury my roots deep inside me until I knew it was safe to do otherwise. Regardless, my buddies looked to me for a clue.

"Look," I explained. "I was a student in engineering school when I got sent here. I know how to get on board a train, any train. I know how to open the doors of any class of car, from passenger coach to cattle, and I know the routine. We go east by rail my friends, even if we have to hop a hundred freights. We go east! Follow me!"

It was an inspirational speech that Commissar Glentz would have been proud of. I only neglected to include some reference to crushing our enemies to be an ideal commie orator. My words invigorated us all, and we confidently set out for the tracks.

The only detail of which we had to be certain was our direction. We could assume no train was headed west, but there were still trains headed north and south, so we had to be careful. It was a massive train yard with a maze of tracks. We roamed around until we heard some brakemen discussing their itinerary, and after fifteen minutes we got wind of an east bound freight. We could have snuck on board a passenger train, but we wouldn't have lasted five miles, which I had earlier learned was as far as they go before collecting tickets. So as soon as our selected freight started chugging out of the station we picked a car with a half open door, and ran along side. We stuck our loaves down in our pants like short sabers, and grabbed hold of the edge of the wooden door and swung in. I was tall enough, as were two of my troops, but the fourth kid was too short to reach it easily so he had to rely on one of us to hold out a helping hand. In short order the four of us were sitting inside an east bound train, eating a continental brunch. We felt good. It was early in a long summer's day, and we had food enough to last the rest of it. That loaf of bread was easily five times what we might have been given back in jail. Plus, the train could easily make hundreds of miles before nightfall, so we were probably far ahead of the game and the advancing German army.

Our movements now had strategic consequences. We had to compare our movements with those of the wermachte, but we had no idea what its plans were. What we knew of the war was just what we learned in the last day, and by now that was probably obsolete. What I observed was that modern warfare rolled on wheels. The armies had trucks and tanks and trains, and moved very fast. But that freight car was a news vacuum.

"Maybe they're gonna try and capture Moscow? Some old guy in the yard last night told me that when you capture the capital city of a country the whole place falls. Like, when they captured Paris that was the end of France. And that's why they're bombing London. They're trying to make the British give in."

"So, you think they'll attack Moscow? That's really far!"

"They gotta. That's what this guy told me last night out in the yard."

My three friends speculated for a good while on military tactics as we sped east. I had no idea what was coming, no idea what I should do, no idea if we were putting distance between us and our would be killers, or if they were easily gaining on us and had us in their sights. In spite of our uncertain circumstances we were still giddy over the bounty of the last day and even made time for idle chit chat. And while we were chatting I heard the brakeman on the roof overhead. I alerted my friends to follow me yet again, and led them to the door at the end of the car. Some freight cars had these doors, because they were really converted passenger cars with the seats removed. I figured the brakeman would check this car any moment, as was their custom, and I sought to buy us some time by changing cars. It might have worked fine too, except that the car we walked into was a regular passenger car, and the conductor recognized us for what we were and yelled for us to stop. We retreated to our baggage car only to confront the angry brakeman, brandishing a truncheon. We were going too fast to jump off, and we were inches away from a beating, so I spoke up.

"We expected to be attacked by the Germans, not our own country men. We're just fleeing the Nazis. Let us wait for a turn, and when it slows down we'll jump off."

"Alright, but I don't wanna see ya back on my train. Y'hear?"

We thanked him, but we really didn't understand what the big deal was. Everyone on that train was fleeing the advancing German threat, so how did three extra kids slow their progress? But that was the system. I knew from engineering class that if you let one hobo on, then pretty soon the entire train is crawling with them like insects, and the whole scheme of things falls apart. Still, it was war. Why couldn't they make an exception?

We came to a curve and jumped off. We were okay, and we stood up and watched our transport disappear into the distance. We sat and talked and ate a little more bread, and an hour later another train came along. Like its predecessor it slowed on the curve, allowing us to climb aboard one of the low passenger car platforms. Being a warm day we just sat on the steps. Our butts had become so used to hard surfaces in jail the iron steps didn't matter to us. And so the day went, sitting on passenger car platforms and dodging conductors and brakemen.

Concerned primarily with maintaining our pace, we were unaware of our exact bearings. Although we had planned to head due east we were actually heading southeast toward the unlimited ocean of grass known as the steppes. I only became aware of this from trying to determine the time from the sun. But I figured that southeast might be better, because south means warmth. When I shared this solar observation with the three musketeers they were dumbfounded. The change in topography was so gradual and subtle they did not discern any change, not that it mattered to them. As long as we didn't hear any German guns we were in heaven.

After riding a couple of hours a brakeman found us and suggested we get off at the next stop. Not being thrown off was a pleasant and considerate change, and when we arrived at the small station we got off and explored the town. It was bigger than Sieniawa and had a nice market. My friends seemed to be experienced thieves and had no qualms about swiping some juicy summer fruit. I hadn't had any in so long it was an even bigger treat than the bread. We found a pump and drank our fill of water, and even washed up a little. We hadn't slept in two nights due to the bombing raid, and it was startling to realize that so much had happened in just thirty six hours. But it was catching up to us now, and we searched around for somewhere to sleep. The moonlight revealed a barn and we snuck in. The smell of the hay and the livestock was earthy and friendly, and we collapsed on the straw and quickly fell asleep after allowing ourselves the civilized luxury of removing our shoes first. It was the softest surface any of us had encountered in ages, and it gave us our best night's sleep in memory. Whatever dreams came our way served to lull us deeper asleep and let us appreciate our lives for the first time in too long.

The owner of that hay woke us in the morning when he came in to milk his cow, and he wasn't at all upset by our presence there. The robust farmer hadn't been affected much by either the revolution or the war, and he was a satisfied soul. He was generous in his nature and didn't begrudge us a nap in his barn. He even gave us a little fresh milk. It was warm from the cow's udder, and its nut like richness reminded me so much of Sieniawa I almost cried from sheer sentimentality. My cohorts fell silent as well, confirming my suspicion that they were country boys like me. Too bad I didn't feel comfortable enough with them to share my origins, but I knew it wasn't wise. These Ukrainian rednecks had probably been taught to hate all the people their relatives had hated for generations, and that could include me. No, I'd have to bury my true self deep down and lock it shut for a long time to come.

We ate the last of our bread with the milk and it was the best breakfast since being incarcerated. I offered some of my bread to the farmer before eating it myself, but he declined, slapping his belly to indicate the presence of a recently enjoyed breakfast of his own. The sounds of the barnyard animals, the sweet smells of the plants, and the kindness of the farmer made jail seem a distant memory. Thankfully, that was all behind us. The war however was just beginning and we had to move on. Smiles and contentment filled the humble stable but we had to continue our journey east. I feared for this sweet man, and hoped the Germans had no design on his little corner of Heaven.

We strolled through the town which was already busy, despite the early hour. That's how country towns were back then, uncomplicated by the presence of electrical energy. It was early to bed and early to rise. But I had been thinking a lot about Sieniawa and similar places the last two days, and I imagined that this war, with its mechanized armies, was going to change them, most definitely for the worse.

I heard the train whistle and I urged my friends to hurry. The lazy rhythms of country life were attractive for the moment, but the Nazis would not respect it, and we had to flee east at a more urgent pace. We got down to the station, and saw it was another combination freight and passenger train, just like the one that had dropped us off last night. We crossed the tracks and hid in the high grass on the north side of the rails. I knew from my training that conductors usually anticipated hobos from the same side of the tracks as the station. In this case it was on the south side of the east/west bound rails, and they kept their eyes on the crates on the east side of the building for potential hobos. Distracted by their vigilance we easily leapt aboard from the opposite side. We were comfortable for about fifty miles when we got booted off by a cagey young conductor. But it was near another village, and we availed ourselves of their provincial hospitality. Bereft of suspicion, their guard permanently down, it was hardly a challenge to distract them and make off with a small piece of bread or fruit. It probably wasn't even necessary to run as we did. It was just part of the routine of chicanery that I learned from my experienced partners in petty crime.

Being the middle of June it was strawberry season, and I just had to have some. Filching such tiny things however seemed ridiculous, so I considered my very first honest purchase. I would hold out my twenty ruble note like an ignorant rube, not knowing what to expect, and be delighted to get change back. I had witnessed such transactions between my mother and her customers, so I'd be comfortable doing it. But I was nervous about spending the entire twenty as I had no knowledge of the price of summer fruit. Upon sharing this confusion with the three musketeers they mocked my honesty and went through their usual distraction game, stealing the much desired delicacy for me. We walked off to the side of the road, sat in the soft summer grass in the shade of a leafy elm tree, and feasted on those strawberries, one by one, licking our fingers at the end. We had made good time so far that day, and the day before as well, so I tempted the other musketeers to take a dip in a nearby stream. People there didn't seem to be in a panic, fleeing from any invading hordes, so we felt tranquil enough to sport in the water for an hour, wash our clothes, and even sunbathe while they dried. The warmth of summer was delicious, and we dared to forget the war for an hour or two. But, in the back of my mind the threat lurked, and I had the premonition that I better enjoy this while it lasted. Guilt over this lark however, was utterly absent. After all, I had just been incarcerated for most of a very harsh year for no good reason, and I deserved a break.

The sun warmed me to my soul, and I lay there like an innocent naked babe, thoughtless and carefree. But as much as I wanted to escape it was only my body that cooperated. The mind would not ignore the situation, and a theoretical problem arose in my mind. Our plan to flee east would only work for so long. Geography class taught me that Russia was vast, but it did eventually come to an end. And when it did it met the Pacific Ocean. The text books showed us that just a little sliver of blue separated Russia from Japan. Some prison guards told us that Japan was now allied with Germany, and that just thirty years or so before, this country had defeated Mother Russia in a war. Tiny Japan beat enormous Russia, and they were with the Nazis? We were trapped in the middle. They were still four thousand miles away, but wheels would bring them here sooner or later. I cursed my awareness. Why couldn't the mind behave like the body and leave me in peace? Then I was gripped by an unsettling realization that forced me to forget World War Two. Our clothes hung on bushes and my nakedness might betray me. Athos, Porthos and Aramis however had surrendered so fully to the all encompassing sun that they had drifted off to sleep, never noticing my circumcision. I nonchalantly rolled over and completed my siesta face down. Had they spotted my proof of the covenant between Abraham and God? Perhaps they were so unsophisticated that they didn't know what it was. Or maybe they just didn't bother to look at another man's privates? I was lucky they hadn't woken up yet, but I promised myself not to tempt fate by repeating such a mistake. I also made a pledge to myself to come up with a course of action beyond merely fleeing. I needed a satisfactory plan to confront this dilemma.

With no mental agitation more complex than sun worshipping to keep them awake, the musketeers continued dozing, allowing me time to retrieve my dry pants and secret once and for all the evidence of my uniqueness. I dressed quickly and sounded revile.

"Come on comrades, the Germans are on our tails!"

They rose and dressed, gaily chatting like song birds. Before long we were jumping aboard our next freight, or so we thought. It turned out to be a cattle train, and we ended up standing among herds of gently mooing bovines, lazily chewing their cud, as clueless as my companions were to impending doom.

For two more days we traveled on a series of trains, sauntering through small town market places in between, availing ourselves of any poorly guarded food. Once, as we were hiking down a road, we passed a sign that announced available work on a nearby farm. It looked like a good opportunity for me to do something besides staying on the lam. We had gone about four hundred miles east, and getting involved in something new and constructive seemed safe. On the other hand, Athos, Porthos and Aramis were happy with life on the road. So, they went their way, possibly to confront the Japanese army, and I turned right toward the collective farm at Salse. I was now truly on my own, and would have to depend on my wits from now on. There was no family, school, friends or institution to fend for me or see to my needs. I had the clothes on my back, a few rubles in my pocket, a false ID, and the secret knowledge of who I was. I also had lessons inside my head of many kinds. My father had imparted to me an education of the most elevated kind, and jail had given me a master's degree in street smarts. And now I had to assimilate and implement it all in order to be able to confront horizons broader than anything ever imagined back in Sieniawa.

THE COLLECTIVE FARM

VII

A narrow dirt road was the only route to Salse, and the old reliable leg power would have to suffice to carry me there, though my year in jail had actually put my body in worse condition. For fourteen years I walked everywhere, but now my young muscles rebelled with each step. And while it was a pleasant surprise to find those shoes in the prison yard, the truth is they were not exactly a perfect fit. As a growing lad, this footwear might have been ideal for me a week earlier. Now they were quickly growing obsolete. In any case, they were valuable, so I tied the laces together and tossed them over one shoulder. I also removed my shirt and tied it to protect my head and neck from the overfriendly Soviet sun. To complete the classic look for the well dressed ex-convict war refugee of 1941 I rolled up the legs of my pants above the knee. Tom Sawyervonovitch was on his way to work in the first summer of the war.

The dirt was soft below my feet. It didn't seem to have been impacted by any wheels in a while. Experience with our old family cart told me that routine travel of wagon wheels will make a hard smooth surface out of a dirt road. So, the soft dirt meant nobody had passed here in a while. This worried me for a minute. Maybe that sign was old, and the farm had long since closed from lack of attention. But I came up with an alternative scenario that was more inspiring to my trek. I concluded that the Russian winter made the farm inaccessible. The spring thaw had turned the road into mud, and the summer sun dried had caked it. A series of wagon trips, seeking provisions for the coming planting season, broke the caked mud into the soft dirt I now trod. Further traffic, which might harden the road, was unnecessary. All hands were needed full time on the farm.

The road to Salse was flanked by stands of white birch trees and their high leafy boughs called out to me more than once to take refuge under them from the heat. But I was determined to get there quickly, and could afford neither the luxury of rest nor the risk of missing a rare passing vehicle while I napped. Besides, hunger was looming large and it would not be mitigated by rest. Hunger just keeps getting bigger, idle or active, and common sense told me that the closer I got to the farm the closer I got to food.

With little to engage the body, besides putting one foot in front of the other, a million mental images invaded my overactive mind. What of my former travel companions, my jail mentor in Kiev, my family, the German army? As these thoughts flew in and out of the bored space between my ears I was startled to discover that they were all in one language. Imbued with local culture for so long I no longer even thought in the language of my birth and rearing, much less spoke it. I was a Russian. For no particularly reason that I could surmise this gave me even more confidence and I quickened my pace.

Telling time by the sun is something any farm boy can do, Jew or Gentile, and I knew that the soft dirt and my soft feet had been meeting regularly for about five hours. The road and I had become close companions and nothing had come between us for too long. And just when discouragement started to threaten this relationship the wheat came into view. The stands of tempting shade trees were long gone, and the flat topography was now uninterrupted by a blanket of young golden grain. It was evidence of humanity, and I knew I would soon see further proof. Encouraged by the yellow expanse before me I prepared myself to be among mankind again. The shirt went from my head to my back as the top of a silo loomed into view. My pants came down below my knees as a barn's weather vane joined the skyline, and I stopped to put on my shoes just before the first farm hand waved a greeting.

City folk are inured to the gift of human contact due to the never ending river of faces that flow by them. But country folk treasure each and every visitor as the rare commodity that they are. No people are friendlier than peasants. A short red haired fellow strode toward me, loudly calling out to his coworkers to come and greet a visitor. By the time he was close enough to shake my hand a dozen more farmers had materialized behind him, all smiles, and eager to feel my grip.

"Welcome comrade, welcome. I am Yuri."

He grabbed me by the arms and pulled me toward him, kissing both my cheeks. It was a little surprising. We didn't do that in Poland, and jail inmates never displayed such warmth. Clearly this was Russian social custom, and I had to get used to it. I would also have to get used to learning Russian. After Ukrainian it wouldn't be so hard. I was also careful to hide the wide eye look of dismay, worried that it would tip my hand, as surely as in prison. It wouldn't be wise to let them know that I wasn't really one of them. My immediate discomfort stemmed from the fact that I didn't know the proper way to respond or in what dialect. For the moment I was just going to let myself be on the receiving end, and smile in response.

"Welcome comrade," said another, and grabbed my arms. It felt natural to grab his as well, making the contact more mutual. So far, so good. Then, a torrent of huggers and kissers followed, including women. I hadn't received such affection since leaving home.

"Welcome. Welcome. Welcome."

Finally somebody with a more expansive vocabulary stepped up. And even though he turned out to be the official government representative, he was as jovial and outgoing as the rest of them.

"I am Commissar Trupopkin. On behalf of the people of the Union of Soviet Socialist Republics and our glorious leader Joseph Stalin we welcome you to collective farm eight hundred and thirty one!"

This inspired a little bit of applause, and I felt equally inspired to join in. Again, it turned out to be the right thing to do. In Russia when one person applauds everyone does. If you clap for a singer he claps back for you in appreciation. So far, so good.

"We here at collective farm number eight hundred and thirty one raise wheat to feed the hard working people of the Soviet Union. And now we feel a special pride because our wheat will feed the glorious Red Army, defenders of Mother Russia"

This inspired more enthusiastic applause, mixed with shouts. I was struggling to understand the speech, and kept a simper plastered on my face to keep up the good will.

"Even now they are preparing to drive the odious Hun back from our borders and punish him for his vile treachery!"

This brought about as thunderous an ovation as two dozen people could muster. Up until now they had done all the talking, and I knew it was my turn now. A Soviet politician is a tough act to follow, so I summoned forth from my memory the oratory of Commissar Glentz back in Sieniawa and the teacher at engineer school. It seemed as if their political system engaged people based as much on their ability to make speeches as for any other talent. They were expert bullshitters, and I couldn't let them down. But I had to deliver my won address in Ukrainian and hope for the best.

"I am Arturo Arkadivonovitch, and I volunteer my services to help you in your glorious efforts to feed the glorious troops of the glorious Red Army!"

With the possible exception of over reliance on one certain adjective, I felt I had done as good a job as was expected of a farm laborer, so I fished out my identity papers and presented them to their leader.

"Comrade Arturo, We are all delighted to have another hand here. May I know how you have come here?"

I was delighted that the particular Slavic dialect I spoke was not upsetting to them, so I forged ahead with my planned phony biography.

"I was living in Kiev, studying to be a railroad engineer, when the Germans attacked. The school was ordered closed and half the city evacuated. I was too young to join the army so they told me to go east until I could find something useful to do. I was walking down the road when I saw your sign."

This impressed everybody greatly and I was immediately glad I had eliminated the part about jail. So far, so good. Commissar Trupopkin ended the impromptu ceremony and everybody disbanded and went back to their duties.

"Oh, but you must be tired and hungry. It's a long walk from the main road. Forgive us for our lack of hospitality. Comrade Marina of the People's Committee for housing will escort you to your quarters, after which she will show you the dining hall where you may eat a well earned meal. Tomorrow you'll pay for it with your honest labor."

Comrade Marina led me through the small collection of buildings that constituted the working heart of the farm. They were concentrated in this wooded area, which was like an island in the vast open fields of wheat around it. There were several tall silos, a barn for livestock, a few other low buildings, and some idle combines which would be put to use when the fall harvest came. But I was not as interested in the barns and combines as I was in Comrade Marina. I had seen buildings and machines before, but I had not been alone with a female since my last tango lesson. Any healthy sixteen year old can't help but take notice of any woman under the age of thirty who isn't utterly grotesque. Sex was a popular topic back in jail. Although ninety percent of us were probably virgins we all bragged about fictional conquests. But now that I was actually standing near a woman its affect was intoxicating. She was part of the ad hoc welcoming committee and hugged and kissed me as enthusiastically as the others. When she did I caught a whiff of her hair, and when our leader assigned her to be my guide I was elated.

Comrade Marina was a chubby country girl with rosy cheeks, a big bright smile and no undernourished or undeveloped parts to her anatomy at all. Her blond hair was covered by a colorful kerchief and spilled out behind her head and down her neck. She wore a long skirt and blouse that fit snugly around her curvaceous body, and her honest perspiration made her glow a little. Of course, I was far too timid to speak to her of anything beyond the matters at hand, if I could even manage that. She led me to a low wooden structure that was little more than a shack. Inside were bunks and I was invited to pick one for myself.

"You have nothing with you? No bag?"

The truth is my entire estate was visible to the naked eye. I hadn't thought of it until that moment, but I was an absolute pauper. Back in Sieniawa I had a home, clothes, books, and the usual collection of objects accrued in the life of even a humble boy like me. But now I was more destitute than the *schnorers* father brought home on shabbos.

"The Germans didn't give us much time to pack."

Comrade Marina looked at me with pity and bit her lower lip in empathy. She said, "We'll show them, Comrade Arturo. Just you wait and see!"

Her sympathy felt wonderful, and I basked in the warmth of her femininity.

"Now, let's get you something to eat."

She led me to another much larger building which my nose readily identified. She sat me down at one of several long tables in the room, and disappeared into what could only be the kitchen, returning soon with a generously sized plate in either hand. One held a bowl of bright red borscht, and the other a colorful collection of things I was eager to investigate. She sat down across the table from me and invited me to dig in. I thanked her and did as she suggested. It was the first home cooked meal I had eaten in almost a year. The engineer school's food was plain and institutional. Jail cuisine was unspeakable. And food on the road was catch as catch can odds and ends. But this was cooked with the purpose of not just filling an empty stomach, but inspiring and enabling people to work hard as well. Maybe the cook even had some pride in her efforts, or even cared about her charges. There must have been some sincere motivation in that kitchen because this food was hot and delicious. There was a little bit of meat along with carrots, potatoes, turnips and radishes. And the borscht reminded me of my father's. I was so overwhelmed by everything a tear escaped one eye and betrayed me. Such a thing had been impossible for a long time, but Comrade Marina did not consider emotion a sign of weakness. She put her hand on mine. "It's alright comrade. You're safe now. We're your comrades. Never fear. And if you want to cry for the relatives you left behind or were killed by those Nazi bastards you go right ahead."

I had not wept in memory. I had not been free to. But now Comrade Marina had removed any pretext of embarrassment or false pride. Her timing was ideal as I was probably about to open the floodgates anyhow. I put my hands over my face and let it flow. My shoulders and chest heaved as I sobbed and I drenched my cheeks and even my neck. All the while dear Comrade Marina patted my back. She could not know all the things that inspired this emotion, but what she imagined was probably not so very far from the truth. Finally she had me lean into the protective warmth of her ample bosom and let me cry myself out. Although I had felt a longing for her our embrace was one of the platonic sort. She was my surrogate mother, sister and best friend. And although she was clearly an ardent proponent of her Motherland's revolution, and probably an atheist to boot, her kindness enveloped and saved me. When I leaned back she produced a handkerchief and let me wipe my face and blow my nose. I meekly thanked her.

"Good," she said. "Now you eat."

After weakly smiling I nodded and picked up my spoon. Then, after breathing the mother of all sighs, I dug in for real.

Food, friendship and therapy. I felt better than I had in a year. But it had been a year that felt like ten. I was a fourteen year old kid from a protective Jewish family in a tiny hamlet in the middle of nowhere, ripped from my home and thrust into a political totalitarian machinery about which I knew nothing, and then subjected to deprivation and isolation. Only war, something even worse than all that had gone before, freed me, and ever since I had been running and living a lie. But in some respects it was not a lie. For all practical purposes I really was Arturo. I hardly remembered Polish at all, and I thought and dreamt in Ukrainian. In addition to that, the word comrade fell from my lips as comfortably as shalom had a year earlier. If the communists were guilty of brainwashing they had done a number one job on me. They put me in a cement box devoid of sense gratification, starved me, and practically the only topics I heard were Marxist ideology, Lenin and Stalin. Of course the result was not the eager beaver Commie they wanted. I had no interest in their political philosophy at all. What I had become was a brute. My heart and mind were not swayed by the content of what I was exposed to inside those walls, but rather by the walls themselves. I could have been locked in a cell in any country, in any culture, and ended up the same. My incarceration was like boot camp to take on life on any terms, not necessarily a socialist one. But the crazy part of it is I was thinking that the communists might have saved my life. I kept my gratitude on a conditional level because I really didn't know for sure what happened back in Sieniawa when The Germans swept through. But everyone in Kiev said that the Huns were killing and destroying everything. If that's true then I might have been killed too. The engineering school was in Poland, conquered land. The fact that I broke a school regulation and was harshly punished for it was typical Soviet discipline, but it saved me. I was miserable in Kiev, but I was far from the Nazi army. And when they bombed the jail they let me out and wished me well. The end result was a changed person. A year ago I was some fourteen year old kid name Ovram, apprentice fish monger. Now I was fifteen year old comrade Arturo. If I could change things and be back in Sieniawa with my family, and make the war disappear that would be my choice. But, considering the reality at hand, I was grateful to be alive, and appreciated Collective Farm number eight hundred and thirty one. One last sigh. So far, so good.

My first day as an honest laborer went well. First, I ate a substantial breakfast in the company of a bunch of gung ho proletariats who spoke boisterously about doing their part to feed the troops who would chastise the invaders. They boisterously spoke in the Russian language however, and I was going to take a crash course in molding my Ukrainian lingo into the mother tongue of the Soviet Union. There were hundreds of workers on this immense farm, but many had left to enlist, so Commissar Trupopkin was grateful to anyone who showed up to pitch in. That accounted for the high proportion of young men there. He set me to do odd repair jobs that would have taken time away from the extraordinary efforts of the essential workers who ran the farm. The wheat was already planted, and the people who knew about soil, irrigation and insects were out in the vast fields nurturing the fragile shoots. But there were a lot of small things that needed to be done to keep things ship shape. That's where I came in. They made me the handy man, jack of all trades. Even though my experience with tools was limited they had confidence in me. Besides, there was no one else. Their previous fix-it man had joined the army, so to them I was a real find. With fewer experienced men in the fields taking even one away for routine maintenance was a crime. So little by little, I learned to use a saw and hammer. I even laughed to myself how I was already using a hammer and at harvest time I'd probably be using a sickle. I was a real commie. Basically though, being out in the sunshine, getting exercise, and eating regularly, was a dream vacation compared to jail. And whenever possible I caught a glimpse of Comrade Marina. She probably only felt a maternal affection for me, but I had a full blown crush on her. Of course she might have considered my romantic emotions to be vestiges of a self indulgent, petty bourgeoisie life, because she was a true believer in the Marxist cause. Like the women on Communist propaganda posters she was noble and determined, and I couldn't help but admire her for that. But my attraction to her was not based on politically altruistic ideals. She was buxom and pretty, and I lusted after her.

In the evenings after dinner the workers remained in the dining hall and socialized. As there was little to do but chat, and as I was the newest thing around, they were curious about me.

"So, Comrade Arturo, what did your father and mother do?"

Of all the things to anticipate a biography was not one of them, and comrade cat got my tongue. They were just being friendly, but I was so conditioned to fear any kind of interrogation, no matter how casual, that I thought I was in jeopardy should a mistruth be suspected. A sigh escaped my lips, and a great big fabrication about my father the bookseller was about to fill the room, when Comrade Marina came to the rescue.

"Poor Comrade Arturo has had it rough and it's still a little painful for him to talk about his family. Let's give him a little more time."

Dear sweet Marina had given me the perfect alibi for remaining silent on the topic, as well as allowing me plenty of time to invent a really good story, should the need to have one arise. To her credit, her purity persisted, because she really believed what she said. It also gave me more time to improve my Russian. I was speaking it almost constantly now, and getting more confident in it by the day.

After my second week there another volunteer showed up. Of course, being the first person to come to the farm in weeks they grilled him for information about the German advance. It wasn't good news. The Nazis had sent a huge army into Mother Russia with plans of doing nothing short of conquering and subjugating us. This caused great lamentation and vows of revenge among us. I fell silent, thinking about my family. Perhaps the German army had indeed passed by Sieniawa in its great hurry to invade Russia. Of course, it was terrible that the Nazis had invaded, but if it meant they had ignored my family in their rush to do so, I could live with it.

They gave the new guy a day of rest, as they had done for me, and then put him to work the next day. Also like me he was young, but he was a lot more experienced at handy work and demonstrated it his first day on the job. I didn't mind if he shared the tasks, and he could even do it all if he wanted to. Life for me at the farm was like a holiday, and even if they sent me out into the fields to cut wheat it wouldn't matter to me. For now they had me on odd jobs, like bringing water to thirsty workers. After all, someone had to do that too. Of course I was a bit concerned over my loss of prestige in the eyes of Comrade Marina. One afternoon my replacement was taking a break when he reached into his pocket, pulled out a comb, and set to beautify himself. When I saw that vestige of refined civilization it was not good grooming that crossed my mind, but something else entirely. Actually, it was the first comb I had seen since Lvov, and I was interested in it at once. There was plenty of paper around, so I knew I could pull it off. That night when we were all sitting around conversing, as there was nothing else to do, I asked to borrow that comb. Back then such things were valuable, so he was reluctant. If I broke it where would he get another in this remote spot? In spite of his uneasiness he eventually handed it over. Perhaps he wanted to avoid being labeled a bourgeoisie. I already had my paper all set and I was poised to make music, perhaps impressing Comrade Marina as well.

For my audition back in the jail in Lvov I had to play before a most hostile audience. Here though I felt loved, and I confidently wrapped the comb and raised it to my lips. Drawing a deep breath to sustain me through my first measure I launched into a wedding waltz. There were some supportive oohs and ahs, and when I finally finished there was sustained applause, something I never got in Lvov. I peeked over at Comrade Marina and she was gleefully applauding along with everyone else. I was elated.

As it turned out my beloved was also responsible for keeping up worker morale. It would have been ideal for her to have some of the workers play their accordions or balalaikas in the evenings, but as unbelievable as it may seem to those who trust in clichés about entire nations, there was not one musician among this group of typical Russian peasants. So my impromptu kazoo recital was like a blast of angel trumpets from above, had they believed in such things. I was an even bigger hit here than in Kiev. There was probably equal appreciation for the arts in both places, but here they were free to express it. Other similarities persisted however. For example, they also reacted with requests. That was more problematic than in my previous venue. Jailhouse musicians can just snarl at their fans and warn them of the strict no-request policy, but among rural friends such nastiness makes no sense. There was no choice at this juncture but to be honest, sort of.

"We didn't have much music in our home back in Kiev, so I just picked this up on the road. I'm afraid I don't know many popular tunes. But if you teach me I'll play 'em."

"Good idea, Comrade Arturo," said my sweet Marina. "Whoever wants to teach Comrade Arturo their favorite melodies please do so."

Confidence filled me, and I couldn't wait to expand my repertoire. Some mystic power entered my soul and I started to play the clandestine tango I had heard so often back n Sieniawa. I hadn't even thought of that song since then, and it mystified my eager new audience. A few of the more rhythmic serfs tapped an accompanying beat on the table top, and a couple got up to sway to the first music they had heard in a long time.

I couldn't help but sneak furtive glances at my favorite comrade, and it was delightful to see her finding such favor with me. Little did she suspect that, while I was entertaining the workers, I was specifically serenading her. At song's end the contented workers applauded, and I nodded my thanks. I ignorantly committed the faux pas of not clapping back, but the jubilation of Arturomania obviated all boundaries of cultural courtesy. That night the workers went to bed happier than they had been in memory, or so said Comrade Marina, chief morale officer.

"Arturo, we love your music. It's the best contribution to our efforts you can make. Our new handyman is fast, and I'm certain he can take care of all our repair needs, so I want you to play music for us every night as a morale booster. In the day you can do light jobs like bringing water. But your main assignment is to continue with your music. You know, Papa Joe is a great lover of music. He would commend you for this service."

Nothing can squash romance quicker than name-dropping Stalin, but I still loved sharing those private moments with Comrade Marina. And maybe if I had been a real Russian the signs of receptive womanhood might have been obvious enough to encourage me to take our relationship to the next plateau. But the knowledge of my true identity curtailed the running of any risks. A legitimate goy might have risked a slap in the face to get a quick kiss or suggest more. A phony one though had to play it more conservative, despite his raging hormones. So, it was only through socialist sacrifice that I was able to share anything with pretty Comrade Marina. In the day I had light duties, just as she promised, and at night I played music, eventually expanding my repertoire to include Russian and Ukrainian folk favorites. Unaware of any particular musical talent on my part I seemed to have been born with the ability to sing on key and remember melodies. With a comb and paper that's all I needed.

During one of my nocturnal concerts, which by now resembled sing-a-longs, I noticed another female giving me the once over. Marina had captured my heart, but this other woman, probably old enough to be Marina's mother, was more in control of her emotions. Where Marina gave into her political passions this lady had the calm demeanor of a veteran of many passions, and was no longer swayed by them. Most remarkably, she didn't break off her gaze, and seemed to project her mood onto me. It embarrassed me, and I sought out Marina's less threatening presence. At the end of my concert Marina came to me and confessed her special fondness for the tango. Overcome by familiarity, perhaps inspired by the other matron's spell, I brazenly spoke up.

"You know Comrade Marina, the tango is not just the name of that song. It's the national dance of Argentina, where this music comes from."

She was fascinated by my tidbit of information, and wanted to know more.

"Well, I don't know anything more about the music, but I know how the dance goes."

I was too shy to suggest a dance lesson, but she insisted on it by herself. So, with my arms outstretched in invitation, she stepped forward as an eager pupil. With no Victrola or even kazoo I had to hum the music to lead her through the steps. It was a very formal kind of stance, with our bodies well separated, but our hands clasped, and we each had a hand on the other's back and shoulder. It was basically the same routine as Sieniawa, but this was a totally unique physical experience for me. For the first time in my life I was under the spell of lust. I longed to kiss her, and for all I knew she even wanted me to. But I was too timid. Our lesson ended abruptly, with Comrade Marina courteously thanking me, and then leaving me alone in the vast empty dining hall. It was my first truly romantic encounter, but it only served to provide me with my first overwhelming physical frustration. But destiny had no plans to frustrate me that night. As I sighed and pined after the plump Marina a figure in the doorway, hazy in the residue of hundreds of smoking soviets, caught my attention. It stood there, blatant and confidant in its bearing. After a second I discerned it was female, the very same matron who had been ogling me earlier. As my hormones were still raging from the tango lesson the presence of this other female was warmly welcome. She confidently strode forward and spoke.

"You play very energetically, Comrade."

She spoke with an air of confidence approaching authority, and whatever I might have said next would have been of no consequence. Conversation was not what she had in mind. Actually, it had nothing to do with anything mental or intellectual either. The little she said had to do primarily with physical longings, and in short order there was no talking whatsoever, except for a few perfunctory instructions on her part. This was one situation where my highly evolved sense of intuition was hardly needed. I would have preferred Comrade Marina to initiate me in the ways of carnal delight, but my professor was not without her own unique brand of charm. Her skin might have been softer and ruddier once, or her hair more peppery than salty, but she was far from dried out or short of vigor. In hind sight I suppose I was far from the only callow youth to stop by that collective and learn something apolitical from that generous woman. She initiated me into manhood in ways that jail absolutely neglected, and it was all so new and overwhelming that I hadn't the sophistication to close my eyes and imagine her to be Marina. In order to have some privacy we used the beasts' boudoir, the forest. Thank goodness it was summer. In any case, while not officially part of the morale committee, that lady did more for mine than anyone on collective farm eight hundred and thirty one!

Besides my unrequited love for Comrade Marina my time in the wheat fields was like a vacation at a spa, with abundant fresh air and sunshine, healthy physical exercise, plentiful food, music in the evenings, and little labor was expected of me. Plus there was the occasional forest tryst to enliven my stay. Even with all that, toward the end of July, when the wheat was growing tall, the need to keep moving east gripped my soul. I had left Sieniawa to see more of the world, but the collective farm was even more provincial than my old home town. What really beckoned me were the great big world and the illusive big city. With Stalingrad still further east I decided to move on. Adieu Collective Farm Eight Hundred and Thirty One. Adieu. They might have considered my exit a form of betrayal, but someone who hums into a comb is hardly the lynch pin in a Soviet five year plan. They must have auditioned my replacement that very night. I hope the winner was the real owner of the comb. Comrade Marina probably thought she understood my exodus best, but she didn't comprehend the depths of my wanderlust. So, I left just after breakfast, with my pockets stuffed with bread, calculating that I'd make the town in a full day's forced march. Once back in civilization I'd go back to catching trains and head into the rising sun. In conversations on the farm I learned that Stalingrad was hundreds of miles from Kiev. Surely, the Nazis would never make it that far.

From 1939-1945 my life was dominated by Joseph Stalin,
so I have to include his cold hearted visage.

The entire village of Sieniawa, including my family,
perished in a scene not unlike this.

STALINGRAD

VIII

The short time at the collective had not diminished my prowess at hoping trains. And, no longer burdened by my old travel companions, I could do it faster to boot. Of course my time with them was not an utter loss. The musketeers had imparted to me the finer points of liberating food from budding capitalist market places. With that knowledge, the twenty rubles in my pockets, along with the other kind of bread I liberated from the collective farm, an air of confidence christened my new venture. The blessing was so strong I caught a train within minutes after getting to the station. The timing was indeed pure luck, but now stealth was no longer a requirement to make it on board. There was a massive movement of refugees fleeing the Axis invaders, and everyone seemed welcome, regardless of ability to pay. The farm had insulated me from the war, but now it was catching up with a vengeance. Refugees of every class were here, including Jews. It seemed like ages since a landtsman had been in the same room with me.

"Sir, madam. Excuse me, but can you please tell me where you're coming from?"

"Minsk, and we've been traveling for days."

"Minsk? But that's over two hundred miles from Poland! The Germans are that far?"

"They were on their way, and we were advised to evacuate. Some planes flew overhead, and even tried to bomb our train."

"You don't know what happened in Poland, do you?"

"All we know is they overran all of Poland, and now they're here. What we do know for certain is what Hitler rants about, and we're not waiting to find out anything more."

"I heard the Germans are destroying everything in their path, and killing everyone."

"We don't know anything exactly, just that we were advised to evacuate. I fought in the last war against the Germans, and I don't want to see any more of it. I hope our army can kick the Germans back across the border."

"But what about Poland?"

"Like I said, Poland's already gone."

Poland gone? A whole country? A meeting with fellow Jews should have elated me, but it was the grimmest ten minutes in memory. My brain fought against the possibility of my family being destroyed. All my life, discussions of Germans always confirmed their pragmatism. So, if you're determined to conquer a big country like Russia it just wouldn't make any sense to split your forces just to harass a handful of civilians off somewhere in a shady grove, devoid of strategic significance. No! That's not pragmatic. So, I tried to visualize my parents among the refugees. Maybe they weren't on this train, but Nikolai must have driven them to that pile of boards by the tracks, and they followed in my footsteps. Maybe we'll even meet somewhere out here.

My common sense formula for survival calmed me enough to let me concentrate on the moment and all the other refugees. These people looked desperate. They had lost everything, what little they had to begin with, and had witnessed what Nazis could do.

They said that German soldiers shot women and children without a second thought. One family from Frolov, on a tributary of the Medvedica, said they had heard such horror stories that they were fleeing even before the Germans got this far, just to prepare a safe life for themselves. I heard this from others as well, but these were rumors. As long as nobody actually saw it first hand my parents were on Nikolai's carriage bound for the rails to the east and safety.

Everyone in the area was convinced that the Nazi blitzkrieg would never dare to invade so far inside the Soviet Union, and that Stalingrad would offer refuge. Also, they had such confidence in their leader they assumed that any place named for him was invincible. So, like medieval peons seeking refuge within the walls of their Lord's castle, a river of proletariats flowed toward the great city, creating a great surge in its population. The further into the heartland I traveled the less Ukrainian I heard, and by now I was getting used to hearing and speaking only Russian.

Like an expanded version of my jail cell I witnessed how desperate the situation was becoming. Along with the common citizens there were thieves of every kind on that train. Constant arguments and fist fights broke out, and it was even worse than jail. Some hardened criminals hid thin razor blades between their fingers where nobody could see, and if anybody objected to their aggression they gave them a nasty slice across a hand, an arm, or even a face if the protest was too determined. Jail had taught me not to interfere in such things. Life is tough. Besides, foiling one robbery assault could evolve into a full scale war with gangsters, who had ruthlessly taken over whole regions of the steppes where the long arm of Soviet law, weakened by their focus on invading armies, had lost much of its control.

We crossed the mighty Don just west of my destination, and it symbolized to me the torrent of frightened refugees heading here.

The region, like the one I had come from, was a continuation of the flat farmlands that stretched westward for thousands of miles. One evening back at the farm, Commissar Trupopkin had explained how the multiple rivers that flow toward Stalingrad make it an ideal candidate for hydro-electrical dams, allowing for massive industrialization. That made it a center for hammers, contrasting its northern outlying areas, employing mostly sickles. However, I was interested in neither. Jail had left its mark on me, and though the farm was a wonderful vacation that put me back in decent physical condition, I still had a chip on my shoulder, and was thinking only of my comfort. No gung ho communism or patriotism for me. Just get me as far away from the war as possible, hopefully where the weather suited me.

Stalingrad sits on a flat plain, so arriving at night it was impossible to tell one end of the city from the other. Since leaving home I'd never really had the chance to see a big city, so walking out of the train yard I got my first real taste of a true modern metropolis. Kiev and its train yard were nothing by comparison. I had to step over a hundred rails just to get to the station, and once inside I was awed by the bright electrical light. It was like daytime, though just outside it was night. The room must have been as big as all of Sieniawa and the ceiling was high enough to fly a kite. Just within this one cavernous room I saw more people at a glance than I had ever known in my entire life. I was thunderstruck. And the wide-eyed expression banned from my face for so long sprang to life and wouldn't subside. My mouth was so agape I could have gotten a dental exam and not taken noticed. So, this is what a real city is like!

My eyes darted to every corner of the mammoth edifice where people of every description and condition walked, shuffled and ran. A loud voice that sounded like it came from heaven announced train and track numbers, and combined with the cacophony of the people, it created a daunting image. Engineering school never taught us about this. It was so intimidating I was paralyzed. Only my neck and eyes functioned. The mouth was fixed in an open position as the eyes darted every which way inside a skull that continually swiveled back and forth. Finally, a strange feeling on my body woke me up.

Thousands of clueless yokels like me came to the big city every day, and just as many locals were on hand to take advantage of us. In this case it was a pickpocket whose hand in my pocket was about to withdraw my entire fortune. How many times had petty thieves in Kiev tried to lighten my meager load in this way? I recognized that sensation at once and immediately reverted to my former feral inmate self, grabbing the protruding wrist as hard as I could and spinning around to confront its owner.

"Whadda ya think you're....?"

I was momentarily stunned to see that this thief was a woman, and the shock almost cost me everything. Every female I had ever known was honest. My mother, sisters, tango teacher, and Comrade Marina all represented the finest that humanity had to offer, and this new wrinkle caught me unawares. It was shocking to me, but obviously all in a day's work for this lady who took advantage of my weakened dismay to jerk her empty hand from mine and run.

The big city was different alright! And there was a lot to learn to be able to survive in it. But it was a valuable introductory lesson. Just as my first moment in prison in Kiev had initiated me into the darker side of life, here too my virginity was violated from the get go. And the spirit of my old mentor came back to me. The inmates were like rats trapped in a cage. Whenever you force too many beings to live together in a reduced space they behave like vermin. Stalingrad was like a giant prison, and their inmates behaved accordingly. And even when the rats were let out of their cages their conditioned behavior stayed the same for a long time. So, I had to be on my toes, trust no one, and mind my own business. With my head now placed straight I left the giant daytime room to explore the nighttime prison house of Stalingrad.

What a racket! Trucks, cars, buses, trolleys and motorcycles choked the air with noisy motors, noxious fumes, and a cacophony of beeping horns. I was raised in the woods, and the only tail pipe I had ever dealt with was the weekly bus. Here I was surrounded by countless vehicles, literally, and there was hardly a tree in sight. Concrete, asphalt, bricks, blocks and endless squares and straight lines composed the landscape, with black wires hanging everywhere, stretching between perfectly straight leafless trees and flat stretches of cement. It really was like an immense prison with walls, walls, and more walls all around. The broad sidewalks and streets were packed with a parade of people, none of whom wore a smile. Could one make a friend in such a place? And who would be my friend anyway? Not a child had crossed my path since arriving. When that thought struck me it became uncannily clear that this city was bereft of youth. What a mystery. Where were the children? Microscopic Sieniawa had more kids than this megalopolis, and the overall effect was totally off-putting. When does the next train leave town?

With my hands thrust into my pockets to protect my few resources, I explored a little further. Within three blocks I broke my record for walking continuously on a paved surface, yet still hadn't found anything noteworthy. With no particular destination in mind the city held no surprises for me, other than its utter sameness block after block. How do people find their houses or anything else? Ignorant of street numbers and addresses, the giant grid was a mystery to me. Perhaps in the day it looked different? For the sake of its residents one would hope so.

Walking on one couldn't help but be impressed by one factor, the immensity of it. Only a tiny percentage of it had passed under my feet thus far, but it already seemed to dwarf the wheat fields of Salse. If my father were caught at one end of this place at three in the afternoon on a Friday and had to get home for shabbos on the other end he'd never make it. He'd hold up somewhere until the next day. But where? My father knew everyone on his route and could always have shabbos dinner in another home. But what would he do here? And what am I going to do? I was getting tired and hungry. The farm had spoiled me with a bed and a reliable flow of food. Now I was on my own, more than a little peckish and in need of a safe place to lie down for the night. After that episode with the pickpocket back at the train station I assumed that taking public naps would invite every variety of thief Stalingrad had to offer. I heard of hotels, but had never actually seen one. And as far as cost, there was not a clue in my head. The occasion for conversation had not yet presented itself, but the need was now urgent. So, I became bold enough to stop a stranger and talk to him.

"Excuse me, sir. Do you know if there's a hotel around here, and how much it costs?"

The man stopped, but looked a little inconvenienced. He regarded me with a brief display of incredulity.

"You're a brave one!"

This totally confused me. It required courage to ask directions of a citizen? Be that as it may he relented and begrudgingly gave me the time of day.

"There are no bourgeoisie hotels around here. It's best if you look near the train station for some place to stay for the night."

Had I not spent the better part of the last year, surrounded by society's rejects, and become inured to their less than warm demeanor, I might have felt rebuff at such brevity. Back in Sieniawa every meeting was reason for friendly discourse. And the collective farm was populated almost exclusively by outgoing country folk. So, this abridged interview was my introduction to urban exchange. My conclusion was that city people were always in a hurry, and didn't dedicate much time to strangers. Plus, I felt a little dumb for not figuring out that the neighborhood that hosted the train station would be the most convenient and logical destination for travelers to find lodgings. An about face and fifteen minutes of dedicated hiking brought me back near the station where several buildings were graced with signs proclaiming the availability of rented rooms and meals. Both sounded fine to me, and I considered my choices. Compared to the charm of my previous address none of them looked appealing, so I picked one at random and strolled into its lobby.

Apparently the train station used up most of the area's electricity, because the lobby's electric bulb was so dim it hardly deserved to be called a light at all. The small vestibule was shadow upon shadow, and one of them spoke.

"I salute you, sonny. Do you want a room?"

How odd that another remarked about my supposed fortitude. I squinted to make out a man about fifty with bad skin and a haircut that looked like the result of a shears and a bowl. He was sufficiently courteous to deserve a response however, so I asked the price.

"It's half a ruble for the night. Have to be out by nine. And a whole ruble if you want breakfast. What'll be?"

My immediate hunger prompted me to ask if there was any fare that included dinner.

"Yeah, two rubles. But we're done for the night. You shouldn't have any problem finding a restaurant right around here. But don't take too long. We close up by ten."

I thanked him and went looking for a place that sold meals, and true to the man's experienced reckoning I found several before going two streets. I spent half a ruble on a meal of borscht, bread and a few potatoes. With no interesting partner to converse with I dedicated my time to reviewing the financial transactions of the last day. It seemed as if a single ruble had some respectable buying power. Even in a supposedly grand city like Stalingrad one of them could secure a room with breakfast. A noteworthy education.

After dinner I went back to the squalid hotel and paid for my room, or more like my portion of it. There were four beds to a room. Privacy was a thing of the past in the Soviet Union. Between jail, trains, the farm and this room I hadn't slept alone in nearly a year. Perhaps they didn't change sheets daily, but at least it was a real bed. My unknown roommates were already snoring, and the combination of their serenade and my fatigue lulled me to sleep at once. In the last seconds before drifting off eerie images of my family invaded my mind. Where they safe? When would I see them again? Would I see them again at all?

There's no such thing as darkness, only the absence of light. And in the golden glow of the early morning sun even an urban landscape like Stalingrad looks better. I joined my roommates for our prepaid breakfast and tried to catch up on war news. This big city had every modern form of communication, and the state radio station had constant updates on the situation. My companions were apparently big fans of the radio, so they were more than informative, even if that information was not so positive. The Nazis had attacked along a wide front, from Leningrad in the north all the way down to here, and they were seriously intent on conquering Mother Russia. Remembering my school text book on geography it seemed, on first consideration, that it was impossible that giant Russia could be defeated by relatively tiny Germany. That was an opinion shared by everyone else at the table.

"This Hitler must be insane. Does he have any idea how mighty we are?"

"Why, Papa Joe will crush him like an insect."

"What does he think? That we're a bunch of pushover Jews?"

That was the first time I had heard a Jewish reference in a long time, but I wasn't really sure if it was an anti-Semitic comment or not. Were Jews synonymous for weaklings around here, or was he specifically citing the fact that the Nazis were attacking unarmed Jewish civilians, an unthreatening adversary? In any case I reasoned it best to just listen, sip my tea and eat my oat cake. Not that they were looking for comments from me anyway, so certain were they of every word they spoke. And such patriotic zeal I had rarely seen. I couldn't help but wonder why they weren't in uniform themselves. But I didn't have to wonder long, because right at that moment a group of uniformed soldiers marched into the tiny lobby cum dining room. Before they even came to a stop their leader launched into his speech. As soon as he began I knew it would be glorious.

"Comrades, Mother Russia is in her greatest hour of need. Why aren't you splendid examples of Soviet manhood in uniform?"

Like dueling gunfighters the manly trio had their identification papers in their hands at once, and it turned out they were all employed in jobs vital to the war effort. Satisfied of their contribution to our defense, they next turned to me. Or should I say, on me?.

"And what about you young comrade? What keeps you from the front lines?"

Too intimidated to speak before such endless eloquence I simply proffered my ID.

"Ah, you're just a squirt!"

This made me feel safe. As long as he recognized the legitimacy of my civilian status insults over my youth and stature were inconsequential. Compared to being on the front lines his taunt was music to my ears. He was however a most determined recruiter.

"Papa Joe recognizes how disappointing it must be for Soviet youth to be left on the sidelines of this titanic struggle, so he has formed the Soviet Youth Brigade. Courageous boys and girls all over Mother Russia are joining its ranks to support our glorious troops as well as prepare themselves for any eventual need to join the fray. Come, my little comrade. You'll get a uniform, food, and feel the pride that all loyal patriotic adults feel, defending their homeland from the vile invaders. Besides, you should have been evacuated by now anyhow."

It was pointless to suggest any alternative plan for my immediate future. This dynamic speech sounded like a sales pitch that one did not have the freedom to refuse. It was war, and free will was not an option. Of course, the offer of food, without even thinking about the rest, was probably enough to convince many a farm boy of the value of volunteering. The truth is there was never any choice but submission. From the moment they marched into the hotel lobby my fate was sealed. Next stop, Soviet Youth Brigade.

On my way down to breakfast I was looking forward to a daylight tour of my first big city, but I never anticipated one by automobile. The recruiters had a couple of trucks parked down the street, and they were already crammed with kids. Seeing them opened my eyes to the real situation regarding children. They were being evacuated. And as soon as I climbed aboard one of the trucks it took off. I stood up behind the driver's cab and held on watching block after block and mile after mile of brick sameness. It was frightening. As far as I could see there was no detail that stood out. I remember when I was marched through Lvov on the way to prison, I could make out a few church spires in the distance, but here nothing distinguished one block from another. I marveled that anyone could find their home if they strayed too far from it. How did the postman find a particular house to deliver a letter? To my eye there was absolutely no difference between one building and another. And I pondered that city folk might find the forest around Sieniawa confounding, what with the trees all looking so similar. All these reflections were my inner thoughts. My fellow youth brigade members had no business knowing what made me tick. Jail had taught me to hold my cards very close to my chest.

The trip was a noisy, bumpy one and a double disappointment

in that it was my introduction to big city life as well as my first ride in an internal combustion conveyance. Why would anyone want to live in such a place? It was suffocating and depressing and I already regretted leaving the collective farm and my musical career.

The truck left the city, and as the millions of bricks receded in the distance it was replaced by a more familiar and comfortable landscape, one populated by trees and birds. Each mile of separation from the city brought more relief to my heart, and I was almost looking forward to getting to my new home at the Soviet Youth Brigade. Maybe they liked kazoo music too. But all mental reflection was replaced by a growing queasiness as the one advantage of city life became clear to me. The round tires of the truck were a perfect match for the flat thoroughfares of a metropolis, but not so for uneven rocky country lanes. The vehicle lurched a hundred times worse than old Nikolai's horse drawn wagon, and it felt like my bones were becoming unglued from the flesh of my body. Only by staring at the unbouncing tranquility of the heavens could my total surrender to nausea be thwarted. And sometimes I had to close my eyes completely and silently pray for it to stop. When the truck finally arrived at our destination my eyes dared to squint open a fraction. We were at a dock by a lake. That was my assumption, at any rate. It was announced that we were on the banks of a river, the Volga. If the Don was mighty, then this was ferocious. It was totally unlike any river in my experience. I had only seen the Don for a few minutes when we crossed it, but my principal familiarity with rivers had always been the San, a leisurely two mile jaunt from the heart of greater Sieniawa. A child could hurl a stone across it and hit a tree on the other side. But the Volga was so wide I doubted if a bullet fired from the barrel of a pistol would make it across. It was the most spectacular sight I'd ever beheld. It's vital for military authority to have submissive troops at their behest, and no better place to initiate that belittling process could have been selected than to be stood up next to this superior statement of nature. Dwarfed by one of her more impressive displays we were humbled, which suited the military man who was next to address us. Through his constant contact with the Volga he had become inured to its majesty, and took it in his stride. But we, his new conscripts, were meek and speechless beside it. We were his ideal audience.

"Little comrades, you all know that the integrity of the Soviet Union has been violated. The treacherous German army took us by surprise and attacked along a two thousand mile front. They are hungry for our land, our natural resources, such as wheat and petroleum, even the power of this very river. Make no mistake. This is not a quick sortie to humiliate us. The Nazis seek to conquer us, subjugate us, enslave us, and even kill us if it suits them. Even now they are doing just that to all of the lands they have thus far rolled through with their *blitzkrieg* tanks and mechanized infantry."

When I heard that my heart stopped. Is he talking about my parents, my sisters? I was convinced that the German juggernaut would not take the valuable time to seek out tiny Sieniawa when they had much bigger fish to fry. Our new leader continued his speech which was not the usual flowery rhetoric. He seemed to be speaking frankly like a friend. Nothing was glorious. Everything was as serious as we expected it to be.

"They are murdering civilians as they move forward, and they are moving further eastward every day. Eventually they want to take Stalingrad, the entrance way to the Caucuses and our rich oil fields. Every Russian citizen must do his or her part to defend Mother Russia, to repel the invader, and destroy him as he would us. Now, we understand that you are young. And that is why you have all been evacuated. Most civilized societies would say that you are too young to perform military service. We do not disagree with that point of view. Soviet communism is indeed civilized. The most civilized, most advanced human philosophy on the face of the earth.

But fascism threatens us far worse than we ever dreamed could be possible. It threatens us even more than corrupt political systems such as capitalism and monarchy. So, we must all do what we can to wage the most aggressive campaign possible against it. Though you are young there are still things that you can to contribute to that effort. Presently, in other parts of the Soviet Union, young men and women like you are replacing adults in their regular jobs so that they can be free to take up arms. Of course, the Soviet authority is a benevolent authority and we also want to protect our children. That is part of the reason why we are going to take you all to a training camp far down the river Volga. Stalingrad is a thousand miles from our westernmost border, and Astrakhan', the city where we are taking you for training, is another two hundred and fifty miles southeast, even further away from the German menace, and safer for you. There the Volga breaks up into many smaller rivers and flows fifty more miles into the Caspian Sea, another one of nature's wonders. Maybe you'll see it. Meanwhile you should be safe there. We have no intention of letting the Nazis get their hands on our Russian youth. And we have absolutely no intention of surrendering Stalingrad, named for our courageous leader. Now we will board a boat and sail down to Astrakhan'. Be brave my little comrades. You are safe. And never fear, we shall prevail!"

I expected glorious but got courageous. Things were different here. And I was about to take a long boat ride, an adventure that never entered my mind even in dreams. And, like true totalitarians, they wasted no time. Within an hour we were walking up a ramp onto a ship. Before my truck had arrived, dozens of other trucks had combed the city and collected hundreds more kids to take to safety and military training, and they all plodded up that ramp with me.

The boat moved and the ramp was our first lesson in acquiring sea legs. But after rocking and reeling in the back of that truck the water craft turned out to be blissfully smooth. It was not fast like a truck or a train, and we were all grateful for that. Except for the meager meals, our voyage down to Astrakhan' was like a vacation cruise. Due to the southern trajectory of the Volga it was warmer than the farm had been. Occasionally I thought about Comrade Marina, and wondered if she missed me. Reflecting on the speech we all heard I couldn't help but fear for my chubby blond comrade. One thing for certain, there was little doubt she'd be proud of me. She would beam with socialist pride for her little comrade. Another thing for certain was the probability that we'd never see each other again. Just one year earlier that kid from Sieniawa would have obsessed over that fecund daughter of the revolution, but now he could put it in perspective. War, jail and travel mature you. I was fifteen going on fifty. So, I put her out of my mind, and watched the southern steppes drift past the bow of our boat.

We stopped frequently at small wharves to deliver mail and other goods, as well as take on more kids, and it was striking how the further south we went the more Oriental the people looked. These were not the typical Slavic faces of my upbringing. Men, women and children here looked similar to the Chinese people from my old picture books. They had slightly yellowish skin and gently slanted eyes. This exotic countenance reminded me of why Ovram Feder had gone off to engineering school in the first place, to see the world. The voyage of Arturo Arkadivonovitch down the Volga was the unexpected fruition of that dream, and it prepared me for even greater adventures.

THE SOVIET YOUTH BRIGADE

VIII

As promised, The Soviet Youth Brigade gave us uniforms and food. And that was no small task, because there were literally thousands of us from all part of the Soviet Union. Besides political doctrine, the one big unifying factor there was language. Everyone had to speak Russian and it wasn't long before all of my Ukrainian vocabulary was totally replaced by well enunciated Russian. They trained us to respond to military commands, and it seemed obvious that they were preparing us as a last line of defense, should it become necessary. We hadn't been given arms yet, but that's all that was lacking. We marched in formation and had our senses dulled by endless hours of civic instruction, which was just communist indoctrination. We sat in classrooms and were taught that Mother Russia had invented nearly every practical, medical, and technical marvel that benefited humanity. The airplane, automobile, sewing machine, printing press, gunpowder and miracles of modern science were just some of the advances of modern civilization which the Soviet Union had developed first. They also had us perform some practical functions, such as putting together first aid kits for the front line troops, or assembling some nonessential field survival gear, like mess kits, or sewing canvas together to form pup tents. As we labored we were told to be proud of our contribution to the war efforts. One of our instructors always reminded us of the story of the ancient knight whose horse threw a shoe. There was no nail to reaffix the horse's shoe, making it impossible for the knight to fight in the battle, and the war was lost. Apparently, the lack of a pup tent was going to lose the war against Hitler for us, so our chests were supposed to swell with pride over our great sense of accomplishment and our glorious contribution to the war effort. After several months though we mostly felt bored. Word was reaching us that the Germans were being held at bay by our glorious troops. In private however, officers whom we trusted revealed to us that The Nazis were actually doing quite well in their war of aggression, and that they were dangerously close to Stalingrad. The Soviet Union had been taken by surprise, was ill prepared for the invasion, and would take a long time to catch up. Then we received some very strange information. One officer told me that ever since we had been invaded by Germany, the United States of America was sending shiploads of supplies to our northern ports. They weren't fighting, but they were sending boats crammed with military supplies and food to the Baltic Sea. Civic instruction continually criticized the USA for being capitalists, the enemy of communism. Yet, here they were, aiding our war effort. To me, America was this big mystery in the middle of our school book on maps. It seemed huge, filling up the space between the Atlantic and Pacific oceans. Also, we had heard that many Jews had left eastern Poland and western Russia to build new lives there. Outside of that, little knowledge of that place had penetrated this far east. It did look big, so maybe with their help we would defeat the Germans. For the sake of my family I hoped so. Secretly and silently, I prayed so.

When we weren't assembling nonessential war goods we were allowed to enjoy the pleasant summer. We played soccer and communed with nature. It was the middle of July and the warm sun made me forget all worries. Just as I had done in Kiev on the day of my early release, and as I had done my whole life in Sieniawa, I stood in the grass, face lifted toward the sun, letting the delicious warmth envelope and purify me. With no one around to chastise me for bourgeoisie sloth I intensified my sun worship by letting the heat melt my legs. Sliding down into the fecund lap of Mother Nature my body splayed itself out in the lush steppe grass and sur- rendered to her gentle caress. As my body became one with the land a most unexpected sensation came to compete with the warmth. A vibration was emanating from the core of the earth, not unlike the vibration of a far away train one feels when touching the iron rails. For a second the sensation was not unlike the tingling one gets in a temporarily dormant extremity. But the blood flow in my limbs was unrestricted. No, this was coming from without. My body was not its source, just its receiver. What could it be? There were no train tacks around. At first, the vibrating was intermittent, but then steady. After a few minutes I became aware that others were aware as well. Ah, I was not mad. Soon, it was the sole topic of discussion.

"Oh my God, it's an earthquake!"

"Comrade Sergei, there is no God!"

"For Lenin's sake, it's an earthquake!"

There were kids from all over the steppes, of varying degrees of education, and it was agreed by one and all, that this vibration could not be anything but a tremor starting deep within the bowels of the earth, perhaps from its very core. Every kid spouted pro- found scientific data.

"It could be an earthquake hundreds of miles to the east."

"In Persia they have lots of them, practically every year."

"They must be experiencing one right now, and we can feel its aftershocks."

"What a shellacking they must be getting."

"I heard the earth opens up and swallows trees and houses."

With such expertise all around me there didn't seem to be any need for further speculation. And it was a relief to hear that these things rarely lasted more then a few minutes, if even that long. So, it was quite a surprise when the vibration did not go away, even after an hour. And it was an even greater mystery when it did not go away even after several hours. Adding to the ground tremors were the rumble of trucks that started bringing in more children from the docks. More important than the kids was the news brought in with them. These were the last of the evacuees, the ones who had stubbornly stayed with their parents against all advice. If we couldn't confide in the immature hysteria of these new arrivals we could rely on the adults who brought them here. The reports were stunning, horrific, and frightening beyond imagination. The vibrating of the earth was not an awesome display of nature's destructive might, but man's. The shivering earth that had started on July seventeenth was the far away extension of the ground shaking German air assault on Stalingrad. They were carpet bombing the great city day and night, and that's why it never went away. Nature is more merciful than man. She'll make the earth tremble for a few seconds, or a few minutes at worst. Man is not so relenting. He'll keep it up as long as it serves him, and the Germans were determined to pound this center of industry into submission. Over a thousand Luftwaffe bombers unleashed their lethal fury in a display of shock and awe. The city had an insufficient number of antiaircraft batteries, and the ones they had were ineffective. The Luftwaffe rained down death unimpeded. We truly had been taken by surprise. The city named for our peerless hero, the heart of socialist hammering, center of airplane and tank manufacturing, was targeted for annihilation. More than that, the Germans were determined to sap us of our will to resist or wage war. To do so they would reduce the city to rubble and kill everyone in it. Once the rest of Russia heard of this she would throw down her arms, her hammers, her sickles. She would submit to the master race, and Mother Russia would forever be lebensraum for the Third Reich, her peoples its willing servants. Such was Hitler's plan. No wonder they evacuated the children. The Soviet authorities must have had a pretty good idea that Hitler would not make a half hearted attempt to subdue her most hated enemy. He intentionally planned the attack for the middle of summer, comfortable weather to lay siege to a city. He was a student of history, and was not about to repeat the mistake Napoleon made, trying to fight both the Czar and the winter. So, he unleashed over a thousand bombers and an equal number of artillery to ring the city and pound it into cringing servility.

We were told all this by the adults who brought in this last load of children. It seemed incredible however that many doubted the veracity of the teller. But he assured us that military intelligence, based on air reconnaissance, had confirmed everything.

The vibrations lasted a month. It seemed inconceivable that so many bombs existed, that anyone would intentionally hurl them at other people, or that anyone could withstand it. Back in Kiev we panicked over the air raids of small dive bombers, but this was a million times more awful. Just as fearsome was the news that poured in. The soldiers themselves were now being evacuated in order to save them to fight the Germans once the aerial assault ended. They went west and took refuge across the Volga, in Volzskij. The civilian population, minus the children, was obliged to remain in the city. The Soviet high command determined that the citizens would fight to the death to defend their homes, and later inspire the soldiers. This sounded inconceivably harsh to me. Papa Joe seemed practically reptilian in his pragmatism. They had all these trained soldiers, but they were taken out of harm's way, leaving men and women of nonmilitary service age, left with weapons, without being trained in their use, to contend with the invaders. It all sounded insane to me.

They insisted we continue to assemble the nonessential war goods, but we were all too distracted by the constant arrival of news to keep up any semblance of serious production. We were not only distracted. We were frightened. Untrained civilians were going to protect us from the onslaught of the Third Reich? They could bomb us with impunity? Our soldiers ran away? If others were scared I was petrified. They might turn the Russians into their servants, but at least they'd be left alive. There just didn't seem to be any room at all for the likes of me in their new world order. Is it possible these people would actually surrender to the Nazis like the rest of Europe? If I stayed here I was doomed. Maybe I should steal away and keep heading east? Some maps had come before me recently and it wasn't hard to notice that by traveling south one could eventually make it to Palestine. Just put one foot in front of the other, be lucky enough to find a little food here and there, and it was conceivable to follow the plan of our youth group back in Sieniawa. This communism wasn't working for me. And fascism was aiming to do me in. Maybe Zionism was the answer.

One other alternative stayed in the back of my mind. It crept in there based on what some of the adults discussed. Napoleon conquered everywhere he went, but when he attacked Moscow he was defeated. Of course, they said it was mostly the winter that drove him out, but that meant that they did manage to hold out until that season rolled around. Was the same tactic at play here? Of course, we were far south of Moscow, about a thousand miles, so the winter wouldn't be as harsh. And it wouldn't get bad, by even our standards, for several months. Who could stand this trembling for so long?

The summer ended with no significant change in news. The battle raged, but nobody claimed victory. Maybe these people were tough enough to hold out after all? They withstood seven hundred hours of continual bombing without a hint of a white flag. They were made of tougher stuff than I imagined existed. These were the kind of people others join. Maybe Papa Joe's tough tactics were based on such knowledge. Maybe the likes of me would even do my part. Getting involved seemed inevitable anyway. And if the winter didn't turn me numb my job would. After assembling thousands of first aid kits and sewing together countless tent flaps, I was freezing up. The work was just so repetitive and tedious my brain was stalling from lack of engagement. That's when an old friend of sorts appeared. In the middle of civic instruction, or CI as we called it, our teacher introduced a powerful commissar to discuss the war effort. Any recess from CI was practically like entertainment by comparison, so we were glad to lend him our undivided attention. He looked familiar, but as soon as he started to speak his identity was unmistakable. It was Russian, not broken Polish, but I recognized him just the same.

"Little comrades, I am honored to have this opportunity to address you, the cream of Soviet Youth. The work of The Soviet Youth Brigade is famed from one end of the Soviet Union to the other. Even our dear courageous leader Joseph Stalin lauds your glorious efforts. Every soldier that goes into battle in defense of Mother Russia carries with him some evidence of your irreplaceable contribution to our struggle against the vile Nazis. For that and much more I applaud you."

Commissar Glentz clapped his hands together to emphasize his appreciation. Of course, by now Arturo Arkadivonovitch knew to return that applause, and the whole room exploded in applause and cheering.

"My dear Comrades, when our soldiers have the dire need to open their first aid kits they feel the affection of their countrymen. When they eat from their mess kits they know you're here working for them. When they sleep at night, protected from the elements, inside your tents, they feel they are not alone out there, because they know they have your support. They hold more than pieces of metal or cloth in their chaffed and scarred hands. They hold your love. They endure wounds, frostbite and starvation because of your endeavors. When they look down at what you've made these men know what they're fighting for."

By now many students were openly weeping, so affected were they by Commissar Glentz' moving oratory. Seeing this he pressed his advantage.

"These men send you their thanks. And even Marshal Stalin personally wants you to know how much your sacrifice is appreciated."

Now over half the kids had lumps in their throats, and Glentz got to the point, and in so doing introduced a phrase which we'd hear many more times in the years to come.

"We all know how valued your participation is in our struggle against the invaders in this, The Great Patriotic War. We asked for your help and you came through. All of you, to a man. Yes, I say man. It's true you are still too young for military service, but the fight is coming closer to us every day. We sought to protect you, the cream of Soviet youth, by bringing you all the way out here. You are too young to be drafted. Therefore, in the name of your mothers and sisters, and the Mother Land, we invite you to join the Great Patriotic War and drive the invader back from whence he came! Who will enlist?"

After such a rousing recruitment speech the kids cheered and yelled as one, "Me!"

Love for the Mother Land did not swell my chest however. I was just here because I got rounded up and pressed into patriotic service. It was pure self-preservation that motivated my presence in this region in the first place. Of course, there didn't seem to be much choice. The call for volunteers here counted as much on free will as did the call back in Stalingrad. Oddly though, there was one other criterion at play. My time in Astrakhan' had been plagued by boredom. Every day was identical to its predecessor. And with no shabbos within recent memory, knowing the exact day presented a legitimate challenge to my intellect. So, in spite of asking myself if I wanted to live or die, I thought I'd give soldiering a try. The enlistment papers were put down before me and my bogus signature found its way there. Commissar Glentz personally signed me up, and I was eager to talk to him about Sieniawa. As soon as he saw me it was clear that he remembered me, but he was subtle about it. He knew I was Jewish, but he knew the score and played it cool.

"So, young...."

"Arturo. Comrade Arturo Arkadivonovitch. You remember me."

"Certainly. But tell me, young Arkadivonovitch, what are you doing all the way out here? It's a long way from Jaroslaw."

Sieniawa was so insignificant he didn't recall its name, but rather the county in which it was located. To reply to him I made up something quickly, because I wasn't eager to tell anyone I was in jail, even if it was unjust. What I really wanted was news of home.

"Honestly, I left before the Germans swept through. I was already in Kiev when their Operation Barbarosa was implemented."

"Barba...what?"

"Barbarosa. That's what Hitler called his sneak attack plan. He sent his General Ribbentrop to sign a non-aggression treaty with our Molotov before the fighting began, but it was all a trick to take us by surprise. And let me tell..."

"Please Comrade Commissar, excuse the interruption. I understand that you were already back inside Russia when Operation Barberous began, but I hear so many things about it. They say the Nazis killed and destroyed everything in their path. Is that true?"

"Well, like I said, I was long gone by the time they invaded."

He could see the frustration in my eyes, and maybe he wanted to spare me bad news.

"Comrade..."

"Arturo."

"Yes. Comrade Arturo, I've heard some pretty awful things. But rumors are rumors. I've even heard it said that I had a reputation for ruthlessness. Me, ruthless? So, who's to say? I like you Comrade, and I pr...hope your family's okay. Anyway, that place is such a hole in the woods they probably just went right past without even realizing it was there. There's not even a train depot for Krissake!"

I gave him a half hearted thanks, and turned to go when he stopped me.

"Comrade, I know you think I'm a real blowhard. But I really do like you, and to prove it I'm going to recommend you to a crack unit. The Germans want our country, but they're going to have to take Stalingrad to get it. And Stalin has given the order, "Not one step back!" The whole German sixth army is committed to this battle, and they have their orders too. But we shall prevail. And those are not just flowery words. We win or we die. And nobody can hold back. Anyway, I commend you for enlisting. You'll get your orders soon. Remember, I'm making a special recommendation for your assignment. Hope to see in better times, Comrade."

He leaned in to give me the classic Russian double kiss, but as he went for the second cheek he faintly whispered, "Shalom."

No solid news from home. No assurance of my family's safety. No confirmation of their peril. The continued uncertainty just depressed me. I moped around the campsite for a while, but the patriotic zeal intruded upon my mood. The kids started singing folk songs as anthems, and swayed to and fro with their arms over each other's shoulders. Their high morale would have delighted Marina, and she would have been right to feel that way. And she would have been right to try to change my mood as well. I had to get in gear. The Germans really were here, and they really were my enemy. They were the enemy of the Russian and of the Pole and of the Jew, and somewhere among that population I dwelt. In October of 1941 it didn't matter if my comrades told jokes about Jews. As long as they weren't making speeches about how evil they were, as Hitler did. It was time to link arms with the gentiles, the atheists, the Bolsheviks, the casual Jew baiters. We all had to fight the Nazis together. It was a code these people understood. Me against my brother. My brother and me against our cousin. My brother and me and my cousin against our neighbor. And all of us against the foreigner. The enemy of my enemy is my brother. It didn't matter that my name was phony. Inside, where nobody else could see, the real me knew it was time to do my part against the Third Reich.

After a few more months of assembling first aid kits and pup tents, my orders arrived. They assigned me to a brigade of Cossacks bivouacked just to the east of Stalingrad, outside of Krasnoslobodsk. This was the big favor from Commissar Glentz? What a mysterious mitzvah. The only thing ever spoken about Cossacks back in Sieniawa was that they were dyed in the wool Jew haters, and raped Jewish maidens for sport. It was going to take a long time to comprehend the strange kind of good word he had put in for me. But there wouldn't be much time to think it over, because first thing in the morning, in typical totalitarian style, a truck took me and a bunch of the other enlisted volunteers south. Since the outbreak of hostilities everyone had advised me to head east to stay alive, but now they were sending me southwest. Living or dying seemed less under my control than ever. But all of Europe was now ruled by this philosophy, especially Russia. And the man made earthquake that I felt told me that we were facing a threat worse than anything known in our collective experience. I had confronted gentile bullies in public school, received a black eye or two, and gave as many in return. The level of violence in jail had been about the same, but now it was about to escalate. This was no fight to be settled by fists. I would have to learn about weapons, about death that could come in an instant, and about an enemy that believed we had no right to even breathe.

THE COUNTERFEIT COSSACK

IX

The truck ride was as bumpy as ever. Standing on the bed of the truck, holding onto the cab, gave a great view of the endless ocean of grass, but the lurching of our transport made it impossible to appreciate. It was a wonder to me how the driver could stand it day after day. Some people can get used to anything. After one hour in the back of that truck hand to hand combat, as long as it was on flat land, seemed preferable. The truck brought me to the banks of the Volga and a boat ferried me back upstream to almost the same place I had left months earlier. There, another truck picked me up and headed out for Krasnoslobodsk and the Cossacks on a bumpy dirt road that cut through infinite green.

Far off in the distance I spied what appeared to be a pair of riders on the horizon. As quickly as they had come into view they vanished, and after another ten minutes of gut wrenching mechanical bouncing an island of trees loomed ahead, and grew bigger by the second. The truck slowed enough to see without visual blurriness, and it was possible to make out various low buildings. The two riders we had seen just minutes before must have heralded our coming, because now there were dozens of armed horsemen coming at us from all sides, firing their rifles in the air and shouting. Our driver waved his own much quieter greeting with an empty hand, and started conversing with some riders who had pulled up next to him. They seemed friendly and incredibly boisterous, and found our arrival amusing. Did we bring this or that, and how come it's been so long? To one side was a massive herd of horses, more than I ever dreamed existed. Some men were throwing knives and hatchets at trees. Another was playing a strange musical instrument, a big round thing with a hundred strings, and two others danced some vigorous steps by him. There was endless activity all around, and their uniforms were remarkable. Russian martial dress was just practical drab shirt and pants, but the Cossacks' uniforms were colorful and exotic. They wore long, open fronted coats with cartridge loops on the chest. Underneath bright vests popped out, and tall round fleece hats topped it all off. And they sported flamboyant moustaches. Between the clothes and the horses and everything, it was like a Purim carnival multiplied a thousand times. It was the most spectacular site I ever beheld.

The truck pulled in by the buildings and came to a halt. It was like being in an earthquake and having it suddenly stop. It's a wonderful sensation. The driver got out, wished me well, and went off with some Cossacks, probably to get drunk. I looked around from my elevated vantage point on the truck bed and found it be less frightening than imagined. Then a short leap down to the nonjarring ground, and I was home.

As soon as my boots impacted the lush grass the Cossacks swarmed around me, curious about every detail of my existence. Why did the truck drop me here? Where did they bring me from? What was my duty there? Is a fighting unit the place for someone as young as me? Obviously, they were suspect of my arrival. These people are a clan, and not eager to embrace outsiders. Actually that was easy for me to relate to. To quell their interest I presented my written orders which they perused, without taking in too much detail, and then laughed boisterously.

"The situation must be desperate if they are sending us babies!"

"Noncossack babies!"

"We're warriors, not nurse maids. Junior, take your report card and go back home."

Do you want to live or do you want to die? This was the biggest jail cell so far and my self assertion was more important now than ever.

"I am here to fight alongside you in the Great Patriotic War!"

There was nothing else to say so I just stood there and waited, looking from one to the other. Looking at just one could provoke him. That was basic jailhouse diplomacy. Then, to reinforce my position, and perhaps gain favor with them, I repeated my declaration in Ukrainian. This changed their mood and one of them took the initiative.

"*Kazaks*, go on about your business. I will take this patriot to headquarters."

"Yes, *prikazny*," repeated several men. And this *prikazny*, this corporal, led the way.

Headquarters was not fancy. It was just one of the low buildings. On the way over there I noticed that most of the buildings were actually stables. No surprise, with so many horses. We went inside and found a man at a desk smoking a pipe, looking content. He had no hat on and his head was shaven in a way I had never seen before. It was not short like jailhouse haircuts in Kiev. This man had shaven his head as smooth as a reform Jew's face, but left a small pony tail at the back. It reminded me of the rump of a horse, though I didn't think mentioning it would have earned me much affection.

"What do we have here, prikazny?"

"A new kazak. He volunteered. He's a patriot."

He scrutinized my papers with more interest than their previous inspectors.

"You really volunteered to join the Cossacks?"

"Well, I volunteered…"

"We don't doubt that you volunteered. You're obviously too young to be drafted. Besides, drafted people don't get sent here."

I thought I was about to be told how glorious I was, but he set me straight.

"Stand at attention when your superior addresses you. We may be lowly Cossacks, but this is still the Red Army. Or is it not?"

There was going to be a lot to get used to. The Youth Guard had prepared me for a regimented life, but only now was I aware of it as being much more than a game. This time I had been embarrassingly slow on the uptake. I was now a soldier, and it was wartime. So, I snapped to attention and saluted.

"Yes. Yes sir!"

"Kazak Arkadivonovitch. That's what we call privates in the Cossacks. Kazak, do you know anything about us?"

"Uh…you're Cossacks? And you're fighting the Germans?"

"This is not a test. Now pay attention, kazak. We are Cossacks of the Donski host from the lower steppes along the Don River. We are not Kuban Cossacks from the Caucuses or Terek Cossacks, or any other kind of damned horse's asses."

The irony struck me, but the golden rule of silence bade me keep still.

"We have roamed these steppes since before your ancestors walked upright."

I let the proud man speak. Correcting him would have only complicated my life.

"You have the rare privilege of visiting a real Cossack *stanista*. Most noncossacks would only know such a place being brought here as prisoners. That is, if we took prisoners. But now you are our treasured ally."

It was hard not to believe he was mocking me.

"We are two thousand strong. That's two thousand hard riding Cossacks and two thousand horses, all under the command of our hetman, Kazachy General Bogaevsky. Kazak, can I assume your saddle is outside with your duffle bag in which you have your uniform?"

Who could tell what he was talking about? Was I supposed to have a saddle? And as for possessions, nothing new had made its way into my life since leaving Kiev, much less a uniform, and much, much less a colorful Cossack get-up like theirs.

"Sir, I found my way hear from Kiev with nothing but the clothes on my back."

"No uniform?"

"No sir."

"No saber?"

"No sir."

"No saddle?"

"No sir."

Now he looked exasperated and incredulous.

"But you can ride, yes?"

I thought about our horse and cart back in Sieniawa, and decided to be honest, sort of.

"A little."

The poor man looked depressed for a moment, and then spoke to the man next to me.

"Prikazny, can you please explain to me why they have sent us a child with no battle experience, saddle, saber, uniform, or ability to ride a horse?"

The subordinate took off his fleece cap, rubbed his bald pate and looked pensive.

"Don't take me so literally, prikazny. Just take this useless piece of meat outside and use him for knife throwing practice."

The man obligingly grabbed my arm and started for the door, but was halted.

"I would like to, but his orders come from high up and are very clear. So, feed him, and then stick him on a horse, not too wild, but not too gentle, and don't let him get off until dinner. And while he's at it find him something to wear."

The prikazny saluted, and dragged me outside.

"Welcome to the Cossacks, kazak…"

"Arkadivonovitch. Call me Arturo or Arkadi."

The food was typical Russian peasant fare, bland but filling. While I was eating I had to field lots of questions. I was the first new face there in months, so they were curious about everything. According to my identity papers Kiev was my home and I stuck to that. Everything else was invented on the spot. Wherever they were from it was the opposite for me. Who was my father? He was dead, and left me nothing. What did I do with the Youth Brigade? Where did they round me up in the first place? Every facet of my existence fascinated them. All I had was Kiev as a birthplace and my identity as an orphan. Naturally, no mention of jail, Judaism or Poland. Next they introduced me to a horse. It was taller than Babe, our old horse back home, but not as fat. It had a saddle, and they all gathered around, eager to see if I would fall off. Having never used a saddle back home I provided my audience with a merry diversion. It took me three tries to get my foot in the stirrup, all three from the incorrect right side. There was a serious possibility that these particular Cossacks might die from laughter. Each time I did something wrong I got a bigger laugh. Finally, one of the more merciful kazaks instructed me in the basics of mounting a horse, which apparently meant always from the left side. He stayed and drilled me at that one maneuver for an hour. Finally satisfied I could get up on my own, he led me to the wide open spaces and told me to walk around. While it seemed like a reasonable plan of action, the mare had her own ideas and broke into a gallop, depositing me about twenty yards away. Thankfully the grass was as deep and soft as it looked. With every one of a hundred faces around me in hysterical fits, it was time for a Lvov pep talk. Do you want to live or do you want to die? In short order the mare was carrying me again, but a bit slower thanks to the intervention of an older kazak.

When I went to bed that night I had to sleep face up, because my butt and the inside of my thighs were raw and bloody. Only my sheer exhaustion allowed me to ignore the stinging pain. They provided me with blankets, and it was odd to see one of my own tents over my head. But my belly was full, and they seemed like a warm family compared to Lvov and Kiev. Things could be worse.

When morning came it was breakfast standing up. Sitting was out of the question. Watching me eat on my feet provided my comrades with a lot more entertainment. So far, my main contribution to this unit was as a morale lifter. Comrade Marina would be proud of me. Actually, these men didn't look like they ever needed to have their spirits lifted. They were a nation unto themselves and didn't miss anything. The saddle was their home, the horses were like their children, and the steppes had been their home for centuries. Although they started out interrogating me, filling me with dread that they'd learn too much, I switched the tables on them and expressed the greatest interest in Cossack life. While they were clannish they were also proud, and loved to talk about their culture. They had their way of doing everything, and they were really quite lucky to be left intact. As long as they were allowed to live as they did, they were loyal to Stalin and Mother Russia. It turned out though, that some Cossacks were turncoats and fought for the Nazis. They had been loyal to the Czar and hated Bolsheviks and collective farms. The Nazis promised them a place in the New

Order of the Third Reich and they fell for it. They were traitors to Russia, but the Nazis didn't fully trust them. They often raided behind enemy lines and targeted communist generals. They were savage and often cut out their victims' tongues as trophies. There were even a few Donski Cossack units that were disloyal, but they were very far away to the west. But all of the Cossack hosts were equally savage, and they all followed the same system. They obeyed a *hetman,* or chief, also called an *ataman.* Their assemblies were called *krugs,* and their senior officers, *starshnya.* The topmost hetman carried a Soviet General's rank and a ceremonial mace called a *bulava.* They claimed to be Christians and had no use for Jews. However it was not a preoccupation, as it was with the Nazis. In general, they didn't like to be too distracted by anything. They were natural brutes, who scratched when it itched and raped when they were horny. They were not overly fond of bathing, smelled worse than their horses, drank a lot of vodka and smoked a lot of mahorka. The steppes, that lush savannah of southern Russia, was their homeland, and the German sixth army was an invader. But as independent minded as they were, they were still a unit of the Red Army and followed orders. First and foremost they were soldiers, an ancient warrior cult, like Vikings, only on horseback instead of ships. They were living legends who loved weaponry and prided themselves on their marksmanship, horsemanship, and ability to slice a man in half with a sword. At night they sat around the campfires strumming balalaikas and the enormous bandura zither and sang folk songs about Tarus Bulba and their victories over the Poles and other Slavic peoples. All in all, it wasn't hard to determine that it'd be better to have them as allies than as enemies. Of course, around those friendly fires at night, plenty of Jew jokes flew, as well as keen insights into the evils of Jewry. At times like that they could always rely on me for a sincere, "Don't you know it," or "Ain't that the truth."

With the help of some evil smelling balm for my raw ass I was able to slowly get back in the saddle, and soon only a handful could ride better than me. This won their respect, and they loved to pass me the bottle.

"Take it easy, Vladimir, he's just boy."

"He can ride like a man, Sergei. Why can't he drink like one!"

Gales of laughter followed this, and many a morning I ended up hung over. While the horse got comfortable between my legs they also taught me to shoot rifles and pistols. Then they wanted to know what special talents I possessed. Flushed with confidence I related my pastimes at the collective farm. Once they heard all about it they decided to make me their bugler. Of course they still found room for levity.

"You never screwed Comrade Marina?"

"Oh, I went by that farm last year. I mounted that wench all night."

"Me too!"

They were typical and predictable, but they were fearless.

After my first few weeks of training their hetman finally showed up. He had been in Moscow, consulting with the big shots of the party and the army, and was back with his orders. When he showed up he also brought with him dozens of howitzers, the current incarnation of the ever evolving cannon, dragged into battle by large draft animals. As soon as he showed up there was a huge huzzah of Cossacks shouting his name.

"General Bogaevsky!"

Over and over again they called out his name and fired salvos into the air. He was quite oriental looking, like a Mongolian, and the men revered him. General Bogaevsky seemed equally delighted to be in the company of his men again.

"General Bogaevsky," I called out too. Maybe I wasn't a Cossack, but I was a kazak.

The next day I was practicing the bugle which I had taught myself by ear, and it caught the general's ear. When he came to inspect he was surprised to discover it being played by a non-Cossack kid in an ill-fitting Cossack uniform.

"What do we have here?"

I snapped to attention, "Kazak Arkadivonovitch, sir."

"Where did you ever get that uniform?"

"Well..."

"Report to my quarters at fourteen hundred hours."

After lunch I was escorted to the general's office. He interviewed me while going over some paperwork. Mostly he wanted to know about my formal education. Satisfied that I was quite literate, and impressed by my having volunteered at such a young age, he decided right then and there to make me his aide de camp. He instructed his staff to see that a new uniform be made for me identical to his own, but minus insignia. He even specified that identical boots be made for me. Having sturdy, comfortable footwear was something unknown to me since leaving home. Truth be told, in my entire life I had never possessed such immaculate footwear as was ordered by the general. They were warm, and protected my feet from any rocks or stones one might encounter on the ground. They were a wonder. Then he gave orders to find me a horse befitting my position, a member of the general's staff, so they brought me a beautiful, noble, snow white mare. It was inconceivable. After mere weeks in the army I was on the general's adjutant, a position of real privilege. And to match my position the general made me a corporal, a prikazny, so experienced veterans of lower rank, practically everyone, had to salute me. I would still have to join in the combat, but every other creature comfort would be mine. My duties included finding lodgings for the general before getting to our next engagement. That meant reconnoitering each new town for the best residence, and appropriating it for the general. At all other times I was to ride along with him wherever he went. And it must have looked incongruous to the troops, seeing a miniature version of the general in an identical uniform. But it wasn't the wardrobe that was the main benefit of being the general's aide-de-camp. It was sharing the same food and roof. So, as long as a bullet or a bomb didn't find me I'd be as comfortable as any soldier in the army, and more so than most. I was a new recruit, but I lived like a general.

Now that I knew my duties, it was time for the rest of the brigade to know theirs. The general ordered his troops to assemble, and he delivered the most rousing speech I heard in the entire war, and that's saying plenty.

"Cossacks. The German wermachte has failed to take Stalingrad!"

Cheers filled the air as did gunshots. They hoisted vodka toasts to Papa Joe and hugged each other. He took a few toasts himself and then calmed his troops. He pulled out a sheaf of papers and looked around grimly. He then read the statistics.

"But the price was terrible, my brothers. The German sixth army entered the city after a full month of continuous bombardment by their Luftwaffe and artillery."

Expressions of disbelief and curses muttered around the throng, and they spoke of their admiration for those so tough to withstand such an assault. The general let his men express themselves. After all, many had family there. Then he resumed his oration.

"But Stalin personally gave his command, directive 227. Not a step backwards. Do you hear me my brothers? Not one step backwards. It was to be a fight to the death."

More muttering of approval, as awareness of the gravity of the situation sunk in.

"In my hand I have some papers, reports of the fierce fighting."

The assembly fell deathly silent, so eager were they to hear descriptions of the battle.

"The Krauts planned for their infantry to take the city block by block, neighborhood by neighborhood, with their big guns and air support paving the way. But the defenders of the city had their own plan. They fell upon the Hun like lice and hugged them. They got so close that only small arms fire was effective, never further than twenty or thirty meters, sometimes at point blank range. So the kraut air force and artillery were rendered useless. If they used them they would have ended up bombing their own troops."

Nods and groans of appreciation hummed as one from the crowd.

"House by house they had to fight. Russian farm boys, long accustomed to hunting the fleet footed rabbit for dinner, became snipers and picked off the best kraut officers. Back and forth the struggle went. In the course of a single day one building would be captured and recaptured by both sides a dozen times. The airport changed hands hourly for days. The Russian reserves marched across the frozen Volga and flooded the city with fighting men. The factories, pummeled as they were and without roofs, still continued to churn out tanks and single engine airplanes. When a tank ran off the assembly line, they didn't even bother to paint it or put sights on the guns. They grabbed a civilian, showed him how to drive it and fire the cannon, and off he went. Valiant Russian women pilots flew successful sorties against the Luftwaffe and shot down their best dogfighters."

Cheers interrupted the general, and I joined in myself. How could I not? It was a great relief to know that the Germans could be defeated. Since being among these warriors I felt more protected than ever, and this news now filled my heart with valor.

"Finally we trapped their infantry within the city, and they couldn't get out. By then our factories had made enough antiaircraft guns to deter the German air drops to their trapped soldiers. The winter set in and the arrogant Nazis, dressed for summer in what they believed would be the only uniform they would need to defeat the subhuman Slav, were now shivering to death. Starving, freezing, and running out of ammo, I tell you my brothers, I almost feel sorry for them."

A swell of laughter filled the air and more gunshots went off. If half of what General Bogaevsky said was true this was the mother of all battles. And I finally realized that Commissar Glentz had absolutely done me a wonderful favor, a true mitzvah. He assigned me to troops positioned on the far southern perimeter, far from the battle proper. I didn't have to crawl through rubble, pinned down by murderous Kraut machine gun fire. My rations were not a slice of bread, half sawdust, because the wheat had been burned as part of our charred earth policy. No jumping from apartment window to apartment window, firing up through the ceilings at Nazis firing down at me through the same holes. No being thrust into the driver's seat of an unpainted tank and pointed at the enemy. No doubt about it. Commissar Glentz saved my life.

"So, my brothers. This is the wonderful news. The German war machine can indeed be defeated. It just never came up against armed Russians before."

The gunfire was deafening.

"I have more news. Six weeks ago America came into the war."

There was silence. Some of these people had relatives who had immigrated there, and of course we had all seen a lot of boxes of food marked with those foreign looking letters USA. If we ate beans they almost always had that strange insignia on the top of the can. This suggested that they had been sending us provisions all along, though they were not yet committed enough to actually fight. Besides, the Germans had previously professed alliance with us, but then stabbed us in the back with Operation Barbarosa.

Maybe the USAs were the same unreliable kind.

"And they came in on our side!"

Shouts of relief and another barrage of small arms fire lit up the sky.

"But the krauts are not defeated yet. They are retreating, and that means they are regrouping and will surely try to counterattack. That's where we come in."

Now, the throng fell deathly silent, and everyone leaned in to hear their orders.

"We, the valiant Donski Cossack Host of the Zaporovsky Brotherhood, have been given the assignment of carrying out Operation Uranus, engaging and destroying the retreating sixth army, as well as units of their axis partners, the Romanians and Hungarians, between here and Odessa. This is a seven hundred mile corridor that they might try to slip through. Remember, they came this way to get to the Caucuses and its oil. Some of their units might be bold enough to try to slip around the southern perimeter and make a rush to the oil fields. Axis forces that try that will have to pass by us to do so. Such a desperate force would be composed of relatively light units. There would probably be no artillery or air force involved in such an operation. For all these reasons our light cavalry is ideal to intercept them. We will camp in the hills and sweep down to sting them and push them back. We will also cut their supply lines. Until Stalingrad, my brothers, the krauts knew only victory. They swept over Europe like locusts, devouring everything in their path. They say we're inferior beings, fit only to serve them, the Master Race. Now we know, they are master of nothing. We have lived here for countless generations, and we know how to maneuver here. Even our mounts know this land better than all their Third Reich intelligence reports. They will know no more victory here, my brothers, than they did in Stalingrad. The steppes are our home, now and forever, as The Almighty has seen fit."

The Almighty was not a reference to Papa Joe. The Great Patriotic War was such an extraordinary event that Marshal Stalin had decided to put on hiatus the ban on religion, proving once and for all that there are no atheists in foxholes. Full of confidence and fervent piety General Bogaevsky continued.

"Just like Napoleon, that arrogant bastard Hitler will live to regret that he came to rape Mother Russia. We will kill his soldiers here and as they retreat all the way back to Berlin. The Cossack Brotherhood spits on the Axis. Our sabers will run red with its blood. We will be terrible and show them no mercy. And we will drink and dance the kazatsky on their rotten Master Race graves! Zaporovsky!"

Shouts of victory and gunfire filled the air, and even I felt a rush of energy. The Germans had overrun Poland, and very possibly my home town. Even if I didn't know that for certain, everyone assured me that Adolph Hitler called for Jewish blood. So I wholeheartedly agreed that killing Nazis was a good plan, and that these wild barbaric Cossacks were just the guys to do it. And I was one of them now. They had taught me to ride and shoot, and as soon as I got my first Nazi in my sights I would pull that trigger and dispatch him to hell. I was truly not afraid, and I would not shrink from my duty. My Judaism was hidden away from my comrades but I was a Jew ready to fight back.

Part of my duty was to travel ahead of the main force and secure appropriate lodgings for General Bogaevsky. In this particular case, my very first assignment, I had to find adequate facility for him, his wife and his daughters. He knew it would be a long time before he saw his family again, if ever, so he made special arrangements for them to accompany him to Kotel'Nikovo, a hundred mile train trip south. From there our actual military campaign would begin. I found a fantastic two story house and informed its inhabitants of our needs. These people were not our enemy, so I didn't demand its surrender, merely suggested the most reasonable and patriotic course of action. They found themselves housing elsewhere, and we moved in. The general was exceedingly pleased with my first acquisition, and invited me to pick out a nice room for myself. When the soldiers observed the deference with which their beloved hetman treated me they even began to salute me themselves.

General Bogaevsky was mightily pleased with the quarters I had secured for him and his family, and he wanted to know if I was comfortable too. He always acted as if my welfare was of great concern for him. He was sincerely affectionate with me, and was eager for me to meet his family. It's as if he had adopted me. The uniform. The boots. The white steed. The rank. The preferential treatment was absolutely baffling. Before drifting off to sleep at night I wondered why I was so lucky, and it occurred to me that the general only had daughters and might see me, another orphan of the war, as a surrogate son in place of the one he never had. For whatever reason I felt incredibly lucky. My food and living conditions were better than ninety percent of my adopted Mother Land. Actually, mere survival put you on the list of the fortunate. So by comparison, my life was that of a prince. The irony of all this vexed me less each day. At first, it was a constant private joke between me and myself that a Jew wielded such power among the Cossacks, people who might have instigated pogroms against my ancestors. Watch out for the counterfeit Cossack! But as time wore on, I began to see them as real people upon whom I could rely. The Jew in me was buried down so deep it was not even an issue any more. I never thought about shabbos or holidays. There was a war on, and I had to be a hundred percent dedicated to fighting it. Living one day at a time was how to survive this war. I couldn't think about my family, being Jewish, or anything else for now.

As the general's aide I was included in the inner circle of his family and social life. They were going to spend a few last precious days with him before the fighting began, and I was permitted to participate in their amusement. His wife and daughters found me cute and wanted to know all about me. Of course, their keen interest necessitated the usual bunch of baloney about my past. They bit their lower lip and furrowed their brows when I spoke of the bombing raid on Kiev that killed my poor parents. And they grinned when I described the comb and tissue paper episode at the Collective Farm. Feeling right at home with these people, I got the chutzpah to teach the daughters the tango. I sang the song and taught them the steps, and they were as entranced with me as can be imagined. The spell was broken however when the mother walked in. We all stopped, frozen in our Argentine footsteps. If the general wouldn't have me skewered as entertainment for his troops he'd probably send me to Stalingrad on permanent burial detail. But my luck held. The mother's only concern was not missing out on the tango lessons. As soon as she saw us she piped up, "Me too!" So we merrily danced away the afternoon as most of Russia, Europe, and even the world, struggled to throw off the Axis yoke. But my dancing days were about to end. We were ordered to take to the field, and my first taste of combat was at hand.

Typical Cossack, with his hand on his weapon of choice, his saber.

Part of the training to join the Cossacks was learning to ride.
My horse was a noble white steed exactly like this one.

ARMED COMBAT

X

Our company was assigned to a much larger division that also included artillery. Along with our thousands of cavalry ponies we had large draft animals to pull field howitzers, modern cannons meant to discourage any thought of an Axis counter attack. They were small and light and could be pulled by a pair of sturdy shire horses, beasts that were twice the size of our mounts, which were descended from the wild Mongolian Przewalskiwe breed of equines. The howitzers, while relatively light for artillery, delivered powerful explosive shells that wreaked havoc on the temporary encampments of the enemy. They were meant to open fire at the beginning of our surprise attack, and once they fell silent our contingency was supposed to personally engage the dazed survivors of that vicious assault.

Our engagements were of two kinds. The first was to attack on horseback while the Axis soldiers were still in disarray from the artillery barrage. We would ride down on them with small arms and do as much damage as possible with rifles, pistols, and submachine guns, firing from our mounts. We also had the option to briefly dismount in order to fire with greater accuracy. And of course, if any of our number was gripped by nostalgic violent tradition, we had razor sharp sabers to slash them at will. Our secondary tactic was to leave our mounts safely behind in the trees and set up a perimeter of fire which, in addition to our usual small arms fire, included mortars and seventy caliber machine guns. Sometimes, this second tactic was used to initiate encounters in which the howitzers could not be used. In any case we were meant for light quick sorties, to catch small units of Axis soldiers off guard, and annihilate them. Our job was to get in and get out, which meant that we were not equipped to take prisoners. We were assigned to one task and one alone, to kill as many of the enemy as possible. But whatever our overall strategy was it was not shared with the mass of soldiers. They were simply told their immediate destination, and even then with never more than a few days anticipation.

It was early February of 1942, and we were on the march to engage the enemy. To start our campaign off in real style, and with the greatest numbers possible, we were going toward the front by train. Even the horses had the comfort of traveling by rail, and we loaded them onto cattle cars. As each of us deposited our mounts into the wooden car we gave a pet or stroke of affection. Our horses were like family to us, and there was a great emotional bond between man and animal. A Cossack spent the better part of every day on or next to his steed, and it's not far fetched to describe his feelings towards his animal as profoundly deep. Although these people were little more than barbarians, their sensibility for their horses were imbued with all the sentiment of poets. Plainly speaking, they loved their horses, and the loss of one in combat was felt nearly as deeply as the loss of a fellow soldier. Often the display of grief was visibly greater, and they felt no embarrassment over it. Everyone named their horse, and I was no different, calling my beautiful white mare Babe, the first and most natural name to jump to mind

When on march everything that we needed was on horseback. Each kazak carried a rifle, pistol, saber, ammunition, first aid kit, mess kit, blankets, and a few essential and nonessential personal items. Every fourth kazak carried a tent which he shared with three others. Some officers also carried hand grenades, binoculars and submachine guns. There were mules that carried seventy caliber machine guns, mortars, more ammo, provisions for man and beast, and our flags. We had a wireless radio set, a few men with medical training, and a mobile kitchen. We cooked over open fires and hardly anybody ever bathed. They slept in tents assembled by the glorious Soviet Youth Brigade, though the general and I slept in an especially roomy tent. Of course, the general and I were often billeted in real houses, depending on my getting there ahead of time and making such arrangements. That was part of my job, but my full time occupation was soldier. There were armed Nazis out there, and every one of us counted.

Finally we got saddled up and took off in pursuit of our quarry. The snow on the ground was not particularly deep, and the horses didn't seem to be inhibited by it at all. These were hardy ponies from Siberia, and the relatively mild cold of southern Russia was as summer to these beasts, long accustomed to frigid sub arctic temperatures and winds. The oil in the crank cases of German military vehicles froze while our mounts easily trotted forward, oblivious to the very same weather that stopped our foe in their tracks. As we rode along we discussed the tactics of the light cavalry. Mounted cavalry could hardly face entrenched modern armament, so it was our policy to never confront the enemy on the open battlefield. We rode mostly at night towards our objective. In the day their reconnaissance aircraft might spot a force as large as ours, even from a high altitude. In the closest possible patch of forest we hid our horses, and encircled the enemy, taking up positions to catch them in a cross fire. With the first rays of sunrise we would attack and not cease fire until we killed them all or forced their retreat. And with each encounter our force would advance further. Such was the theoretical combat tactics that we were going to put into practice. And they all discussed this as calmly as deciding seating arrangements at a wedding. They were all battle hardened veterans who carried on their bodies scars and other proof of combat. Only one among our ranks was untested. Would my nerves fail me when the moment of truth came? Would I find the courage to face our enemy and shoot true? I must not shame myself. The Nazi troops we were about to confront might well have been the same ones who swept through Sieniawa. For the sake of my family I must be ready to honor them and mete out harsh punishment. Maybe they weren't the same Nazis, and maybe my family was still alive and well. Whatever the circumstances of our encounter in battle I must be sure to acquit myself with honor. One thing was certain. I had done nothing but run away from the Nazis since they invaded Poland. Now they would run from me. Occasionally I gripped my pistol handle or rifle stock. They had taught me to have complete confidence in our weapons, the best in the world. Of course, by then anyone with a lick of common sense took absolute statements like that with a grain of salt. The communists always claimed to have the best of everything, or to have at least devised it in the first place. The entire industrial revolution, from the steam engine to assembly line manufacturing, was the result of Soviet ingenuity, and our weaponry was no exception. Tokarev Munitions made both our rifles and our sidearm pistols. And after learning a little about such things it really did seem to me like we had excellent weapons. They were semiautomatic which meant that we had the option of rapid fire. And they took magazines of ten and fifteen rounds. They taught us that semi automatic guns were plagued with jams from the spent cartridges not extracting smoothly, leaving even the most patriotic and courageous kazaks at the mercy of his enemy. But the Tokarev model 1940 had a specially refined barrel that allowed cartridges to eject from the weapons almost without fail. Even if snow or mud got into the breech it should still function. We were assured it was far superior to the German Mauser. The Tokarev even allowed us the option of full auto which means it could function like a submachine gun. But we were under strict orders never to engage the weapon like that without direct spoken orders from our commanding officers to do so. If not, we'd run out of ammo just seconds after pulling the trigger. Even though it seemed to the uninitiated that a flurry of bullets might kill more Germans it was actually the old fashioned one shot at a time method that was most deadly. It was far more accurate and economical. Why waste ten wildly splayed bullets when one well aimed chunk of lead would do the job? But the full auto option was always there if and when we were face to face with a roomful of adversaries. Having these weapons at our side made us feel confident, strong, and ready to engage. An occasional pat on my rifle stock and pistol grip gave me resolve. No doubt about it. I was ready.

Periodically, we were told to stop and rest the horses. They didn't specifically tell the men to rest however. It probably wasn't meant as such, but it appeared as if there was more concern for the welfare of the animals than the humans. Sometimes we walked along so as to make progress while still giving our horses some rest. At those times I felt an increased camaraderie with these Cossacks. Actually, an air of invincibility had fallen over me and there was nothing less than utter certainty within my heart that victory would be ours. Who could even imagine that one of us would fall? The cold was already dealing the Nazis a losing hand, and we were coming in to mop up the field with them. The snow would turn red with German blood. It was clear to me what General Bogaevsky meant. You could almost feel sorry for those bastards.

The sun goes down early in Russian winters so I rode up ahead with a couple of kazaks to reconnoiter a good location to place the general's tent, and we found a space among a dense stand of trees that was custom made for it. Having authority over these men I had them remove the layer of snow on the ground and lay down the thick lower carpet that insulated the main Persian carpet from the ground and allowed the general some real creature comfort. He could even walk around in his stocking feet, if he wanted to, and not feel cold. After arranging the interior to the general's liking I then went out to find his dinner. We always had provisions to fall back on, including USA beans, but the general liked his fresh meat, so I dispatched a sharp eyed kazak to hunt up anything that moved. He was armed with a rifle with a telescopic sight and silencer, so as not to give away our position to the Nazis. By the time that was taken care of, the rest of the company arrived. The mobile kitchen set up and all the men deployed their four man tents. A scouting party was dispatched in the direction of the enemy with a radio. Depending on the distance they'd signal back if we could light a fire or not. It was a single word, a constantly changing code that told us everything without telling the Germans anything. A campfire could be seen for a long ways, so we had to be sure it was safe. With the silencer and assured campfire security we guarded our approach. Even a general wouldn't risk betraying our position for hot meat.

The scouts gave the all clear signal and fires soon warmed the meals and spirits of the men. I shared some rabbit stew with my commanding officer and he wished me good hunting for the battle to come. It never occurred to him that the dawn would bring about his aide's baptism by fire. He sawed wood all night, and though I was confident about the fighting that awaited me, much of the night was spent reviewing the use of small arms in my head and thinking about my family. If they were alive my actions in a few hours would continue to protect them. If they were dead it would avenge them.

The general was up by three and warned me not to blow revile. It was our first engagement of the campaign and he didn't want to start it off by announcing it. This drove home the reality of the coming battle. They might be close enough to hear a small bugle, and be warned. That's not very far.

We mounted up and headed through the dense woods. Our strategy placed us about five miles away from our objective, a distance which our Siberian ponies could easily close in an hour. Combat was second nature to these warriors so, and as we rode along, they discussed everything except the coming fight. I was grateful for that, because it helped pump up my confidence, as well as distract anyone from speculating on my lack of combat experience. Soon enough we were there.

From now on it was all hand signals. We were silently ordered to dismount and tie up our mounts. Then we marched west through the woods. By the time it was five thirty in the morning we had formed an arc around their eastern perimeter, and stood within a hundred yards of them. We could have opened fire and shot them in their tents, but we preferred to see them and verify our kills. Before long they were waking up and huddling around their campfires. The silent signal to take aim came, and I suddenly realized I hadn't chambered a round in my rifle breech. All the others had done that en route, and now all they had to do was quietly release the safety position from the mechanism. That was the benefit of experience. I hadn't done that, and now I would make a loud series of metallic clicks to get my own rifle in firing mode. It's even possible that a German sentry would hear it across the wide unnaturally quiet expanse of snow. Rather than spoil our surprise attack I decided to wait until the first shot was fired before touching the bolt on my Tokarev. And that was not long in coming. No sooner did I realize my dilemma when the Russian word for fire, *agonya*, was spoken, chilling in its cold blooded and calculated calmness. Our seventy caliber machineguns initiated the barrage, immediately followed by thousands of rifles, and a variety of submachine guns and mortars.

It was a roar such as I had never imagined. Thousands upon thousands of small explosions overwhelmed my senses. It was an awful man made thunder that crashed against my ears, rendering me deaf. So, this was war! With such a din nobody noticed my momentarily muted gun. But as quickly as I had taken the lesson of life or death from my jailhouse mentor, I recovered and the bolt of my Tokarev was in my hand. In a heartbeat my first round was headed home with the others. In rapid succession I emptied the other nine slugs from my magazine and wondered if I hit anyone with my ten large jagged pieces of white hot metal. I was fighting for my survival, and that meant eliminating as many of my potential assassins as possible. What's more, these men had either already killed my family or would gladly do so. They were my enemy and must die. But who knew if I hit any of them? Only the starshnya had binoculars, and a handful of snipers had telescopic sights. Besides them, and perhaps a few other eagle eyed kazaks, nobody else could be absolutely sure exactly where their bullets found their marks after crossing a field long enough for a professional soccer match. Judging by the scores of Germans that were dropping though, it's safe to say our ambush was a fatal success. There were so many guns going off at the same time as mine, to the left and right of me, it was impossible to tell if a Nazi bit the dust because my finger squeezed the trigger or a comrade's. In a few seconds my magazine was empty, so I released it and jammed home another. We were well supplied and under no strict orders to make every bullet count. Our mission was to pour as much hot lead into those bastards as possible. A third magazine found its way into the breech of my rifle, and my trigger finger automatically squeezed off one round after another. This was like a shooting gallery. It was not so much a battle as an immense firing squad carrying out a death sentence and executing a gang of deserving murderers. Another clip went in. A metallic chorus of clattering magazines and bolts were sounding all around me, making a harmony for the thunder of our *agonya*. I glanced to one side, and saw the concentration of the sharpshooters next to me. One or two perceived my regard and shot me a quick look of confidence and controlled glee. They were intent on what they were doing, shooting fish in a barrel. Or so I thought. Barely twenty seconds had gone by since emptying my first magazine and now I became aware of buzzing sounds over my head. Zings and zips were now as omnipresent as the clatter of bolt actions and our own salvos, but what it meant didn't hit home until one of our number cried out. He was hit. The German targets in the shooting gallery were firing back, and the wide eyes, so long suppressed, came back. As another reflex I hugged the ground even tighter than before. But my gun did not fall from my hands and my pants stayed clean. I was a soldier at war, and I emptied my clip and slipped in another, as trained. Bullets meant for us, but falling short in the thick snow banks, kicked up an almost constant flurry of snowflakes and ice crystals. The German ranks also seemed partially shrouded in those white clouds. Our *starshnya*, firing blasts from their submachine pistols, exhorted us to do our duty.

"Pour it into 'em bothers! Drive these weasels from the steppes! Remember what they've done! Don't leave even one to tell the tale!"

The Cossacks are such a gregarious and boisterous lot they talked to their victims too.

"Take that Axis pigs!" "Eat this Adolph!" "Hey krauthead, how do you like the Russian winter so far?" "Whadda ya think of Barbarosa now?!" "Die Nazis, die!"

About ten feet from my position a cry went out and another soldier called for a medic. I didn't think it would do me any good to see a wounded soldier, so I kept firing. By now our mortars were falling within their perimeter and I saw bodies fly up into the air, not entirely whole. Several times our mortar rounds landed in the middle of a group of men and a shower of dark water shot upwards and fall back to earth. Even from this distance I knew it was German blood. Their shouts were easily audible and it sounded like chaos. Several people were screaming orders, but our snipers silenced them whenever they showed their faces, creating even worse disorder among them.

Scum that they were they were still disciplined scum, and they put up a fight. But they were tired, cold, hungry and scared, while we were fresh, well fed and confident. After just fifteen minutes General Bogaevsky felt we had accomplished our objective for the day and ordered our withdrawal. With a ringing in my ears, I obeyed the silent hand signal and stealthily crept backwards until out of range.

Our strategy was followed very carefully. If we stayed too long in the field we risked more casualties than we were prepared to deal with. It's difficult to cope with wounded cavalry as it is prisoners, because the jarring ride on a horse opens wounds. Cossacks have strong constitutions and are a resilient lot, but their flesh is as weak as any when invaded by jagged chunks of hot lead. So, our tactic was the classic tactic of the guerilla. We engaged the enemy in brief skirmishes at close range, did as much physical damage as possible, and retreated before they could organize a defense. Even though we were part of an entire division, our part in it was specific, to kill as many of them as possible and inflict as many wounds in the process. It's a reliable strategy to weaken an opposing army by wounding more than you kill. You kill a man and the enemy loses one soldier. Wound a man and, not only is he probably out of action, but it takes one or more of his own comrades to take care of him. That puts more enemy combatants out of action. Of course, the Cossacks were intent on doing as much killing as possible. You couldn't order them to merely wound, because that required a great marksmen with a sniper's rifle, firing from a hidden spot. But as unintentional as it may have been we kept their medics overworked, and their suffering great. Basically though, our goal was to harass the Axis retreat, discourage any thought of a counter attack and force them to abandon valuable hardware. And our guerilla tactics were the very worst kind of nightmare for them. They had just gone through months of close range fighting with subhuman slavs and wanted no more of it. So we hammered away, killing, lowering their morale, and making them long for the pastoral peace of the Bavarian Alps.

As we returned to our mounts I suggested to one of our marksman to look for something edible to shoot for our ataman Cossack chief. Now that the axis was aware of our presence an unsilenced shot or two more in the distance was inconsequential. Back in camp I reported to the general. He was pleased with how the battle had gone and received word that his young aide had done his duty well. He briefly praised my valor, but his demeanor demonstrated that nothing less was expected of me. The notion of a cowardly Cossack was so oxymoronic as to defy reason. It made me proud to be accepted by these ruffians, and any thought of disguising my Judaism was so deeply buried that it was unnecessary to affect it any longer.

That night we sat around campfires in a joyous mood. There were so many that the combined heat made it almost feel like summer. Our field cook had spent the day making a hearty soup and plenty of bread. Nobody would go to bed hungry that night. And few would go to bed sober. The Cossacks love reasons to celebrate, and today's stunning victory was motive aplenty. They sang songs and told jokes. They bragged about how many kills each one had, and when it came my turn I exaggerated as well as anyone else. Of course my bullets might very easily have felled dozens. After all, my gun was hardly ever quiet and there were so many German targets in that general direction it seemed impossible that none of my ammo found its mark. But I never saw it personally. Some Cossacks lamented the great distance over which we were fighting. They longed to thrust their sabers between Nazi ribs and vowed to do it before this campaign was over. And when a drunken Cossack asked me how I felt about it I echoed his sentiments exactly. I was becoming a Cossack myself, a prikazny of the Donski host.

We were flush with victory and full of glory. We recounted our heroic exploits of the day and also some of those of the recent Battle of Stalingrad, which had now reached legendary status. One of our favorite tales of battle was about Lily Litvak, The White Rose of Stalingrad, a female pilot who shot down more German planes than any of the thousand aviatrix of the Red air force. One time she shot down a famous German ace. He parachuted to safety, but was caught. With classic Prussian etiquette he asked to meet the pilot who had shot him down. When he was presented to Lily he refused to believe it, thinking he was being mocked. But she described every detail of the dog fight, and he knew it was true, that he had not only been bested by a subhuman Slav, but a woman.

As we sat around the fire, telling stories of the courageous comrades of Stalingrad, a fatter than usual kazak ambled by under the influence. His poor physical condition inspired the loud jeering disapproval of several men, and even prompted one to comment, "He's so fat. He looks like an *evre*, a Jew!"

It was meant as an insult, but it drew laughter. It reminded me for a moment who my cohorts were, and it also reminded me to watch the drink. A drunken Arkadi might accidentally reveal his secret obesity too. So, I excused myself as a member of the general's staff. Everyone stood and saluted me and I retreated back to the splendor of our Persian carpeted tent. There was a fire in front of the tent and it provided so much warmth I opened the front flap and let it in. It was my best night's sleep since the collective farm.

We struck camp the next day and pushed on further west. We

were going to engage a larger force, Romanians, but it was going to be a coordinated attack. First the Russian air force bombarded them, using dive bombing techniques learned from the Luftwaffe. During the Battle of Stalingrad the factories there never stopped manufacturing tanks or airplanes. That's an amazing fact, because all the reports said that literally every single building in that city was laid to waste. Not an edifice was left standing. The factories had no roofs and only a few walls, but the machinery for building these machines of war was still operational. The airplanes they turned out were not pretty. They didn't even bother to paint them. As soon as one rolled off the assembly line they stuck in anyone who could fly, man or woman, and sent them off to serve the Motherland. Once the aerial bombardment and strafing had thrown the Romanians into disarray, Red field artillery opened fire on them. After an hour of that these half hearted Axis soldiers were utterly disinclined to pursue further thoughts of invading Russia. Regardless, we were unleashed on them. Our strategy was planned so that we knew exactly when the howitzers would fall silent, and just minutes before that we mounted up. The thought that a bunch of Romanians or Hungarians would intrude onto Russian soil absolutely infuriated General Bogaevsky, and he wanted us to lay into them even stronger than usual, taking away from them any notion of welcome. Exactly one minute before the last round was fired from our howitzers an officer yelled, "Zaporovsky!" We were off.

Even though I had practiced to be their bugler I was not ordered to sound any charge. The Cossacks didn't traditionally use a bugle to lead them into battle, preferring just to bellow out the name of their Host, or tribe, sabers raised high. Now, thousands of us were racing across an expanse about two hundred yards wide. But our ponies were so swift, and the disorder among our adversary so complete, we were upon them in seconds with no doubt of victory. To further bolster our confidence we knew we were up against inferior

Axis combatants. These were not disciplined Germans or Austrians led by Prussian trained officers, but drafted citizens from countries that were obliged to cooperate with the Third Reich because of their incompetent rulers' poor decisions. Their training was not half of what a wermachte regular's was, and they had little stomach for the battlefield. To make them fight their sergeants were positioned at their backs threatening to shoot slackers. Added to that they had grown up on fairy stories of the fierceness of Cossacks, and hearing the war whoops of our Host and the thunder of our galloping steeds, they probably wet themselves.

We had begun our charge before the last cannon rounds were fired, and I felt as if we were riding so fast we might actually overtake them. But the plan worked perfectly. The last shell hit about a hundred yards in front of us, driving the Romanians and Hungarians into utter chaos. Seconds later we were among them slashing and firing.

My comrades were gleeful to be using their swords. The saber was the traditional weapon of the Cossack, but modern warfare had rendered it a relic, found mostly in museums. So, having an opportunity to thrust them into the flesh of an enemy filled their hearts with a grim satisfaction. As for myself I felt safer with my modern sidearm. I rode with the reins in one hand and the pistol in the other.

My cohorts were as fearsome to behold as legend implied.. They rode at a full gallop with the reins between their teeth, a saber in one hand and a pistol in the other, screaming as they charged. Just the sight of them made this enemy flee. They could have stood their ground and taken aim with their rifles, but they were so terrified they were beaten before the fighting began. And who could blame them. If we joked about feeling sorry for our Nazi foes, we might have actually felt real pity for these draftees, victims of their moronic governments' inability to deal with a madman. There was no time for political philosophizing however. They were the enemy, servant of the Nazi, and must die. They were running everywhere, looking for shelter, both to hide behind and to return fire from. I emptied my pistol clip in their direction, holstered the empty gun, and swung my rifle around from off my back and started firing from the shoulder, though with little accuracy. Just as I had done in the previous battle I kept firing my weapon and reloading. All around me the Cossacks were swinging their sabers and firing their pistols, all of them with much greater accuracy than me. I saw what happens when a strong muscular arm jabs a three foot long piece of metal into human flesh, and I'll never forget it. The victim shrieks, grimaces a horrible death mask, and falls away, dead before he hits the dirt. If he's not lucky enough to be dealt a deathblow he writhes around, an uncontrolled and chaotic animal, screaming and crying, with blood gushing from his wound and mouth. Sometimes a Cossack takes pity on such a victim, and shoots him with a coup de grace from his pistol or rifle. And this grisly sight is repeated a thousand times, with the horses neighing their own blood chilling cries, adding to the nightmarish mayhem. I recalled that some adult prisoners back in Kiev had discussed the pathetic Poles counter attacking the blitzkrieg on horseback and being decimated. I suppose that must have been true, but in these circumstances we held the high ground and were the uncontested victors. The Hungarians and the Romanians put up much weaker resistance than the Germans, even though they were fresher troops. And now that they saw that Hitler was not invincible they probably regretted getting in bed with him in the first place. They just wanted to go home. But we were savage, butchering thousands of them. Many of their units hoisted white flags, but we did not relent. We were merciless.

After a mere ten minutes of this carnage we were ordered to retreat. We had learned from experience that there were always some clear headed soldiers who held back and organized a cadre of riflemen and machine guns to fire into us, regardless of the presence of their own comrades. They figured that any of their ranks already in hand to hand with the dreaded Cossacks were dead anyway, so they might as well as fire on the enemy regardless of the effect of so-called friendly fire. It was pragmatic military strategy at a Napoleonic level, and we knew it. So, before that happened we did our damage and rode away. The Cossacks were absolutely elated to have fought on horseback with sabers and yelled nearly as much retreating as when charging.

That night around the campfires they drank and sang more than usual, and were practically solemn in their carousing. They had fought with sabers, were victorious and fulfilled. Our campsite was a *stanista* by the flowing Don. They were louts, and would have probably done me harm had they known my roots, but this was war and I was glad to be among them. But every night, before sleep took me, I thought of my family. My father, mother and sisters were manifest right before my eyes every single, solitary night.

THE BLOOD OF WAR

XI

We continued to march west, engaging different elements of the German sixth army. We covered about twenty miles a day, always repeating the same strategy. But we weren't always as comfortable at night as after our first battle. It was still cold and we often spent nights surrounded by our horses, the heat of their bodies helping us withstand the cold, which was made even more chilling from the unfettered winds sweeping over the open expanse of the Steppes. Animals can provide great warmth. They have a body temperature similar to ours, yet don't need fuel to keep generating that heat. Furthermore, they seem quite pleased to share it. I recall how comforting and warming Babe's breath was. I named her after our horse in Sieniawa, and like all cavalrymen throughout history, Cossack or otherwise, I was attached to her. Sometimes I slept with my face right against hers, and I'm not embarrassed to confess that I felt great tenderness towards my mare. It was a platonic kind of affection, I can assure you, but her soft muzzle and great warmth were a real comfort to me on those cold nights. And she did not suffer from bad breath as most of my comrades did. Actually, no horse smelt as bad.

Whether I woke up next to a horse or in a fine house commandeered for the hetman, the day was spent either traveling toward our next battle of fighting it. Traveling west we snaked back and forth through the outskirts of towns like Novocerkassk, Novosachtinsk, Krasny, Terez, Makejevka, Konstantinovska, Kramatorsk, Marganec, and Apostolovo. We traveled on horseback, hiked, and even used a train when logistically possible.

In tiny Terez, barely fifty miles north of the Azov Sea, the Germans organized a counter attack. We had them pinned down, but by then the weather was a balmy spring, and their oil was fluid. All of those conditions conspired to give them such high morale they tried to take the initiative. Our surfeit of confidence and bravado also led us to make the mistake of moving in too close, risking the danger of the Nazis trying to implement the hug tactic that was their own downfall in Stalingrad. But we still held to Papa Joe's directive not to take one step backwards, and stood our ground. A unit of their infantry flanked us and momentarily gained the advantage. I swiveled to fire on them, and for the only time of the campaign my Tokarev jammed. Of course, being without a rifle was nothing new to a Russian soldier. By then we had all heard how pairs of fresh recruits were sent into Stalingrad with only one rifle between them, theorizing that one would die and bequeath his weapon to his surviving comrade. And more often than not that beneficiary would in turn leave it to whoever retrieved it from the mud or the rubble. I jiggled the bolt but it was useless. And in that moment I let the Germans advance another ten yards towards my position. Hardly ready to rely on my saber, which I had yet to carry into battle, I pulled out my other Tokarev, the pistol I had only fired once since training, at our second encounter, the first cavalry charge against the Romanians and Hungarians. On that day I had only fired a clip's worth of ammo before switching to my rifle. My sidearm seemed puny in comparison with its longer and heavier cousin, and only carried an eight round magazine, but it was all I had left. I fired the first shot with one hand and was surprised by its kick which I hadn't noticed before. So I grabbed hold with both hands and emptied the entire mag as quickly as I could. It's nearly impossible to aim a pistol with any reliability, and no Germans fell from my barrage. Furthermore only one spare mag remained on my belt, and I had to roll on my back to dig it out. It went into the handle of the pistol as soon as I freed it from its sheath, and I was prone at once, squeezing the trigger again. Pop! Pop! Even the sound of it took away my confidence. But I had to keep firing. Pop! Pop! Pop! Each report dissipated quickly and I felt utterly impotent to repel the small kraut unit that had closed the ground between us even more. I could actually make out their ranks now, and only a few shots remained in my pistol. I took aim at what looked like a sergeant, but before I could pull the trigger a hundred high caliber slugs ripped the air over my head flying straight into the Nazis. Several Germans were thrown back by the force of the barrage and I looked up to see the same kazak who had made the joke about the fat Cossack emptying his Tokarev on full auto into the krauts, screaming obscenities as he did. All tolled, a dozen comrades had quickly reinforced my position, taking the initiative to put their guns on full auto without permission. The krauts dove into the mud and crawled backwards, firing as they went, but retreating just the same. It was about as close as I had come to buying the farm since joining the Cossacks.

I fell back to my previous position with my rescuers and dug in, now bereft of armaments. No sooner had we done so when a barrage caught the soldier next to me and ripped him apart. I had never been so physically close to such carnage as this, and for the first time since the fighting began I felt frightened for my life. I actually felt my eyes in the forbidden wide open position and immediately narrowed them again. Even under these circumstances I had to maintain the act. I had actually imagined that I had become one of them, but here was a reminder of my less brutal nature.

We continued to pursue the Germans and reduce both their number and will to remain of Russian soil, and the number of battles we had waged was by now already impossible to enumerate. But of all our encounters the bloodiest by far took place a little north of our usual path in the railway juncture of Slav'ansk.

Reports came back to us that the Germans might try to make a run to Odessa, and we were determined to cut them off. Three days of riding by night and camping in the woods by day, brought us to within striking distance the next morning. We rode to within two miles of the town and sent a scouting party. They returned and reported that the station was empty. No trains or troops from any army were there, so we advanced on it, wary that we might encounter them any moment. When we got to within a mile of the juncture we dismounted. We cleaned our weapons, loaded a few dozen mules down with more ammo, and set off for the abandoned depot. On the way there we got constant updates from our scouts. Still, no sign of the enemy, and we had no reason to suspect that we had been detected. To be safe we split our forces, sending half north of the depot by two miles and around to the western side of the rails to pick off any krauts that might be on that side. From there they would fire at their flanks with a southeastern trajectory. The remaining half of the force would approach the objective from the eastern side, and fire directly into them if we encountered any. Shooting at these angles assured us of no danger of hitting each other with friendly fire.

In about ten minutes we were in the train depot, and it was abandoned. It was an ominous quiet, reinforced by orders to stay silent. Our intelligence was usually reliable, and if they said there were krauts in the area it must be so. One of our officers knelt down on the ground and put his ear to the rail. Immediately he glanced up and nodded, pointing north, then pointing down, indicating that a south bound train was bearing down on us. We didn't know if this train carried allies or enemies, but it's always best to plan for the latter. Actually, intelligence indicated that this train should be ours, but we planned a strong defense just in case. The surrounding trees made it ideal for an ambush, so we dug in with mortars and machine guns at twenty yards. First we would take out the locomotives, so they couldn't escape. There might be engines at both ends, as is usual for military trains, but there was no way of knowing how many cars were on that train. Then we heard it. The chugging of the locomotive grew louder as it drew nearer, and we were all calm, expecting to see a red flag and star over it any second.

We concealed ourselves completely, and listened as the engine got stronger. Finally a twenty car long troop train was in the station. We heard the sound of some boots plopping down from the coach and landing on the wooden platform. Just the sound of that was enough to tell us they were Germans. And a second later their language confirmed it. From our hidden position we didn't know if we were outnumbered or had the advantage. In this case, whoever had the superior force would almost certainly enjoy the element of surprise. Either they'd be put off guard by our presence or we'd be shocked at their overwhelming force. But there was no more time to speculate. The agonya was issued and we stood and opened fire.

The German troops left out in the open were mowed down. Thousands of rounds poured into the cabs of the engines and left little chance of an escape by rail either to the north or south. The Nazis took up defensive positions behind the depot and surrounding buildings. Those buildings though were wooden and afforded poor defense against seventy caliber slugs. Their best chance was to get up a head of steam and escape, but we'd already killed the engineers. Now they had to stay on board the train and fight from a defensive position. Clearly they did not have the great numbers we feared. Now our objective changed from harassing and discouraging theses troops to wiping them out. The coaches were loaded with German regulars, well armed and battle hardened, but they had left themselves no route or plan of retreat. I could now see these *soldaten* closer than any others I had yet seen, and we were firing volleys right into them. The glass windows on the coaches and depot were shattering and splintering while the wooden walls were being ripped to shreds. Their best defense was to get off the train on the western side and hide behind the much stronger raised platform of the depot, but our own forces on the western side observed them and opened fire. At that moment the Germans probably realized they were doomed. On the eastern side our forces moved in even closer. You didn't even need binoculars to see the distorted faces of our victims. We got to within twenty or thirty feet., hugging them like Stalingrad. They did their best to shoot back, but they were so outflanked and trapped it was useless. German soldiers were hanging out of every coach window, bleeding on the sides of the cars, the platform was strewn with their corpses, and no more fire was being returned from the bullet ridden station. By now it was nine in the morning, and our withering barrage had reduced the train to splinters. The best dug in soldiers were under the cars now where it was more difficult to hit them. The shadows afforded them some degree of safety, but every time they fired their guns the muzzle flashes revealed their position, and for every shot that came out from under a coach a hundred of our boys blasted away at it. I must have emptied twenty magazines into the coaches myself, and it was the first battle in which I was reasonably certain my marksmanship must have produced results. Having heard endless stories of Nazi butchery, including shooting unarmed civilians, none of us felt any pity for them. At least they were armed. Within a half hour not a shot was being returned from the train, the depot, or any of the buildings around the station. We ceased fire and approached on foot. Nothing moved. Blood was flowing out of the sides of the cars and pooling on the ground. To make certain they were all dead, we stood at the side of the train at about ten feet and blasted it to bits for another full minute. Then we climbed onto the cars, all of which were crammed with the dead. We had to walk on top of the corpses to survey the damage. Every soldier had been shot through and through, some as many as fifty times. They were like raw meat in uniform. We listened carefully to see if anyone was breathing. In case of that many kazaks and star-shnya had their Tokarev side arms out, ready to deliver a coup de grace. Some even thought that was too merciful.

"Let 'em bleed to death."

Finally, General Bogaevsky personally inspected the carnage. He rode up on his steed, and dismounted. He climbed into several cars, drenching his beautiful high boots in blood. He had a grim look on his face the entire time. This was a lot of carnage even for a Cossack General. He trod the German cadavers with no more concern than walking over rocks or logs. As he stepped on one chest he heard a faint groan. He looked down and saw a soldier who had somehow survived the massacre. The general pulled out his onyx handled semi-automatic nine millimeter pistol and shot the soldier in the head, and the man stopped groaning and breathing. There was a hush through our ranks as the general studied his victim. He returned his pistol to its holster and turned to us.

"He should have stayed home."

Then he added, "Leave everything as it is. This is our calling card."

We had decimated the entire train, perhaps as many as twenty five hundred soldaten, and hardly lost a kazak. We took our few wounded, and left nothing behind but our mountains of spent cartridges as testimony to the perpetrator of this massacre.

I saw a lot of blood in the war, but never as much as the ambush at Slav'ansk.

THE LAST BATTLE

By March of 1943 I was practically a Cossack, or at least I probably smelled like one. Significantly and ironically, I was now old enough to officially enlist. A year had gone by since joining these ruffians and I was older, taller, more filled out, and a veteran in every way. Few could claim to ride better than me, and I was a respected member of the general's staff, not because I was the ataman's pet, but because I had acquitted myself on the field of battle. I was no sharpshooter or hero of any kind, but I had done my duty and nobody could claim I was lesser than they. My survival instincts had submerged my roots so deeply it wasn't even an issue. I was past merely pretending not to be Jewish. Shabbos, Yom Kippur, Rosh Hashanah, challah, and all the rest of it, was buried inside and lay dormant. It never came up, not even in my mind. Self preservation had conditioned me perfectly and I was a Soviet Russian through and through.

As the campaign continued I found myself in battles less frequently, owing to my duties for ataman. In describing those it might sound offensive to refined ears to hear that I also had to supply women for him. We often went for long periods of time without seeing a female, and it was one of the prerogatives of a high ranking general to have his natural force satisfied. It was an intrinsic part of their culture to expect that the females among our vanquished enemies be conquered women in every sense of the word. And if they weren't from the enemy camp, then they should feel such gratitude for their heroes that they should voluntarily ease a soldier's burden. Usually, it was just a matter of finding an occupied house with a likely female candidate and inform the residents that they'd have to temporarily move out to allow the general and his staff some much needed working space. Then I would suggest that the female inhabit of that house remain to accompany the general. Sometimes they were eager to share their bed with such a great warrior, while they just as often resigned to it as inevitable. Sadly, this benefit of rank did not extend to the rest of the general's staff.

During the course of our campaign we were re-supplied many times, and each time we received more stories of the heroic struggle for Stalingrad in the Great Patriotic War. It seemed inconceivable, but they told us that over a million Russian soldiers died there. They probably told us that to instill a greater feeling of revenge in our hearts, and for the most part it worked. Nobody ever forgot that it was a treacherous sneak attack from a supposed ally in the first place that dragged us into the war, and they wanted to insure that our outrage did not abate. A motivated soldier is essential to victory. But, just as tough as we were, so were the krauts. They were disciplined and now feeling a second wind. After Stalingrad anything seemed minor. The house to house fighting, the frostbite, the starvation, fighting in the sewers, it was the worst that any wermachte regular had ever endured. By comparison, being out in the open steppes, where he could see his foe from far off, was like a holiday. And now with spring coming, the weather was less of a threat and he took courage anew. That was why we were assigned to harass them and not let up. Under usual circumstances a bunch of saber wielding cavalry would be a joke to the Germans. When they invaded Poland they mowed down the same kind of adversary. But the Donski host followed a different strategy, dogging their footsteps and keeping them on their toes. And our campaign had produced great results. The Germans had not gained an inch since Stalingrad and they were now five hundred miles further west than when they started. Ever since their commander at Stalingrad, General Palus, had surrendered, Russian morale had been sky high. And it never diminished. We glorified General Zhukov, the hero of Stalingrad and the Great Patriotic War, and wrote heartfelt poetry about him and all the Soviet troops.

With so much to build on the Cossacks planned their campaign to take them all the way to Odessa on the Black Sea. From there it was just a little more than a hundred miles to Romania, an Axis stronghold. First we had to take Nikolajev.

Nikolajev was about seventy five miles slightly northeast of Odessa. The Germans, reinforced by Romanian troops, had a small air strip there on the far western side of the town, about twenty five miles away. They had Stukas and Junker dive bombers and they controlled the area. They also had some artillery and tanks. We would hit them in our usual guerilla fashion, inflict as much damage as possible, and withdraw. We were also going to meet up with other Cossack forces and have a much larger presence. I went ahead and secured a first class dacha for our hetman, and had a feast of venison, potatoes, and some spring vegetables waiting for him when he got there. It was one of the best day's work I ever did for him, and he showered me with praise. After eating, he addressed a group of several hundred men with his ceremonial bulava in his hand. As always he was ready with the latest statistics of our successful campaign. When he read them it always impressed me how so much energy was invested in destruction. And this day was no different.

"My brothers, Marshal Stalin sends his greetings and praise! You have become the reincarnation of the Zaporovsky brotherhood! The word Cossack once again inspires terror in the hearts of our enemy!"

Shouts of agreement resounded and every eye was on their beloved ataman.

"You know, maybe the Germans aren't so bad after all."

His troops looked a little bewildered, but had faith in the words of the hetman.

"Yes, I hear that they are sorry."

He had the attention of every eye and ear.

"They are sorry they ever set foot in Russia!"

Raucous laughter and more shouts.

"And we have been good hosts. We have done all we can to help them retreat by lightening their load. Since February of last year we have relieved them of much of their burden. Listen well. Besides killing well over three hundred thousand of these assholes we have thus far captured fifteen hundred tanks, sixty thousand trucks, eight thousand machine guns, ninety thousands rifles, sixty seven hundred pieces of field artillery, fifteen hundred mortars, and three armored trains!"

Deafening applause answered every statistic, and I clapped as loud as anyone.

"But not so long as one Axis soldier remains in Mother Russia will we relax our grip on their throats. Tomorrow we begin our march to Nikolajev and victory!"

As high as our morale was already, our ataman's speech raised it even more. We felt invincible and couldn't wait until the next encounter. We all knew we had a long ride ahead of us, so bottles were passed around and mahorkas lit up.

After a few minutes with the troops I had to report to the general, and as I walked over there I reflected on the report of the captured munitions. It was absolutely staggering. Up until the Communists made their passive invasion of Sieniawa I had not in my life seen two guns together at the same time. Growing up I saw an occasional hunting rifle, and a policeman or two armed with a pistol. When Commissar Glentz and his occupation force showed up they carried some guns, but never used them. The jails I was in were juvenile facilities so the guards didn't carry weapons, and there were some limited arms in Astrachan, also unused. Since joining the Cossacks I had see many weapons, but the numbers recited that evening were unimaginable to me. The invading Nazis had brought them with the intention of killing as many Russians as possible, Jew, Christian and atheist alike. So, it was encouraging to know that such vast amounts of armaments would not be used against us any more. But I didn't kid myself. There were ten times that many out there aimed right at us.

The general went over some brief details about the coming campaign and quickly excused me. It wasn't cold and the house had comfortable beds, and as it would probably be the last real one my body would know for a while, I made it a point to take rest early and enjoy it. It was as plush and soft as a baby's blanket, and it made me wonder what kind of person usually lived there. My speculation was short lived though as the gentle comfort lulled me into a deep sleep.

With no more snow on the ground we thought we could easily make twenty miles a day. But the ground was nearly frozen and the weather was continually rainy and windy, not very hospitable conditions for riding. But our victories, and the natural courage of these men, still kept our morale high. I shared pleasant conversation with soldiers of every rank as I continually rode back and forth between the general and other members of his staff. Our hetman was almost like Julius Caesar in that he could call by name so many of his troops. Such personal treatment, plus the fact that he went into the field with them, earned him the trust and unwavering obedience of the entire company. There was nothing they wouldn't do for him, creating an atmosphere that was more like an extended family than an army. And for now I was part of that kinship. They did not threaten me as my co-prisoners had done. They did not badger me like so many refugees did. And they did not fear or shun me like the citizens of Stalingrad. It was impossible not to feel protected and confident among these devils. Many speak of the camaraderie of men in arms, but one must live it to truly appreciate it. Death is everywhere, but your comrades will defend you. Our esprit de corps was unmatchable.

We were riding through wide open spaces by night and camping in the forest by day. By the end of our second night we had covered fifty miles, ten more than planned, and we calculated that we'd come to the forest outside Nikolajev shortly after sundown. We were ahead of schedule and anxious to get back into action. It was a clear day and the weather was unusually mild for March. A few of the ponies seemed spooked by something, but we couldn't tell what. Animals can often sense things before humans do, such as natural disasters. The horses were right. We heard the airplanes and immediately understand what had upset them. About two miles out we saw a Focke-Wulf circling around us, its buzzing motor splitting the tranquility of the morning. In half a minute he was over us, and many unsheathed their Tokarevs and fired at it full-auto, with permission. So many fired I wouldn't be surprised to learn that we actually hit it. Our volleys were ineffectual however, and the reconnaissance craft turned back to the west from whence it had come and was gone in seconds. This was serious. We had been spotted by the Germans. General Bogaevsky called for his staff and they had to decide what to do.

"We should turn back. We depend on the element of surprise, and we've lost it."

"We need to make a break for the forest."

"Is camouflage an option?"

Finally our general said, "We have been spotted. That's a fact. We received poor intelligence, because we should have known we were this close to their air base. No forest is in sight, not even with binoculars. If we go back we're just as exposed in the open as we are here. We should disperse and not provide them with one big target. Break up our company into platoons and we'll assign a path for each to take. We'll regroup as soon as we spot any protective stand of trees."

Individual units went off in all directions. If a plane came at us now the pilot might be confused as to where to attack first, buying most of us a few more precious seconds of retreat. But what came at us was immune to human contemplation. Fired from several miles away, so far we were unaware of it, an immense artillery shell whistled right into our midst with devastating impact. There was barely time to yell, "Incoming!"

It was the first incoming explosion I had experienced since Kiev, but now I witnessed it in all its awesome fury. I saw men and horses blown to bits. I galloped away in the opposite direction in full retreat, as eager to save my horse as myself. But the German artillery was faster than any mount. The whistle went over my head this time and landed another seventy yards ahead of me. But the force made my horse rear up and I was thrown off. Even as I fell I heard several more incoming shrieks. I lay as flat as I could, truly frightened for the first time in recent memory. The ground shook from three more impacts, tremors far more terrible than those I felt at Astrakhan. I found enough courage to look up, hoping to find Babe. But she had run off with the hundreds of other riderless mounts. Men were scurrying everywhere, arms at the ready, hoping to confront a human foe. But already more Cossacks died here than in our entire campaign so far. Hundreds lie on the ground, dead or writhing in agony. I had a quick thought that the Germans discovered the railway station at Slav'ansk and plotted this revenge.

It was impossible to decide where to run to, but the exact opposite direction seemed the only logical choice. The landscape was changing right before my eyes, with gigantic wide craters in the ground. At the edges of the holes were limbs blasted off my comrades and their ponies. There was booming thunder, the shrill whinny of a thousand maddened horses, and men screaming threats to enemies too distant to hear them. And on I ran, only turning when I heard small arms fire. Airplanes were coming in at us now and we were firing back with everything we had. They were Messerschmitts, first diving to release their two hundred pound bombs, and then strafing the area with seventy caliber machine guns. Men and animals were falling like wheat, and I was afraid Babe would get hit. But it seemed futile to run. The fighters were roaring past us at two hundred miles an hour, spitting death. My heart was pounding as I pumped my legs as hard as I could. The engine, high and over my shoulder, got closer and closer, firing at me. The ground was torn in a straight line, each bullet kicking up a mound of dirt. Just before they got to me I changed direction and the barrage barely missed. A hundred horses and another artillery shell flew past, and a moment later they were running through a new crater, some stumbling and breaking their legs. Another bomb, smaller, but better aimed by a dive bomber, hit a unit of riders and mutilated countless ponies. I dropped from exhaustion and looked up to see a plane banking my way. Hundreds of men were firing their full auto rifles at it, but the unscathed Messerschmitt flew past them, headed straight toward me. I got to my feet and continued my pathetic retreat when I heard the immense bullets ripping my way, accompanied by screams and more explosions. My boots dug into the dirt, my heart pounding, and I saw another crater not fifty feet in front of me. The thought that its rim might offer me some protection from the incoming planes entered my mind and I charged at it as fast as I could. But just as I was about to dive into that crater an explosion behind me sent me flying. I landed in that crater just as a bullet hit me in the foot. It caused me to flip like a rag doll and roll over and over until I lie face down. I pushed my self up and turned over, still in shock. I noticed that there was a lieutenant in the crater with me, but he wasn't moving. Then I looked down where the impact gripped me and saw that my right boot –my custom general's aide boot- was torn wide open. The shiny brown leather had its own crater and was smoldering. Was that my boot, my foot? Everything seemed to stop for a moment as I stared at it. The right boot's outside edge was blasted off and smoke rose from it. Then a burning sensation shot up my leg and blood gushed from it. It wasn't just my boot. It was me. I was wounded. Blinding pain tore through my body and I jerked around in convulsions. A four inch long chunk of red hot lead, fired at a thousand miles an hour, had grazed me, and now half my right foot was gone. And there were still bombs going off all around me, and more planes dive bombing and strafing. I couldn't move, so I hugged the crater wall and tightened my eyes against the pain. Every part of me trembled, and I violently shook. The spasms gripped me so totally self control was impossible. I vomited and screamed and the pain was so blinding a quick death seemed more merciful. I felt as if my heart might explode and I threw up again. Then blackness overcame me.

When I awoke I was aware of activity around me, but I was not in control of my senses. There were human voices, but nothing cogent. And a great numbness, with an incessant tingling, had control of my lower body. Slowly, my eyes opened all by themselves, and they observed men carrying wounded soldiers. The men were gingerly placed down on the ground all around me, and they were all bleeding. The other men were wrapping bandages around them. Their heads, their arms, their chests, hands, legs, every part of the anatomy. Then I understood the first fully comprehensible sentence.

"Radio for medical supplies. We're running out. Give them a full report."

"This is a catastrophe. How did we ever let ourselves get caught out in the open?"

"Half our force is wounded. How are we going to evacuate them?"

"Can any of them ride?"

"Vladimir, these aren't small ordinance wounds. Most of the men are suffering from concussion trauma from the artillery they unleashed on us. They need surgery. Who knows what shape their guts are in? We need some flights out!"

"What about prikazny Arkadivonovitch here?"

They were talking about me, but they were talking about me as if I wasn't there.

"We gave him a couple hits of morphine. But he's gonna probably lose his foot. If it gets infected he'll lose the whole leg and maybe even buy it."

"Ataman loves this kid like a son. We better do what we can for him."

"Morphine's all we can do. And everyone's screaming for that."

"Wait a long as you can before his next one. And get some flights headed this way! He needs to be evacuated."

I was only vaguely aware of what was going on. Movement and speech were eerily not within my dominion, but a warmth I had never known now enveloped me. It's impossible to know how long I lingered in that condition, but I saw through misty vision General Bogaevsky look down at me and say some soothing words, commending me for my so-called bravery, and told me not to worry. Then the blessed blackness returned.

Someone was lifting me up, and horrific pain shot through me, causing me to go stiff, then limp, then stiff. My hetman cut through the haze.

"Prikazny, the krauts shellacked us. We lost a lot of men and horses. But we'll get 'em back. You'll see. Look, Arkadi, they're gonna fly you and some others back behind our lines to a field hospital. I hear the USAs sent us some new kind of medicine. Fix you right up! You'll be back in the saddle before you know it. Don't fuck too many nurses."

I barely understood him, but I managed a weak salute as they lifted up my stretcher. He snapped to attention and gave me the sharpest salute I ever saw him give anyone. It made me smile, in spite of the pain. As soon as I was in the fuselage they revved up the giant motors and the whole plane vibrated tremendously. Within moments we were airborne, and I was off on my first ride in an airplane. The general gave special orders to keep me comfortable, so they gave me morphine at the proper intervals. After a couple of hours we landed somewhere called Sverdlovsk to refuel. Then we continued onto the field hospital at Volzskij, just across the Volga from Stalingrad. It was like a refugee tent city, teeming with sick and dying people. As Stalingrad itself had been flattened the survivors, both civilian and military, were installed there. I had lost a lot of blood and was half dead, but people there were far worse off, including many others who were also highly recommended by other generals, admirals, commissars, and supposedly Papa Joe himself, all waiting for desperately needed medical attention. The war was going much better for us than it was just the year before, but the Nazis were not throwing in the towel just yet. Both of us were still waging all out war.

I was surrounded by the survivors of the Battle of Stalingrad, and the stories they told me were horrific. Now I was getting it first hand, and it was startling. As bad as I thought it was these stories put everything into a much clearer perspective. The Germans wanted nothing less than to utterly eradicate the city, wipe it from the map. In the past few months we had been waging a guerrilla campaign against the Nazis that caused us to joke about feeling sympathy for them. But meeting these survivors it became clear to me that we were doing the right thing. The Nazis deserved exactly what we were giving them. They came all the way over here for the sole purpose of doing harm, and killed millions of Russians who had never done a thing to a German. Absolutely, those bastards had it coming. We just needed to ambush more train stations.

Because of the congestion in the field hospital in Sverdlovsk I wasn't much better off than in Nikolajev. Round the clock their inadequate and overworked staff was operating to save lives. As long as I was alive and not bleeding, my case was a low order of priority for them. I was missing a few toes. Big deal! There were people there missing hands, eyes, noses, feet, and organs. As far as they were concerned I was practically a malingerer. The main things they did for me were to keep my wound clean and give me morphine. In spite of their earnest efforts to keep my bandages changed I still developed a bad infection. And after a month of morphine I couldn't live without it. Finally, they carried me on a stretcher to the railway station and shipped me off on a seven hundred mile long train trip to Baku on the western bank of the Caspian Sea. The train was full of badly wounded war heroes, and was fifty coaches long. I was so addled from morphine not a memory of the four day trip remains.

BAKU

XIII

Baku was not a way station on the way to some place better. It was my final destination. That was fine by me, because the train, though little more than a blur in my memory, was a nauseating blur, practically a repeat of my first ride from Sieniawa to Lubaczow, only a thousand times longer. Another reason to celebrate my arrival was the fact that the hospital, as well as the city, was utterly untouched by the conflict in the east. There were no air raids, falling artillery shells, or fighting of any kind. And most important of all, they offered proper medical treatment. Within hours of my arrival I was being prepared for surgery. A young nurse came in and cut away all my clothes with a scissors. No longer under the stupefying sway of morphine my nakedness embarrassed me in front of this lady, and I thrust my hands down over my private parts. The nurse was all business and bathed me everywhere, even pushing my hands of modesty aside to make sure I was as clean there as my public parts. It was routine for her, but might have caused me even more shame had it not been for the fact that the water was cold. By then my Judaism was so far from my mind it never occurred to me that she might discover my mark of Abraham. Doubtless she saw it, but took it as much in her stride as seeing any other version, aroused or otherwise. What was probably most embarrassing of all was just being so filthy in the first place. The Cossacks seemed as unconcerned with personal hygiene as the rest of the forest critters, and being in constant combat it was even tougher to bathe. Being raised to be a clean person, it always made me feel uneasy to be so continually filthy. Even having the advantage of an occasional bath at some commandeered dacha fell far short of the standard of cleanliness of my rearing. Anyway, those baths were almost obviated by having to put back on the same unwashed uniform. So, the ministrations of this nurse, though potentially scandalous, were greatly appreciated. It was the first tender care I had known since the collective farm.

They operated on my foot, and attacked the infection with the miracle drug penicillin, courtesy of our friends, the USAs. But the infection was so advanced they had to inject it directly into my spine. My foot was under local anesthetic, but not my back, and the hypodermic needle went right into it without the benefit of any prior localized pain killer. It was agonizing and I begged for morphine. By then I was used to having only one symptom treated, the pain. These doctors however were intent on actually healing. They told me that the pinprick in my back was just temporary, and I had to expect some discomfort. Characterizing my excruciating pain as mere discomfort was something I found cold heated and insane. I had to protest.

"But comrade doctor…"

"Comrade, you got hit by the biggest bullet the Nazis can throw at us, and it came to within an inch of tearing off your whole foot. If that would have happened the loss of blood would have killed you on the battlefield. And if you would have survived that then the massive infection that would have almost certainly set in would have killed you in the field hospital. But providence sent that bullet one inch the other way and only grazed you, slicing off two toes, and it's doubtful you'll die from that. So all in all, Comrade Arkadivonovitch, I'd say you were quite lucky. And with all that you should not be surprised that you experience some discomfort."

"But in Volzskij the doctors gave me something for the pain."

"Comrade, they're overwhelmed in Volzskij. Practically every single person in Stalingrad was either killed or wounded. The entire population and half our army is in the hospital. And thanks to our American allies, decadent capitalists though they may be, one thing they have aplenty in Volzskij is morphine. It's strange; we're supposed to have invented it, but the Americans seem to have all of it. Keep that to yourself, comrade. Anyway, it's the easiest way to deal with cases like yours. But now you're in Baku. And in Baku we heal. Turning you into a dope addict is hardly the way to go about that. Morphine kept you sane for a month comrade, that's true. But now we have to wean you off of it. It'll be unpleasant for a few days, but in the end you'll walk out of here…that's right, walk out of here….a healthy person. Now, I have a hundred more patients to see. Maybe more. So, say thank you comrade doctor, and let me go. I'll be checking up on you regularly. Some general really favors you. Meanwhile the nurses will take good care of you. Baku nurses are the best."

I thanked him as ordered and he vanished. I was grateful for his help, and especially so to my old hetman, the ataman Kazachy General Bogaevsky. Putting me on that medical supply airplane literally saved my life. In spite of all that my body ached to get more morphine. Besides the throbbing of my wound I now had to endure the gut wrenching torture that came from not getting it. It was most definitely not within the realm of my experience to know anything about narcotics, let alone such advanced scientific notions as dependence and addiction. I really wasn't any more educated than when I had left Sieniawa. Even though I had traveled fifteen hundred miles from my home, and met many new people, I hadn't learned anything new except for basic military survival skills. My academic education was still that of a fourteen year old boy from the sticks. So, topics like medicine were just as foreign to me as ever. What did I learn from jail? To be tough and cynical. What had my time at the collective farm taught me? That music hath charm to soothe the peasant breast. The Youth Brigade and army exposed me to Soviet propaganda. All that together added up to a lot of street smarts, leaving most intellectual knowledge far from my grasp. One thing for sure, there would now be a lot of time to think all this through. My hospital bed was probably going to be my home for a good long time while I recuperated, and my thoughts would be my most steady companions. In my room were two other beds that saw a lot of patients come and go. Some were amiable, others were tight lipped. And in the morning some just didn't wake up at all. But, thanks to my nurse, loneliness was not an issue. Her name was Ana, and she was as positive and cheerful as dear old Comrade Marina. But Ana was not given to political fanaticism. She didn't call me comrade or make me call her that either. She called me Arkadi and I called her Ana. Of course, she was still a patriot, and was proud to serve the gallant veterans of The Great Patriotic War. There were a hundred soldiers on her ward, and she constantly visited them, serving in any way possible. She bathed us, changed our bandages and bedpans, brought us lunch, and even read to us. One of the most courageous and empathetic things she did was sit by my side while I went through the withdrawal pangs of morphine deprivation. She clasped my hand, wiped my brow, held the bucket while I threw up, and constantly encouraged me.

"Be strong Arkadi. It'll pass soon. It'll pass and you'll feel better than you ever did in your life. You endured so much, and you can take this too. By tomorrow it'll all be a bad memory. Hold my hand. I'm with you. The war will be over soon. We're winning. The war will end and you'll go home and see your family. And they'll throw a grand party in your honor. Everyone in the village will come out to see the great patriotic war hero. And there'll be music. Music, Arkadi. And you'll dance. Yes, you'll dance."

I gripped her hand so hard I feared I might hurt her, but she said nothing. She had probably gone through this with other soldiers, but I was so racked with pain and starved for this affection that only she and I existed in that moment. There was no war or other patients. It was a selfish night, with her giving and me taking, and it saved me.

The first morning that I felt totally free of the craving for morphine Ana came in with a wheel chair. She helped slide me into it and wheeled me onto an open air veranda overlooking the sea. It was the first time I had been aware of anything outside of my ward, and it was a revelation. Baku was paradise. The whole area was landscaped with trees and bushes and flower beds. It was mostly a desert country, not lush like the forests of Southern Poland or the Steppes, but it was lovely in its stark simplicity. There were palm trees and other exotic plants, and the yellow sand was dazzling in the daytime. But immediately my lack of formal education came back to haunt and embarrass me. I looked out across the endless expanse of briny water and remarked.

"Is that the Pacific Ocean?"

Losing all sense of time on the long train trip here it seemed reasonable to speculate that we had gone all the way to the Pacific coast. After all, the name Baku meant nothing to me. And seeing a body of water that stretched to the horizon convinced my puny intellect that it had to be either one of the two great oceans. Knowing that we'd have to traverse all of war torn Europe to see the Atlantic I concluded that it could only be the Pacific. My sound logic was charmingly mocked by Ana.

"Arkadi, that bullet hit you in the foot, not the head. This is the Caspian Sea!"

"It's not the ocean? But it's so huge!"

"It's the largest inland sea in the world, corporal. This is where Russia gets most of her salt. And it's the city you were defending by holding those Nazis at bay. This region has the biggest oil fields in the Soviet Union, and Hitler wanted to get here more than anything. And if they'd have made it then nothing could have stopped them. That's what they say. But we held them at Stalingrad. And you and your Cossacks kept them in check. You saved the world, corporal."

As we sat out there Ana educated me about Baku and a lot of other things. She seemed so educated, refined, and willing to share. And the more I talked with her the less of a Cossack I became. And she saw to the emotional needs of all the other men in her care as well. Of the hundred men on our ward it was a safe bet that every single one of us was madly in love with her. I was among their number, and when she was with another patient I was consumed by jealousy. I counted the moments she was away and my nights were filled with dreams of her. As an eighteen year old, as gripped by hormones as ever was a man, not all of my dreams could be related to a child. That's part of growing up.

Once I was free of the grip of morphine I had to come to grips with the new and different appearance of my foot. When Ana changed the bandages next time she gave me my first good look at it. The wide eyes came back without shame. Two toes and a portion of the adjoining area of my foot were gone. Gone! They told me at Nikolajev, and again at Volzskij, but the drugs prevented it from sinking in. But there it was. Or wasn't. Oddly, seeing it made it hurt more. My eyes clamped shut to fight off the vomit rising in my throat and I started to tremble. Ana quickly covered it with a clean bandage and said, "Arkadi, you know how lucky you are?"

I faintly nodded.

"Everyday I treat young boys like you who are missing whole

feet and legs, hands, eyes, and some who'll never be whole men again. But I can tell that you will learn to walk again so well that nobody will even notice it. And when you get out of here and go back home you'll find yourself a nice girl and get married. And Arkadi, you listen to me. You will dance at your wedding."

I felt ashamed for being so squeamish. I shuddered, and a tear or two released my tension and let me back to Earth. Ana was right. It was nothing compared to so many others, or what it could have been to me.

After a couple of weeks they told me that my foot was knitting well, but it was still an uphill battle against my infection. So they had to give me another injection of penicillin in my spine. The hypodermic was no less excruciating than the first one, but I no longer begged for morphine. Anyway, Ana kept me distracted with news of the USAs and their war in the Pacific. On top of all her wonderful qualities Ana had a great sense of humor. So, when she told me about some recent battle with Japan she would point toward the Caspian and say, "Oh look, there's the American fleet now!" This made her laugh, and even though she was making fun of me I knew it was all harmless, and I laughed as hard as she did. Sharing those moments with her was blissful. She made my convalescence smooth, and I was almost grateful to have been wounded.

Except for a short respite at the collective farm, all my interpersonal relations for the last three years had been an ever intensifying exercise in macho bravado. I had to pretend to be mister tough guy in two successive jails, surrender my individuality to become a cog in the Soviet Youth Brigade, and then transform myself into a Cossack warrior for a year and a half. Furthermore, it had been necessary to disguise my nationality, change my name, hide my religion, and learn a new language. For so long every moment of my life had been a test. And it was a challenge that offered me no respite. But chatting with Ana was such a family like experience that my tough guy layers peeled off, allowing me the freedom to become myself again. Of course, once changed you can only go back so far. If I hadn't ingrained some true degree of viciousness within me then survival might not have been possible. The other inmates would have dominated me, and my foes on the field of battle, as well as my comrades in arms, might have gotten the better of me. In order to confront the world on its own terms I had summoned forth that flinty nature within our people, developed over millennia of adversity, to cope and even prevail. Just as my father taught me, we got what it takes. And if we got a fighting chance we'll muddle through. But now, that macho persona, maintained for so long, was subordinated to the resurgence of my soul. I'd continue to maintain my phony external identity, but my long buried sentiments could now resurface without fear of negative consequence. And being in possession of my emotions again I dared to take the freedom to miss my family. Soon I was motivated by little else but getting better just so I could return to Poland and seek them out. For too long I had been forced to play the role of Arkadi. I was the son of Yisroel Ben Yehuda Feder, and I wanted to see him again, eat my mother's shabbos dinner, and visit my sisters.

Modern science and my iron will to get better cooperated, and the infection was defeated. Ana taught me to walk on crutches, and the wheel chair was now a bad memory. Finally, after five months of treatment, convalescence and therapy, I was ready to be released. It was the end of June, 1943 and the Great Patriotic War was going much better. The Nazis failed to take Stalingrad, Moscow or Leningrad, and every day they were being pushed further west. Word was sent to many of us at the hospital that we would be welcomed at the Kremlin and personally cited for valor by Papa Joe himself. It seemed inconceivable that a little *pisher* from a Polish shtetl would be invited to the Kremlin to have a medal pinned on him by the maximum authority of the Soviet Union. Ever since my first exposure to Soviet bureaucracy all I ever heard was the glories of Joseph Stalin. He was revered as a God by these people, so it was unimaginable to me that this superman wanted to personally decorate the counterfeit Cossack as a war hero. Before the medals however there came a most welcome and credible reality. As the war was going so well it was determined that Mother Russia no longer required the services of those already crippled in action. The maximum military authority decided we had done our bit, and offered us all honorable discharges. Of course, those who were utterly consumed by patriotic fervor were welcome to carry on. I for one was not so inclined, and gratefully accepted the transfer to civilian life. But they were insistent that I first make my way to Moscow to accept their medal of gratitude. Sieniawa was my real goal, but it was a long trip and the Cossack Host had no pension plan. To go by plane to Lwow, the closest big city to Sieniawa, was a fifteen hundred mile flight, and would probably take only six hours. However, my access to that luxurious mode of transportation was nonexistent, so I had to plan a land route. I could travel the twelve hundred miles to Moscow by rail and then have only an eight hundred mile trip by land vehicles to Sieniawa. The Moscow portion of my trip was a courtesy to all winners of The Medal of Stalingrad. From there I'd be on my own, and there was certainly no chance of hopping freights with crutches. But I was determined to make it. So, I tearfully said goodbye to Ana, my angel of Baku, and headed north.

Although I had been on many trains over the course of the last two years I hadn't actually sat in train coach seat since being taken to jail in Kiev. The last four years had been fraught with great anxiety, none worse than being in the dark about my family, and the week long rail journey to my rendezvous with Papa Joe gave me plenty of time to reflect on my life. Through prison, life on the road, and military service, I hadn't done anything worse to shame the name of my family or discredit myself than steal some fruit to keep from starving. And I think that even the bureaucratic Bolsheviks who judged me so harshly for petty truancy, would wipe my slate clean for my service with the Donski Host. So, there was no reason not to return home with my head held high. This gladdened me, not for the sake of my ego, but for how it would make my parents feel. And they're all I thought about. Did they look older? Did they suffer hunger and hardships? Are my sisters married? Is Marisha still with them? I was so obsessed with mental images of my family I even wondered if Babe the mare was alright. And what of Sieniawa? What happened to the public school, the cheider, and the two shuls? Did those gentile bullies join the army and bully the Nazis? I was so gripped by this all consuming passion to get home I even begrudged Joseph Stalin his award ceremony. And after a week of watching the monotonous flatness of central Russia drift by me the train arrived in the grand capital city of the Soviet Union. Next stop, the Kremlin.

STALIN AND THE TRIP HOME

XIV

It was late August of 1944, and the clinging warmth made for a hospitable reception to the grand capital city of the largest country in the world. Compared to the wasteland of Stalingrad the hard fought city of Moscow was a pristine showcase. The Germans had done a lot of bombing here, but the winter prevented them from invading the city, so there was still plenty to see. Huge government buildings and cathedrals were everywhere. And while pre-invasion Stalingrad was just a mass of bricks and cement, this city had style in the classic European sense. In all my travels I had yet to come upon a place that reminded me of the pictures that were in my geography book, until now. The avenues were broader than any I'd ever seen and the buildings taller. Although I saw my visit here as little more than a detour on the way home, I relaxed enough to enjoy the sights. And for a poor class of tourist such as me, looking was all that was in my budget.

Even though I had no finances, everything so far had been a courtesy. Back in Baku they had provided me with a new uniform and a bit of extra wardrobe. The boots didn't quite match those of my Cossack days but I was comfortable. The train fare was complimentary as was the food on the trip. And the local room and board was arranged for all of the heroes of the Battle of Stalingrad. Part of that included land transport to the hotel, and we begged the driver to take it slow and let us take it all in. I had left home years earlier to see the world, and now I was finally on my first sight seeing tour. Most of the other honorees were yokels like me, and we all enjoyed craning our necks.

The next day I made my way to the Kremlin, as instructed. It was so immense it dwarfed the Stalingrad train station. But that depot was utilitarian, while this place was an ornate palace. Nothing in my text books rivaled it. When I collected my senses and forced my mouth shut I hobbled over to the reception desk and showed them my credentials. Everyone was extremely courteous to me and I was escorted to a large hall. My mouth fell agape once again and my eyes bulged out of their sockets. It was the most gorgeous room I had ever been in. From the floor to the ceiling it was full of exquisite and intricate detail. It had large mirrors, chandeliers, red velvet on the walls, and massive paintings. There were no words in my meager vocabulary to tell myself what I was looking at, and I knew I'd never be able to do justice to it when I got home and tried to describe it. It was hard to decide where to look first, but such decisions were forgotten as soon as they announced the arrival of Marshall Stalin.

After hearing nothing but solemn adoration for him since my first meetings with communists, I was trembling with anticipation over the prospect of seeing him. One doesn't meet a God every day of the week. Along with everyone else, I stretched my neck and stood on one tip toe to get an early peek. Some order was imposed upon us, herding the overenthusiastic back, and I was finally able to spot him coming my way. He was shaking hands, saluting, and pinning medals on chests. There were veterans with their arms in casts and slings, and some with empty sleeves, neatly pinned to their epaulets. There were dozens of wheelchairs, and more men on crutches than I could count. Some held a single crutch next to a folded and pinned up pant leg. Men had their heads swathed in white bandages, patches over eyes, and whoever didn't figure into any of those categories leaned on canes. There was hardly a whole man among us. There were even a few women waiting to meet their hero and get decorated.

As the great man worked his way toward me there was time to take a good look at this living legend. Considering his reputation and the reverence with which his name was always intoned, the actual event was mildly disappointing. He was not a big man, though a little taller than my five feet, six inches. And one could hardly call him handsome. His skin was terribly pock-marked, and neither his nose nor ears were nicely shaped. And his eyes were mere slits as if he was always looking into the sun, or at someone with suspicion. He did have a thick and healthy head of hair and moustache. He also had a broad chest which made him appear somewhat powerful, though his body was not very gracefully covered by his uniform, which was drab. As I was taking all of this in he was working his way toward me. One by one he stopped, received the medal from an aide, pinned it on the chest of the proud recipient who puffed it proudly out to help, gave the double Russian kiss and moved on. Some men saluted after receiving their medal, but he was too busy to return it. Then it was my turn. He repeated the processes, looked at me for a fraction of a second and moved on. He was not particularly charismatic and the whole experience was far less than what was anticipated. Perhaps meeting anyone would've been a disappointment after having had my senses conquered by the stupendous Kremlin. Before considering any of this, a man in a much more impressive uniform, covered in medals, made a short speech. He thanked us for our patriotic sacrifices, applauded, and allowed us the time to return the hand clapping. Then, we were ushered out of the great hall to make room for the next contingent of medal receivers.

I thought I might run into other Cossack heroes there, but I didn't recognize a single face in the ceremony, or anywhere in the entire city for that matter. It seemed as if that chapter of my life was truly over, and that notion just made me all the more eager to see my family. So, curtailing my tourism, I left Moscow and its museums behind and started out on my homeward bound Odyssey.

There was no plan or itinerary other than the general direction. My route would take me five hundred miles south to Kiev, and from there three hundred miles west to Lwow. Once there I'd be less than a hundred miles from Sieniawa. All in all, it was going to be a journey of about a thousand miles. I had no funds, papers of authority, and only limited use of my body. I had two concerns, one long term and the other short. My long term goal was, of course, that tiny house in the woods of Jaroslaw County. My short term goal was to eat. To accomplish both objectives meant utter reliance on the good will of the simple Russian people. They might respect my uniform, recognize my sacrifice, and share what little they had. I'm not big, and being on crutches I expended little energy, so I wouldn't need much to eat. I just had to have blind faith that I would somehow make it.

More than anything else I had to have the will to get here. In my youth I had learned the cliché that a journey of a thousand miles begins with a single step, and I was struck by that being my exact situation. With no train fare in my pocket I leaned on my crutch and stuck out my thumb.

Hitchhiking was new to me, so I didn't really know what to expect. A few cars passed me by, and I got momentarily discouraged. Then, in unison, both my jailhouse mentor and father reminded me of how tough I really am. They were right of course. Why should I be discouraged? It was mild climate, I had eaten enough the day before, my bandages were fresh, and I had no enemy to evade. And, while still counting my blessings, a truck pulled over. The driver got out and happily helped me into the cab. He drove very fast, which suited me fine, and he wanted to know all about my wound and war experience. It embarrassed me to have him faun over me, but he absolutely begged me to tell him about the combat. I tried to be humble, but he'd have none of it. Seeing how truly disappointed he was over my reticence it seemed my patriotic duty to satisfy his curiosity. So, he heard my life story in return for driving me fifty miles.

Five percent of my trek was already behind me and it was still early in my first day of travel. Unfortunately, my first ride hadn't any food to share. But my next was an ambulance and they offered me coffee from a thermos along with some bread and cheese. It cost another go-round of my autobiography, but it was worth it. All the components of my mobile breakfast were relatively fresh and it gave my host real pleasure to see a veteran eat his fill. The reaction of everyone who heard my story was always the same, utter horror over how I came to be wounded, and then how lucky I was to have survived. These tidings were well timed as I had lately become a little vexed over hobbling on crutches. These people were right of course. The number of men hit by seventy caliber bullets who lived was of a low order, and it made me think about the ceremony back at the Kremlin. There were so many men there who were forever crippled, legless, blind, deaf, armless, or a hundred other horrific conditions. Being reminded of my luck was not a bad or unwelcome thing.

On my next ride I forced the driver to do some of the talking and I got an update on the big picture of the war. Although I'd learned plenty in Moscow, the war could have changed overnight. After all, I was hobbling because of a counter-attack. But that was over a year before and the Germans now seemed truly doomed.

Every day they retreated more. They were headed back to Berlin and Adolph, and that was exactly the goal of the Red Army. They planned not only on kicking the Nazis out of Mother Russia for good but also dogging their trail all the way to their Fatherland and annihilating them there, once and for all. While I was glad to hear of our success I still kept one selfish thought in mind, of standing before my parents and sisters. I felt that if I could stick to my itinerary of pursuing the retreating German army, I'd make it.

As different rides informed me of the war's progress I learned that much of Poland was still under Nazi control. That worried me greatly. If the Germans had sped past Sieniawa on their rush to conquer Russia, now they were held up in Poland with nothing but time on their hands with which to investigate every nook and cranny, and discover shtetls like mine. Resentful over their debacle in Russia maybe they'd take revenge on the defenseless citizens there. Such reflection depressed me, and it was a much needed distraction for me to talk to my hosts about Cossack exploits. My first day's travels ended with the truck pulling over into a stand of trees where other truckers had formed a camp and built a fire. There my crutches caught their attention, and I escaped into my autobiography yet again, this time bolstered by borscht, potatoes and vodka. There was a stream by our campsite and I cleansed my foot and changed my bandages as had been ordered before leaving Baku. Lying down someone tossed me an apple, and biting down I calculated I had traveled about eighty miles that day. So far, so good. Nine hundred more to go.

It was a pleasant night, so I had no objection to sleeping outside on the soft grass. Now, many men might think that it was a pathetic situation. I was broke, had no roof over my head or anything reliable to count on for food. But not a glimmer of such self pity could penetrate the armor that had been custom designed for me by my squadron of life coaches. My father, prison mentor, Comrades

Marina and Nurse Ana steeled me against all adversity for good, and my cup would never be less than half full again.

My second day was not unlike the first. My crutch, bandage, uniform and medal stopped more trucks and I retold my life many more times. I was a bit hungry at times, but a day did not pass without food. Nor did a day pass without news. Our army had crossed into Poland, but was not engaging the enemy or moving forward. The capital, Warsaw, was only a hundred and twenty five miles west of the Russian border, and there were rumors of armed insurrection by the citizens. But there were no tales of more Soviet victories or Nazi retreats. Could the wermachte be mounting a counter attack? Is such a thing possible? Maybe the Germans, vicious and clever, had been pretending to retreat all this time, merely to lure the Red army into a huge trap in eastern Poland? After all, if Poland was a Nazi stronghold why wouldn't it have a huge fresh army waiting to pounce on the Red army? These thoughts invaded my consciousness, but I dare not breath them out loud for fear of making them manifest. And as nobody else speculated along those lines, I kept my fears to myself.

After five days I made it to Kiev. This destination was unique for me in that it was the first place I had seen in years that I had previously known. Of course, I only knew the prison and the railway station, so it wasn't much of a reunion. Athos, Porthos and Aramis briefly flitted through my mind, and I wondered if they too had served Mother Russia. But the town held no nostalgic draw for me, and I was merely anxious to continue my journey. Then I had a stroke of luck by running into an army unit. I had a conversation with some of the troops and learned that they were being sent to reinforce the army chasing Hitler back west. Everyday our army was getting bigger, and everyday his was getting whittled down more. But he was far from throwing in the towel and the world was still at war. As I was not officially a soldier any more it was against regulation to let me tag along. But they didn't care if I followed behind as closely as I wanted. So I continued to hitchhike with some of the supply trucks. Often the trucks would reach their destination and have to turn around and return for more supplies. At those times I would just wait. And sometimes, just to try and strengthen my leg and foot, I would walk as much as I could. It was painful, but Ana had taught me that constant therapy would accelerate the healing. By this time there was no chance of my wound tearing open. The bones were knitted and the skin was completely healed over. The muscles had atrophied a bit, but they could be stretched back out. And if I was going to dance at my wedding I figured that I'd better get back in practice as soon as possible.

Mostly, I was able to get rides with supply trucks. My story was constantly reiterated, but in exchange I got updates on the war. I heard what the Americans were doing in the Pacific and how the British were holding out against the Germans. It struck me that Russia was fighting in Europe and America in the Pacific, and that is seemed balanced. After all, who wanted Japan to attack from the east and surround us?

My focus was so narrow, to get home, that I didn't dwell on anything else. A few times we passed some shuttered Synagogues, and I might have expressed some curiosity, but I made no inquiries into Jewish life or anything that might distract me from my mission. Those thoughts however could not be purged from my mind. For a long time I had been aware of rumors of harsh Nazi treatment of civilians, especially Jews. They were just rumors, so I didn't want to depress or discourage myself. After all, there was no evidence to the contrary so it was reasonable to assume that my home town got passed over. One can hardly imagine the German high command planning the conquest of the key cities of Stalingrad and Sieniawa. It had no reserves of oil to interest the Third Reich, and the most advanced industry was a fish farm, hardly adequate to feed a platoon. Surely, they must have passed it by. Anyway, I needed to concentrate on the present, and my immediate short term goal of finding food. Once or twice I had to stop hitch hiking just to find something to eat. As generous as the simple serfs of Mother Russia might be, if they don't have it they don't have it. The Red army had taken most of the food and the people who had once been the Czar's chattels were starving. Most of the food reserves went west, so on a few occasions an entire day went by with no food on the horizon. Fortunately it was never two in a row.

With uncounted days of hitchhiking, sleeping out in the open, and making do with an occasional piece of fruit, Lwow was only ten miles away. Only the sign was spelled oddly. It wasn't Lwow, but Lvov. I asked the driver about that and he explained what I had forgotten, that the Communists had peacefully invaded here in 1939, but had never gone away. The Nazis had forced them out, but now it had reverted back to the Soviet Union. In any case it was no longer Poland. We were still in the Soviet Union in its new westernmost city. From my youth I knew that this city was about half Jewish. The truck driver filled me in, speaking in a matter of fact way, which made it all the more chilling.

"Oh, they took the Yids away a long time ago. There's hardly any left here at all."

I remained silent, but inside I was gripped by terror and panic. The rumors were true after all! My poor parents! My sisters! The shuls. Home! Could they be so savage? Of course they could. And why not? Wasn't my own old army unit that barbaric? What about the train station at Slav'ansk? Maybe Germany was outraged by it. Perhaps it had become a rallying cry for the krauts, and they stormed shtetl after shtetl with the battle cry, "Remember Slav'ansk!" in the air. Maybe their most beloved citizens had been on that train, adored patriotic musicians playing for troops at the front, and the annihilation of Sieniawa was part of their revenge? This was war and any barbarity was conceivable.

While I speculated on the worst case scenario for my family, the truck driver babbled on until we came to the city limits. But I hadn't heard a word since he mentioned the yids, and now I needed to get my bearings again. So, when he pulled off to the side of the road to take a piss, I asked him how much further to Jaroslaw.

"We chased the krauts out of there weeks ago. It's about ten miles straight that way."

He was pointing toward the setting sun. Everything was clear. Years before I was obliged to head east, constantly east. Now, it was all turned around. Everybody and everything was headed west. The German army, the Red army, the road, the sun, and me.

My destiny lay a mere ten miles west, a short hop away, but my ride wanted to bed down for the night. My eagerness to cross into Poland was so strong though, I nagged the driver to take me to the train station.

"Please comrade, I have to catch a train there. You've been so kind I hate to impose, but I don't think I'll be able to sleep tonight knowing how close I am."

He frowned, scratching his head, and finally, owing to my heroism, relented.

"Okay, but don't be shocked if your friends are gone. The krauts were pretty rough there. You gonna be alright with those crutches, *tovarich*?"

"*Spaceba*, comrade. We'll meet in better times."

Though I was just ten rubles short of the ten ruble train fare from Lvov to Jaroslaw, my uniform and medal provided me with a hundred percent discount. I plopped down in the first seat on the coach and nodded a greeting to my new traveling companions. Across the way from me sat what could only be some returning refugees, a man and a woman in rags. I was so eager to learn more I couldn't resist starting a conversation.

"Are you from Jaroslaw?"

"The man frowned a little, shrugged and said, "Nyet Ruski."

Reality reminded me that I didn't have to speak Russian any-more, and I slowly and clumsily shifted linguistic gears to remember the language of my upbringing. I hadn't spoken a word or Polish in years, but it was time to remember. They related their flight from Poland and what they did in the Soviet Union for four years. They also shared their hopes for the future. They seemed to be gentiles, but they were the first Poles I had met in a long time and I was overwhelmed with curiosity about my people. So, I casually opened the topic of the Chosen People.

"I've heard some pretty grim stories about the Nazi occupation. What do you know about the Jews of Jaroslaw. There were so many of them."

Everybody in that part of the world had been living under one kind of totalitarian government or another for a long time, so they were naturally skittish about strangers and their questions. These peasants were no different. They looked at me as if trying to analyze if I was up to any mischief, and after inspecting me and my ban-daged foot, decided that I must have been harmless, and worthy of a response.

"Well, I've heard bad and good. I heard a lot were taken away. But now I hear they're coming back. I even met someone who told me they have a restaurant of their own right in town."

This sounded mostly positive. Of course, a Jewish restaurant in Jaroslaw should hardly be news. Anyway, hearing that made me practically drool. Still, there was something about this report that sounded like something was missing. The man looked down after speaking, as did the woman. Well, maybe they were typical Poles, never keen to discuss Jews. Then again, they did discuss them, and without including the usual comments about their filth. Anyway, I thanked them, and continued my journey, looking out the window.

The landscape was looking familiar now, just like home, and I was getting nostalgic.

The train pulled into the little station, and there was plenty evidence of fighting there. The truth is I had no idea which way to go. All I knew is I was finally back in the county I grew up in. I saw people walking around, so maybe the rumors were exaggerated. There was hope. One thing for sure. Being back in this part of the world after four years, I was finally prepared to satisfy some deep seated need to seek out something of my Jewish roots. It was finally time.

JAROSLAW

XV

Since the Russian invasion of Sieniawa I had traveled nearly three thousand miles round trip, leaving home and now returning. Of course, it was now just conquered Soviet territory, but it still looked, smelled, and felt like home. I was in Jaroslaw, the capital city of the county of the same name, and just about thirty miles from one of its smallest towns, Sieniawa. It seems like several lifetimes ago that I missed that train back to engineering school. Four long years without a word from my family, and no word to them about me either. Or was I wrong? Did they know I was a war hero? Did Commissar Glentz send word? Or was anyone there at all to receive word? Were there any Jews in Sieniawa or even in Jaroslaw? Some of the people passing by looked like they could be landtsmen, but I was hesitant to speak to anyone. Four years before the odds would have been fifty fifty, but now I had no idea.

It was well past seven, but it was that magical time of year when the summer evening stays light even after the sun plunges below the horizon, and there was an inviting and friendly atmosphere. After hobbling a few blocks I finally decided to take a chance and stop a woman, using my recently reborn Polish.

"Excuse me ma'am, you wouldn't happen to know if there is a restaurant with Jewish food here? Someone on the train from Lwow told me there was one here."

She looked at me for several moments, but without changing her demeanor. I thought I sensed a touch of pity in her expression, but it could have been my own perception. At least she didn't look hostile.

"I think if you walk down a few blocks along this avenue you'll come to it. But it's getting late. I hope you make it before they close. You know…"

She stopped in mid-sentence and I waited for her to continue. But she seemed to think the better of it and said nothing more. Again that faint look of pity.

"Good luck, sir."

I was simultaneously thrilled to hear that there was indeed a Jewish restaurant there, but at the same time worried about that lady's odd behavior. In any case I knew she was right about the hour so I started hobbling along. All of the people I passed in the street seemed tense. The Germans had left only a few weeks before, so maybe they were worried about a counter attack. Or maybe it was something else, something strange, something that infected the entire region. And the more people I passed with this same somber countenance the more concerned I became. Even though they should have been gay to have overthrown the yoke of fascist tyranny they were subdued. There was no music or laughter emanating from any window, and people were not given to light hearted greetings on the street. It was as if the whole town was in shock. Nobody was ill tempered or mean spirited. They were just numb. If I offered a pleasant evening's salutation it was received with a courteous nod. The enemy had been routed, no bombs were falling, and the weather was lovely. Where I had just been that would have been more than enough reason to hoist a toast of vodka. But not here. Instead, a most unusual mood permeated the atmosphere. There should have been celebration, but fate seemed to have a totally different kind of homecoming in store for me.

I limped forward on my crutches until I spied some people sitting and chatting at some tables outside a simple storefront. At one table a man and two women were sipping tea. Were they landtsmen? Was this the Jewish restaurant? The aroma of cooked food coming from that place answered my question. Its familiar smell made my mind reel, and my feet couldn't move another inch. That scent froze me in my tracks, and I started to sob. I was home. It wasn't Sieniawa, but I was close enough. The smell of that food was definitely kosher. So, it wasn't true. The Jews weren't taken away after all. Here they were, just like always. Maybe they knew my family. I got a grip on myself and limped on. As I got closer my premonition was confirmed. It was a miraculous sound I heard, one that had not landed on my ears for a very long time. It was Yiddish. Yiddish! Jews were still here! My parents were alright! I was afraid for nothing! The rumors were wrong! Thank God! Now I was practically running, talking as I went.

"*Bist ein Jude?*"

They seemed afraid. Maybe it was my uniform, so I continued.

"*Ich bin landtsman.*"

I gushed on in broken Yiddish, and they finally saw that I really was their landtsman.

"Yes, we're Jews. Where are you from?"

I'm from Sieniawa, but I was taken away by the Russians four years ago over some trivial nonsense and I ended up way past Stalingrad where it's practically desert. I'm so excited to be back. I haven't seen my family of communicated with them in all this time. My father's a fish monger. Maybe you know him? Yisroel Ben Yehuda Feder? I'm so happy to see you all!"

While I was babbling they remained passive, occasionally glancing at each other. I finally stopped blabbing out of sheer exhaustion. The man invited me to sit down and offered me a cup of tea. I gladly accepted it, and its old familiar taste made me nostalgic, and my eyes glazed over again. How wonderful! What a relief! Here I was, sitting down with some fellow *yidlach*, enjoying a glass of tea with sugar as if nothing had happened. Now, one of the women spoke up.

"You say you were taken far away?"

"I ended up at this hospital on the Caspian Sea. Lost a few toes"

There didn't seem to be any reaction to my wounds. No recoiling or grimaces.

"And this hospital had no radios? You have no war news?"

"Well, I know we've been pushing the Germans back. I even heard that the Americans landed in France. We've got them whipped for sure now!"

At this the woman gave a slight grin, almost ironic. And then the other woman talked.

"You mean, you've heard no news about the camps? About… us?"

This utterly confused me, and I looked from face to face. Since approaching them they had not been anything but serious, and now an even graver pall hung over the table. I had to confess my ignorance.

"What do you mean?"

All three regarded me with such a melancholy as I had never known, and my chest tightened up. They regarded me for several more seconds and then the man spoke up.

"You don't know?"

There was nothing for me to do but shake my head like a complete ignoramus. He looked at me quietly for several moments, as if to give me a moment to imagine the worst and prepare myself to hear it.

"They murdered most of us."

"Who?"

"Who? Who do you think? The fucking Nazis! They set up huge concentration camps with gas chambers and shipped most of us there. They murdered millions. Women, children, the old folks. We still don't know how many."

Millions?! Children?! Speech failed me.

"It started as soon as they invaded Poland, but even we didn't know about it until it was too late to flee. We were a few of the lucky ones. We were strong enough to work, though they tried to work us and starve us to death. But the Russians got there in time."

"But why? How?"

"Why? They hate us! They hate everything. They killed Poles and Gypsies too. But they made us, the Jews, a real project."

They just stared at me without emotion. The man verified that I was from Sieniawa.

"Don't go there. Nobody's left. They marched them into the woods and shot them all. The whole town."

"My parents. My sisters...."

"They're all gone. That was back in forty one. It was a regular invasion. They even shot the Russian soldiers there."

"But somebody must have escaped."

One of the women answered.

"Yeah. One. My husband, Abe Kestenbaum."

I thought his name over in my mind until I remembered.

"He was a butcher in our village."

"One of the goyim let him hide in his barn. It was all so fast. Soldiers just poured in. Who knows? Maybe they could have hidden more. Abe told me that they marched in around two in the afternoon and by five it was all over. So, there's no need to go to

Sieniawa. The two of you are all that's left."

My mind was reeling. Had I not been sitting I would have fallen down. My vision went dark and all sound seemed muted and far away. This was beyond mere shock or disappointment. All this time I had been convinced that my family was alright. There had to be an alternative! Surely, some fled. Some escaped. How could they talk so casually about the lives of my family? My father, my mother, my sisters? They just stared at me, calmly. They didn't offer me a shoulder to cry on or even say they were sorry. I tried to talk, but failed.

"How...how..."

Their expressions did not change, but they lowered their tone.

"It was like a factory for killing. You know how methodical the krauts are. And if they found you out in the open they made you dig your own grave, and then shot you right then and there. But most got rounded up and put on trains to the camps. Places like Treblinka, Auschwitz, Bergen–Belsen, all over Poland. When the trains got there the Nazis told everyone to take a shower so you could be clean to start work the next day. But water didn't come out of the shower heads. Poison gas did. When everyone was dead they dragged the bodies over to the crematorium. Giant ovens burned them up and got rid of the evidence. Day and night the showers and ovens operated. They tried to kill us all. Six more months and they would have."

I sat there, paralyzed. It was inconceivable. Unimaginable. My vision blurred, and I started to gag. My whole being began to spin. My condition prevented me from running off to the side to throw up, so I just turned and vomited on the street. My breathing was labored and I rocked in my seat with my head in my hands. But there was no relief. At that moment I knew with utter certainty that my family was gone. This barrage of dire news was too terrible to contend with and I just started to sob. The man continued.

"Don't go to Sieniawa. There's nothing for you there. Actually, we're not out of the woods yet. The war's still on and there's vigilante groups of fascist Polacks running around killing everybody but other fascist Polacks. They hate Germans, communists foreigners, Gypsies and Jews. They hide in the woods, and come out at night. Until they're pacified we stay right here. I suggest you do the same."

I still couldn't talk.

"I suppose you have nowhere to go?"

No positive pep-talk from any of my past mentors could snap me out of this. The man got up and brought back a bottle. He poured a small shot and pushed it towards me. It calmed me a little, and I held out my glass for a second. As he poured it he introduced the element of mundane reality again.

"Okay, have another. You need it. But I'll charge you for a third. This is our business."

"Whadda ya mean?"

"The Russians helped a little when they liberated us, but we're on our own now. Gotta eat, so we opened this restaurant. The few landtsmen left eat here, and an occasional sympathetic Pole or Russian. You hungry?"

Everything was moving so fast. Not a minute ago they were describing the murders of a million of our people, but now they were back to business.

"I haven't any money," I mumbled, still numb.

The fellow looked at me coolly, evaluating me.

"That's quite a uniform."

"I was a general's aide and he had it made for me."

"I see you have a medal."

"I'm no hero. Everyone who fought near Stalingrad got one."

"You shoot any Nazis?"

"I shot at a lot of them. Maybe I hit some."

"Sounds heroic to me. Dinner's on the house. From one landts-man to another."

"Thank you. Maybe I can repay this favor to you."

"Maybe you can."

Everyone here was quite blasé. Doubtless there had been plenty of time to let seep in what I had just learned. Also, the drinks were taking affect now, and I was trying to focus on this fellow. He shoved his hand my way.

"I'm Joe Glicksman. I run this place."

I shook his hand and almost said that name that I had repeated for the last four years.

"My name if Ovram."

The women went to get my food, and one of them came back in a minute with a plate laden with warm potatoes, vegetables, and a little piece of brisket which smelled like my mother's kitchen. She placed it down gently, and just as gently said, *"Essen."*

Slowly, I lifted the fork. I held it in my hand and studied it. It was not like the practical institutional utensils I had seen and used for the last four years. This was ornate, doubtlessly part of a set of fine shabbos flatware that was once a treasured part of someone's household. It reminded me of our own back in Sieniawa, and I stared at it, transfixed. Joe Glicksman tried to snap me out of it. He cajoled me into tasting the food, and I slowly lifted a morsel of the brisket to my mouth. As soon as I did a thousand Friday nights came rushing back, and with it a thousand tears. My face dropped to the surface of the table and I banged on it with my fist in rage. I was no longer merely weeping in stoic silence, but openly sobbing with my chest heaving. For the first time my hosts showed empathy and made physical contact with me. The man put his hand on my shoulder and let me cry myself out. Having already gone through it themselves, their own tear ducts had long since dried up. While Joe consoled me he educated me more.

"They dragged me and my family away in September of forty one. They killed my wife and babies the first day. But they thought I was strong enough to get some use out of me, and they put me to work. Back breaking labor. And I struck it out for almost three years. When the Russians liberated the camp they gave me a pistol and said I could kill as many of the guards as I wanted. I shot at least a dozen right in the head the way they liked to shoot us. I was like an enraged animal. The Russians hung a bunch more. Finally, I figured the best revenge was just my survival. Now eat, soldier. You survived too. That means your family survived. Not all of them, I know. But your father's name is yours and you gotta carry on. So, eat up. You got a life to live. After all, whadda you want, to live or to die?"

I lifted my head up and looked at him, tears still streaming down my cheeks. He didn't know how hard those words hit me. I looked at him for another moment, and then down at my food. I filled my fork and then my mouth. I was weeping, but chewing and swallowing. I ate another forkful and then another. With a piece of bread I wiped the plate clean. Without hesitating I had the chutzpah to say, "More please."

The man smile broadly and warmly said, "Sure. Why not? But you'll owe me."

So, I ate that second plateful and accepted one last small drink, both on credit. Now Joe was all business, eager to know as much about me as I was willing to share. Once he was satisfied he revealed to me that he had another business besides the restaurant, and wanted to make me an offer. He said, with my being an honorably discharged Russian war hero, dressed in such an impressive uniform, I was free to go wherever I wanted in Russian held territory without being badgered. He went so far as to say that I fell from heaven. His offer was simple. I take some of his merchandise to Lwow, or Lvov, as it was now known, and upon my safe return he pays me one hundred zlotys. It was the largest amount of money I had ever contemplated in my life, but the whole situation was too soon for me to consider. I refused, but he asked me to think it over. Meanwhile, he guaranteed my tab at the restaurant, eyeing me as a future investment.

I was only about twenty five miles from Sieniawa, and bursting to go there, but I trusted what they said about the situation. So, for now I'd stay put, and keep locked in my heart the desire to go there as soon as possible. The woman who had served me returned. She looked at me with an odd mixture of exasperation and kindness.

"I suppose you have nowhere to stay?"

She showed me to a small storage room in the back that had a small cot. I thanked her and lie down. But that night it was impossible to sleep. The ghosts of my parents and sisters were in my heart, and I had to breathe fresh air to stay sane. It was a clear night so I hobbled outside and looked at the stars. There was only a quarter moon and it was fairly dark. The street lights were still not functioning, so I was able to stare up at the stars as I often had out on the steppes. Casual astronomy is always calming to the nerves, and I forgot my woes somewhere between Ursa Major and Cassiopeia. The air was very still and all I heard was the wind. There was a strong chill in the air, heralding the approaching winter, and I had my blanket wrapped around me. Once or twice I thought I heard something move, but I was alone. Then a woman's voice broke the sacred silence.

"How did you get wounded?"

I had a start. Shaking the constellations from my mind I lowered my line of sight from the distant universe to the silhouette of a mysterious female in the shadows of Jaroslaw. It rendered me speechless. The silhouette spoke.

"Ooh, I'm sorry. I didn't mean to startle you."

Unaccustomed as I was to being in the presence of women I

was tongue tied. This mystery lady had to keep up the conversation on her own for a while.

"Was it in a battle with the Nazis?"

My eyes became adjusted to the dim light provided by the quarter moon, but I definitely determined that this voice belonged to a female that was both young and pretty. She also seemed determined to pursue this conversation.

"Does it hurt?"

She sounded so innocent, and I was glad for the company. It's true that I had been asked these questions a hundred times in the last few weeks, but always by smelly truck drivers, and never by anyone so pleasing to the eye. She was a welcome intruder, and appeared to me as an amalgam of Comrade Marina, nurse Ana, the daughters of General Bogaevsky and every other female I had seen from a distance over the last few years.

"It throbs a little sometimes."

"Was it a battle?"

"A pretty big one, but it was kinda one sided. We got a bad shellacking that day."

She looked disappointed, so I immediately told her of our division's previous success rate, and she seemed more enlivened. Everyone around here had lost their families, and an occasional word of revenge on the Nazi scum was most welcome. So, I told her all about the Battle of Stalingrad and the exploits of the Donski Host. She was attentive and looked at me with admiration.

"Those Cossacks are real anti-Semites too. Did they know you were Jewish?"

"No. They thought I was someone called Arturo or Arkadi."

She repeated my phony name but modified it to the less exotic sounding Arthur, which had a nice ring to it.

"Were you shot?"

"By an airplane no less."

She looked horrified and drew in her breath in a quick gasp.

"Took off two of my toes. But I was lucky. Half inch more to the left and I would have lost my foot and bled to death. What about you?"

She looked thoughtful, and I regretted making her relive something painful.

"Of course, I don't want to make you remember…"

She cut me off and told me it was alright.

"We were mostly lucky. We're from Krasník, near Lublin, about fifty miles north of here. When the Nazis came into our town my father sent us all into the woods. He told us to run and not look back while he stayed behind to stall them. I fled into the forest with my mother, sister and brother. That was my sister Regina that brought you your food. She's older than me."

For a moment I was embarrassed that she had been sitting nearby and perhaps seen me cry, but she made no such comment, and continued with her story. She told it in a straight forward manner without looking for pity, and I couldn't help but relate to her and appreciate what she had gone through. She had a very melancholy demeanor, but frank and innocent at the same time, as if she could just look at you and know if you were sincere or not. Her skin and eyes were as clear as a baby's and her neck and shoulders had a graceful tilt. Most captivating of all was her shy though comforting smile.

"They got most of our family, my father and uncles and everyone else. Anyway, we ran until we met some Polish partisans. Some were Jews, though most were goyim. But they didn't care if we were Jews. They were just out to fight the Nazis, sabotage them in any way they could. They had guns and they took care of us."

This fascinated me. As tough as the Cossacks were we had no women among our ranks. I told her how impressive that was, and begged her to go on.

"Well, I didn't fight. My sister and I were so small we couldn't even carry guns. Once they handed me a rifle to schlep, but it was so heavy I kept dropping it. Anyway, whenever they went out to fight we girls stayed behind, collecting fire wood and cooking. After a while the partisans considered us more of a liability than anything else, so they found some Gentile farmers to hide us. They had to drop each of us off at different farms of sympathetic goyim. First my mother, than my brother Nathan, and than me. Until a few days ago I had no idea where they dropped off Regina. When we got liberated she got word to me that she was in Jaroslaw and had married a man from Sieniawa. So I came down to see her just yesterday. But we still haven't heard anything about our brothers."

She had only mentioned one brother up to now.

"Brothers?"

"When the Nazis invaded so did the Russians. They promised to educate all the young men of our village, so they took them away to the east. His name is Itzhak, but they called him Isaac. He was only thirteen, and we haven't seen or heard anything from him since that day."

We had barely known each other fifteen minutes but could see that we had so much in common. Of course, as much could be said for millions of Jews at that time. Not a single one had come through the war unscathed. But there were so many different depths to the wounds. Some lost their jobs or fortunes and survived by hiding. Most could name murdered friends and cousins. Too many witnessed the deaths of spouses, children and parents. Countless survivors were physically maimed or permanently traumatized. Even Jews that lived secure lives in far away places like America agonized over the shared persecution and mourning. Beyond the immeasurable abstract torment of millions was the individual heartache for loved ones. And this young woman and I both knew it with an intimacy that is indefinable and inexplicable to the stranger. This last detail about her brother Itzhak put us in a box so exclusive our meeting felt like destiny, and when she heard that I had also been taken away under exactly the same circumstances, she became hopeful. It made her cry a little, but she stopped as soon as the first tear welled up in her eye, as if she had already promised herself not to succumb to any more grief. Her will to stem the salty flow was almost mystical. The tear vanished. Instead, she took a deep breathe.

"Anyway, it's late. You must be tired. Goodnight, Arthur."

I had been Ovram, then Artur or Arturo. Now, this kind, pretty girl adjusted it and dubbed me Arthur. It sounded natural, and I liked how she said it. More importantly, I was eager to learn hers. This soul had been on a collision course with me since who knows how long, and I had to hear and pronounce her name.

"Goodnight… ?"

"Esther. Esther Apthekar."

"Good night Esther."

This was a day like no other, and everything changed for me forever. I finally made it home only to find that there was no longer such a thing as home. I was devastated to find that my family was gone, and found it unbearably ironic that they had been gone for years already, without my even knowing it. It was overwhelmingly sorrowful, but it gave me a smug satisfaction to know that I had participated in dispatching as many of those bastards as we did. And finally there grew in my heart a resolve to do the memory of my father justice. I would choose life over death and carry on. I reflected on all this and realized that a new era for the world was at hand, as well as for me. Part of that was meeting someone who made me feel utterly normal, and gave me hope for the future.

Esther and her sister Regina with Polish partisans.
Approximately 1942.

Our official wedding portrait.
We were both just 19.

GOING BACK

XVI

Joe Glicksman converted me into a businessman, at least for the time being. I was technically not a soldier any more, which meant the Soviet government wouldn't continue to feed me on a regular basis. For the first time in my life earning a living was my own personal responsibility, and the Black Market seemed as good as any place to begin. I took Joe's merchandise to Lwow, dropped it off, came back and got paid. Basically, I was his mule and, being a decorated veteran on crutches, I was a damn good one. I was absolutely above suspicion. Anyway, the black market didn't traffic in anything more sinister than cigarettes. It thrived mainly on common luxuries like sugar and silk stockings, things that were normally for sale in stores, but just too hard to come by in the shadow of the war. My smuggling was usually done in quick round trips, leaving in the morning and returning by evening. Sometimes I even got lifts from the same military police whose job was to crack down on the black market. But I was hardly a dedicated criminal. More and more I looked forward to returning home where Esther waited to accompany me over the hot meal that Joe provided as part of our common enterprise. She had already dubbed me Arthur and I called her Eda, the nickname her sister Regina used. There didn't seem to be any-one else around to compete for her affection, and I counted myself lucky. Mostly, I counted myself lucky for what had really happened the first night we met. I had behaved rather crudely toward her, but she considered my war experiences and decided to give me another chance. What I did shames me, but confession is good for the soul so I'll share it. Ultimately, I'm forced to acknowledge that the war took its toll on my character, and I have Eda to thank for making me realize it. Here's what happened, and I hope whoever reads this cuts me as much slack as dear tolerant Eda did that night.

As you already know the Cossacks were a rough bunch of char-acters, and didn't intellectualize about anything. They scratched when they itched and raped when they were taken by sexual urges. They were never conflicted about anything they did, relying more on basic instinct than any other type of human barometer. Later, I even heard that one group of Cossacks liberated a concentration camp up north, and were so aroused by their first sight of women in two years, even emaciated and filthy camp victims, that they raped them. Knowing them as I did, it hardly shocked me. What did shock me was that I seemed to know their character better than my own, or at least what mine had become. After being with them for a year and a half, the period of time during which I graduated from boyhood to manhood, a degree of their nature had rubbed off on me without my even being aware of it. It only surfaced when I met Esther.

It was that first starry night. We had exchanged life stories and were alone. It was my first non-medical encounter with a woman practically ever. Comrade Marina had sexually frustrated me on the collective while the older woman there relieved me of it. Since then no other such opportunity had arisen. I danced the tango with General Bogaevsky's daughters, but had I so much as touched one of them a saber would have skewered me through and through.

To add to my frustration it was my duty to repeatedly provide the General with amorous company while ignoring my own natural urges. Nurse Ana in Baku excited me even more than Comrade Marina, but there was no older nurse there to remedy that situation. Since then, no opportunity for amour had presented itself. So, when I found myself in rapt intimate conversation with a pretty, sweet, clean, healthy woman all alone at night in a sidewalk café in liberated Jaroslaw, it was enough to make me explode, and I couldn't resist suggesting she share my cot. I was so blinded by animal lust it hadn't dawned on me that I was no longer on the steppes. She might have taken all that into account as she attempted to educate me with her civilized reply.

"Please! What kind of a girl do you think I am?"

Now, a young man on the make may hear a female's rebuff without taking it seriously, attributing it to false modesty. Furthermore, I had just spent several years among men who never exercised the formality of asking for sex in the first place, and thus influenced, persisted in trying to satisfy my animal lust with this innocent Jewish maiden. In furtherance of that singular goal I resorted to a tactic that shames me to recall.

In order to understand my base behavior you must know about the behavior of the conquering Red army and their peculiar obsession. Besides killing Germans they were dedicated to two principal activities, liberating the population from the strangle hold of the Third Reich, and then the watches from the wrists of those whom they freed. The Soviet Union had made impressive strides in industrialization, but at the cost of forsaking all bourgeoisie luxury. Wrist watches were considered prime examples of that middle class status symbol, but no amount of communist indoctrination could cure Russian soldiers of their mania for them. Whenever they killed a Nazi they relieved the corpse of its watch, and whenever they freed the victims of fascist oppression they introduced them to the

Russian language with the phrase, "*Dai svoi chasí*. Give me your watch." To their credit they even tried to learn to say it in the language of whatever country they happen to be rescuing at the time. The average Red soldier had his or her forearm, wrist to elbow, covered in them. It was like an extra medal of valor, well earned and gladly paid by the benefactors of merciful Red heroism. So, at the instant when I was attempting to crudely seduce Esther my mind went on auto-pilot and I intimated that there might be one of those coveted time pieces in it for her if she changed her mind. Actually, instead of a wrist model it would have served me better at that moment to have a stop watch with which to measure the fraction of a second that elapsed between my brazen offer and the swift slap in the face she gave me. That blow knocked the macho warrior's belligerence out of me, and I was never anything less than a perfect gentleman around her again.

She forgave me, and we continued to keep company, talking for hours every night after dinner. We were becoming close, and in the back of mind I was thinking about what life would be like married to her. We had everything in the world in common, and she's exactly the kind of girl my parents would have chosen for me. I found her lovely, and her disinterest in watches let me know her high moral character. We were both still in our teens, she just four months younger than me, but mature beyond our years. My affection for this delicate creature was beyond doubt, but I was concerned over the whole notion of supporting a family. Until meeting Joe Glicksman I had never earned a zloty in my life, and I was not particularly attracted to continuing those covert Black Market activities. Then it suddenly struck me that I was selling my uniform far too cheaply. I was exploiting the good will of the uniform for the Black Market without estimating its real intrinsic value. It was being used to disguise certain activities when in reality it was worth more at face value. After all, a man in my position could be of real value to the new regime. Flawless Russian, Ukrainian and Polish languages were on my résumé, and my war record showed that Corporal Arkadivonovitch was someone who could handle responsibility. After all, I was on the general's staff of the division that carried out Operation Uranus. On top of that I already had the uniform. No doubt, some kind of administrative position could be mine. Before approaching the local Soviet authorities however, I felt it prudent to visit Sieniawa and feel things out. I mentioned it to Eda.

"Eda, I'm not cut out to work with Joe Glicksman and this black market thing. I think I can get some position with the new government, at least for the time being. First, I want to see what's going on in Sieniawa. If it's safe I want to spend some time there to see if I can find out any details about what happened to my family. If I don't at least try I'll never rest easy. Anyway, if I think it's safe I'm gonna try to get assigned there as a base of operations. I should be back in a few days. Will you wait for me?"

She leaned over and gave me a kiss on the cheek.

"Don't be too long."

I rented a horse and wagon for the return trip to Sieniawa, and marveled that I'd be returning in exactly the same kind of conveyance that carried me from there. No automobile was at my disposal anyway, besides which I had never driven a car in my life.

In my recently cleaned and pressed uniform, with my medal all shined up, I climbed aboard the wagon and set out for the town of my birth. By now my wounded leg was getting stronger and I carried a single crutch.

The route was an easy one to follow, looking like so many trod before by my father and his cart on his fish route. So many bends in the road were familiar to me, and a mood of great nostalgia overcame me. Traveling through open fields and stands of trees, between sun and shade, brought me back to my childhood, riding on Babe's back while my father recited verses from scripture. I could hear his mellow voice talking of Queen Esther and I anxiously wanted to tell him about the girl I loved who was named for that ancient Persian queen. I was so distracted by my sentimental musings I neglected to consider the real dangers at hand. Though the Red army had purged this area of German soldiers there were still cells of ultra nationalistic Polish partisans hiding in these very same woods. For years various groups of resistance fighters had fought and sabotaged the Nazis. Mostly, they were dedicated to badgering the Germans, such as the group that took in Esther and Regina. But there was one radical group called the Armia Krasnia, generally referred to as the AKA. They were against anyone they considered foreign. They hated Nazis of course, but they were fanatics and were equally against Russians, Jews and a long list of other so called subversives. They didn't share camaraderie with people whose common foe was Germany. They were vicious and killed whoever was on their list, not even feeling pity for the millions of Jewish victims of the Nazis. They just hunted and killed Jews with the same dedication as their other enemies, real or imagined. If they caught me out here I'd have no chance. I had a pistol with me, but my physical condition made me vulnerable. Even though they didn't know I was Jewish they would have killed me for being Russian. But I wasn't thinking about that or anything else. I was lost in childhood memories. Actually, it was pure luck we didn't cross paths.

While I wasn't ambushed by physical enemies, an attack of a less threatening nature awaited me in Sieniawa. All this reminiscence was setting me up for heartache, because there really wouldn't be any homecoming at all. Abe Kestenbaum, Sieniawa's only other survivor, and now possibly my future brother-in-law, assured me that nobody else was left alive. And what is home without family? And if I wasn't really going home, then wasn't this really just a fool's mission? There would be no boisterous greetings, handshakes, slaps on the backs, hugs or toasts. My one sane thought was to see if I could possibly find if there was a responsible party for bringing the Nazi murderers to our town.

I had long theorized that the krauts would have passed by many of these out of the way shtetls if not for the vicious betrayal of some Polish gentiles, eager to please their new Aryan masters. It was my own madness, but I had little method to pursue it. I was not a trained policeman. Regardless, it was a justification for going back.

My lurching cart entered Sieniawa and I had to steel myself against shedding a tear of nostalgia. Practically every building looked as it had when I left. Except for demographics it had not changed an iota. I even noticed that certain fences that had been in disrepair still lacked the same slats, nails and paint. Anyway, misty eyes would hardly befit a representative of Soviet authority, so I took a deep breath, sat up straight and guided the horse toward my house. Before the cart slowed to its stop several people came out to see their latest visitor. As provincial as ever, the residents took notice of everything new in town, and it was easy to tell from their sourpusses, most of whom I recognized, but none of whom recognized me, that the authority of the Soviet Union, herein represented by a decorated war hero, was only begrudgingly respected. It momentarily chilled me to see my old house, but I kept a stiff upper lip and climbed down. Nods passed for greetings and soon enough the gentile Polish family that lived there came out. I immediately recognized the master of the house as an old schoolmate named Bodek, but he didn't know me. I spoke Russian and pretended not to speak Polish, though I understood every word he said. I told him that I had been assigned by the regional Soviet authority to assess the area, and needed to spend the night there. Though they couldn't express themselves in Russian they seemed to have warmed their ears to its sound these last four years, and obeyed without delay. The one Russian word everyone knew was *hodosho*. It meant good or alright, and they used it constantly to demonstrate their subservience to Russian authority. Having no choice, they made a temporary bed for me on the floor in the corner of my old living room, in the same spot where our old maid, Marisha, used to sleep. The house had not changed its interior any more than its exterior, and it was immeasurably harder for me to hide my emotions. The dark favored me with success in that endeavor, but it was one of the toughest and most uncomfortable nights of my life.

As I changed my bandages in Marisha's corner I wondered if I might be able to learn anything about the circumstances of my family's demise, and if any locals might have had a hand in it. They'd probably profess utter ignorance of such things, but I'd have to investigate fully just the same. If there was someone around here responsible for tipping off the krauts I wanted to know. Anyway, for now it looked like it would be safe for me to be here. My old schoolmate had no idea who I was, but was quick to curry favor with me as the latest Soviet big shot, and he offered me dinner. I accepted with an air of bureaucratic indifference and then lie down for my first night's sleep in nearly five years in the very house in which I was born and raised.

As I lie in Marisha's corner I wondered what became of her. Mostly though my sisters, parents and old boyhood friends filled my memories. To keep from going crazy I thought about the present and Esther. As long as I stayed focused on her I'd stay sane.

In the morning my hosts were anxious to know if they were in any kind of trouble, and I assured them they were not. Their main fear was that I might move them out, but I was infuriated by the way they phrased it. They didn't want to be put out of their home. '*Their*' home. All the houses of the murdered Jews had been taken over by the gentiles of the town, and they were content to have new free residences. I had to control my righteous indignation and tell them in fake broken Polish that they were safe. I left, warning them that I'd be back soon.

I got back to Jaroslaw the very next day and went straight to Soviet military headquarters to offer my services. Even though the Germans had fled just a few weeks before, the efficient commies had already established offices. Ever the pragmatists, they merely moved into the recently abandoned Gestapo headquarters. They tore down the swastika and raised the red hammer and sickle up the flagpole. They used Hitler's portrait for target practice, and replaced its honored spot on the wall with a gigantic likeness of Marshal Stalin. Everything else stayed the same, including the file cabinets, desks, ink pads, chairs and fans. The Germans even left behind a wall calendar and for fun the Russians left it up, making it the butt of countless jokes. I hobbled in on my crutch and greeted them, catching the whole staff by surprise. As soon as they spied the Stalingrad medal on my chest they snapped to attention. They even applauded for a few seconds which naturally I returned. I momentarily considered making one of those speeches full of glorious references, but decided just to present my papers. As they studied them in great detail I explained that I was actually from nearby Sieniawa. They were mightily impressed by that, and that I had learned Ukrainian and Russian so well. All in all, they seemed both pleased and impressed, and we got right down to business.

"Corporal Vonovitch, you're just the kind of person we need in Jaroslaw County. We want to root out the Nazi sympathizers that we suspect still live among us. They're called volksdeutsche, a fancy sounding word for suck-up. Even though the fucking krauts invaded them these pathetic cretins still kissed the hands of the master race that slapped them and tried to become like them, so-called Aryans. They even turned on their own countrymen. And don't think that any of us are exactly thrilled to be seating on the same chairs those SS assholes farted on. Anyway, these volksdeutsche are not actually military personal, but they're still wanted as war criminals. I guess you know about the concentration camps. Anyway, you speak their lingo, so you'd make the ideal administrator for your old home town. You'll be appointed Commissar Vonovitch, if that suits you. Maybe you can find out more than we have. Our front line troops were here first, but you know how they are. Shoot first, then shoot some more, and don't ask too many questions later. Well, they're well on their way to Berlin now to personally shoot that paper hanging son of a bitch right between the eyes. So, it's up to the occupation forces to administer and keep order. When you find any volksdeutsche you report them to us. If you arrest them yourself, which I realize might be difficult in your present physical state, you turn them over to the military police. They'll try them and hang them. It's all very proper I assure you."

I told them about my need of a certain house, and they approved its appropriation as my headquarters. If only Commissar Glentz could see me now. Actually, I was given even greater authority than he had. There was no place in the county beyond my jurisdiction, as long as it was within the boundaries of Soviet law. Part of my duties also included monitoring black marketers, but that held no interest for me. The war was still the overriding concern, and I was assigned to ferret out Nazi collaborators, the volksdeutsche who fawned on their Nazi masters in order to be accepted in the New Order. Sometimes that meant something as inconsequential for me as exposing a woman who had granted sexual favors to the krauts in exchange for her own safety. But it also meant finding Poles who had willingly assisted their Nazi overseers in alerting them to the presence of small out of the way Jewish communities, like Sieniawa. Without the help of collaborative Poles the German army might have easily passed by such hamlets. Anyway, before starting on my military mission there was a civilian mission to undertake, asking Esther to marry me.

She was at Joe Glicksman's restaurant. I was thrilled she had waited for me, and told her so. It's never good to show women you take them for granted. We chatted about how I felt going back, but all the while I was just trying to get up the nerve to ask for her hand. When the conversation lagged she just looked at me. Actually I had to catch my breath, because I was so nervous. Then a ghost from long ago gave me a nudge and I blurted it out.

"Eda, I love you. You know I do. Marry me and come to Sieniawa with me."

She stood there studying me, peering through my eyes into my soul. No wrist or stop watch could calibrate this ticking of time, because its passage was now being measured solely by heartbeats. Her face softened and she leaned in, putting her arms around my neck, still looking deeply into my eyes. We were alone, below the same stars under which we first met. She simply whispered, "Yes." Then we kissed.

Since meeting, it had really been my assumption that we would always be together, but it was pleasing for me to hear that she had always assumed it too. The next morning we went down to the magistrate who wrote up some paperwork and declared us man and wife. Regina and Abe Kestenbaum, recently married themselves, and now my in-laws, were our witnesses. Joe Glicksman, though heartbroken over my leaving the Black Market, made us a luncheon.

Although we had no formal wedding we arranged for some nice civilian clothes in which to pose for a formal wedding photograph. Although such finery did not reflect our true financial condition at the time, I was determined to achieve and even surpass it. This was a silent oath made to myself and on behalf of my lovely young bride and children yet unborn. Money or not, at that time we were just glad to be together. Our union was one of love, and it also symbolized that our families survived through us, and that we would live on as a single, strong unified family. The Feder and the Apthekar clans united. It was a merger made in heaven.

A KOSHER COMMISSAR

XVII

Eda and I loaded a wagon with all our worldly possessions which amounted to a change of clothing for each of us and a few photographs. Ironically, we were bound for a place where I was a man of property, but whether or not I could reclaim it remained to be seen. For now our load was light, and we enjoyed the leisurely ride to Sieniawa, relishing the clear day as much as our company and conversation, recapturing the innocence stolen from us by the war. Our pockets were empty, and we had nothing between us but each other, yet we were full of confidence. After all, we had nowhere to go but up.

As soon as we got to Sieniawa I lowered the boom on my old schoolmate and told him to hit the road. I found another house for him, and my new bride and I moved into the Feder estate. This was our family homestead and should continue as such.

The house was complete, and all Esther had to do was find some groceries, which she did with the credit traditionally extended to the local commissar. We celebrated our honeymoon exactly where my parents had, though I confess it made me a little inhibited.

After taking a few days off, my first in years, I rode the wagon around town, acquainting myself with the people who now lived there. The houses looked familiar, but the faces in the windows were totally different. I vaguely recognized many, and it amazed me that absolutely nobody knew me. I had lived alongside most of these people for fourteen years, yet I was a stranger to them. Of course, I had left a boy and was now a man, but I still found their lack of sensory acuity abysmal. Once I had satisfied my curiosity I started concentrating on the task at hand, the reason that brought me here. I wanted to see if the German army stumbled on Sieniawa or if somebody had led them here. If I found that out it wouldn't require the help of the military police to deal with it. I'd shoot them myself.

Only about ten percent of prewar Sieniawa was gentile, which limited my list of suspects to a few hundred souls. Visiting their houses didn't turn up any incriminating evidence. After all, as soon as they heard the Reds were on their way, any volksdeutsche would have burned or buried every swastika, portrait of Hitler or copy of Mein Kampf. Now they all professed to like Jews and Stalin. Anyway, I wasn't trained in the methods of police investigation, so every day the task seemed harder and harder. But I persisted, and was at least able to uncover evidence that led to the arrest of a few Nazi sympathizers who had previously escaped Soviet detection. I summoned the military police to arrest them and help me interrogate them. First, they had to explain where they were when the Germans invaded. We spoke to them one at a time, and then compared their stories. They corroborated each other's versions, but the MPs said that they sounded rehearsed. And none of them knew anything about murdered Jews. So, we recorded their names and the MPs led them out of town. They were doubtless hanged without ceremony in the nearby woods, possibly from boughs hanging over the grave of my family. The only way we were able to accomplish even that much was due to the voluntary betrayal of their fellow citizens. Eager to keep their skins, neighbors informed on neighbors. The volksdeutsche were condemned by the same kind of infamy they had earlier committed. It was perfect justice, but I feared that the man who might have betrayed my family had slipped between my fingers and was already swinging from a tree. If that was the case then justice was served, but not my desires for revenge. The odds were so remote I might find him I was probably wasting my time. But I had to try. Sieniawa was so remote someone must have led them here.

By now I was walking with only a cane. Esther and I were constantly talking about where we might go, because we really didn't feel that we would stay in Sieniawa. We didn't feel welcome there, and for that matter we didn't even feel welcome in Poland. Few Jews did. We knew that the Germans were being pushed back daily by the Red army, and the radio serenaded us with exhilarating reports of the unbeatable Americans doing the same from the western front, sweeping through France. The Nazi defeat was a foregone conclusion, and we were determined to stay as close to the Russian front as possible in order to affect our ultimate refuge in the west, whether that meant France, England or even America. We were also seriously considering Palestine. As youths in our shtetls we had both heard the very same traveling Zionists glorify our native homeland. Echoing their arguments we found they made a lot of sense. Imagine, being in a land of only Jews. No anti-Semitism. No pogroms. We could do as we please. It was like a dream, and being young we entertained all dreams. On top of that we both had relatives there, and the thought of being among family again always made us happy. So either way, in the west or Middle East, we'd be content. As long as we were together.

While searching for the betrayers of Sieniawa a particular group of people turned up whose presence surprised me even more than discovering my quarry. Out of nowhere eleven Jews materialized.

They had been hiding for years, and we were so ecstatic to find them I dropped my act. In such presence, enough Jews for a prayer quorum, I made no further pretense of being anything but what I was, Jewish. Now there was no secret that the chief Soviet administrator of Sieniawa was a Jew.

To celebrate this joyous occasion Esther and I decided to get married again, only this time with a Jewish ceremony in the company of landtsmen. There were eleven at hand, and we also invited Regina and Abe and Joe and all the regulars from his restaurant that had become our friends. We had a Kosher feast prepared, Joe brought wine from Jaroslaw, and the gentile who had commandeered the house where I learned the tango sheepishly offered us the loan of the Victrola. One of the eleven cut some green boughs and fashioned a hoopah, and we exchanged vows in Hebrew under it. I put my good foot to good use, stepping on a glass, and then, just as that doctor in Baku predicted, I danced at my wedding. It was just a slow waltz, but I danced. It was New Year's Day, 1945, and we saw this solemn and festive occasion as an auspicious new beginning. The gaiety was made a little bittersweet by the ghosts of our families, but it also contributed to our commitment to each other and to continue living as Jews. That would have made our parents content, as it did us. After the ceremony, which many of the townsfolk witnessed from afar, Bodek approached and congratulated me. His jaw hung agape with a slight quizzical grin as he had a realization.

"Aren't you Ovram Feder from school?"

He was perplexed and stupefied to learn that he was right, but he was still friendly. Of course, now more then ever, he had real reason to suspect he'd lose the house for good. That's all anybody there was worried about. They were just concerned for their stolen real estate, and felt no shame over it or anything else. And there was little doubt that someone among this collection of Quislings would tip off the AKA. My feeling about that was confirmed when a couple of the eleven Jewish survivors came to me with chilling news.

"We have to talk with you about something important, but we wanted to wait. We didn't want to spoil your wedding or distract you from it."

They were very grave, and I begged them to go on.

"We think that a couple of local goyim went and told the Germans about Sieniawa. It was not by accident that they came to such an out of the way place as this."

My body temperature must have dropped ten degrees. I felt absolutely frozen. I had to talk to keep from getting worse.

"You know, for years I was out on the steppes; and all that time I was thinking that my parents must be safe, because they were in such an inconsequential and remote shtetl such as Sieniawa. Do you know their names?"

"No, but I know their faces. By sheer luck we saw them coming. We were out in the woods foraging for wild berries. We heard a large group of people coming our way, so we ducked down."

"But we could see them through the leaves and hear them pretty well."

There was nothing for me to add, so I just bid them continue.

"I recognized the faces of the goyim. There were two of them and they were talking to the officers and telling them that it wasn't much further…"

"And that there were thousands of *zyids* there."

"They would have gone right past us."

"Those two goys informed on us."

"We didn't even return home."

"We were friends with some truly Christian farmers, and they hid us."

I was stunned and angry.

"Where are they now?"

"We came back over a month before you got here."

"We looked everywhere for them."

I was now trembling.

"Did you speak to anyone else about this? You get any names?"

"One."

"Konstantin Jonjac."

I thought about the name, but it didn't sound familiar.

"Are you sure? How old is he? What does he look like?"

Such was my anger that my thoughts were unclear and my words mere babbling.

They described him as best as they could. He was about thirty, five foot, six and average build. He had blond hair and was fair skinned. In other words, he looked like every other Pole. No facial scars or limp. Nothing special to distinguish him from anyone else. They explained that they asked about him all over Sieniawa and for ten miles in every direction since then.

"Nobody ever saw him again after that day."

Had these landtsmen reemerged just a month earlier I would have had vast numbers of troops at my disposal to aid in the search. But now that the area was pacified of Axis combatants all of the Russian soldiers were sent to reinforce the Red army in the west. They wanted to guarantee the speedy demise of the Nazi war machine and were mounting an army that dwarfed even the immense force the Third Reich had treacherously hurled against Russia four year earlier. They were not out to defeat Germany, but annihilate her. They wanted to exact revenge so complete that Germany would never rise again. And if they had to put a torch to the entire country and kill everyone in it to accomplish that end, then they were more than up to the task. Anyway, with the troops rushing west to assist in the defeat of the Third Reich it meant that the Soviet presence switched from military to civilian, and from conquering bodies to conquering minds.

Poland was slated to become another state in the Union of Soviet Socialist Republics, regardless of how she felt about it. Fascism had been booted out only to be replaced by communism, and groups like the AKA, though barely operational, were resentful and determined to make some sort of statement in protest, no matter how last ditch and futile. Sadly it wasn't long in coming. As they were neither brave enough nor tough enough to take on their real tormentors, they went the usual route of picking on some defenseless scapegoats which in this case, as it had been for eons, were yet again the Jews. The Poles never tired of accusing us of being communists and subversives, though the utter lack of evidence to support this supposition didn't deter their madness. Polish paranoia convinced them that the Jews, even decimated as they were by the Nazis, were somehow mystically taking over their country, and my presence only convinced them of that certainty. The bottom line was that we were not considered Poles and therefore not worthy of living on their precious dirt. Some friends, including Bodek, even warned me that they might target me specifically, the most powerful Jew in the county. Maybe he was right. That possibility became less of a speculation and more of a threat, when just a few days after our wedding, while we were still giddy, the fanatical AKA made the last eleven Jews of Sieniawa vanish. I got the reports from so-called sympathetic gentile citizens, and Esther and I were disturbed to the core of our souls. I had barely begun my own investigations into the whereabouts of Konstantin Jonjac when I was faced with solving this immediate crime. But I didn't even turn up the bodies. Then again we never saw the bodies of the two thousand killed here years earlier. The situation was unbearable. The ultra nationalist mania to purge their country of anything perceived as foreign knew no satisfaction. Not the deaths of the entire population of this town, nor the murder of millions sated their fanaticism. Their mindset suspected everyone of subversion, and they were intent on killing every suspected enemy until only their notion of the true Pole was left standing. That was their fiendish philosophy and only their eradication could prevent them from carrying out more heinous plots. But the troops necessary to put the pressure on the local populace to cooperate was marching toward Berlin. Eda and I discussed this tragic dilemma.

"I have to find this bastard. He killed my family! He killed every Jew in Sieniawa!"

"Who understands how you feel better than me? I wish you could catch him. Probably, the same thing happened in Krasnik, but what can we do? You heard what they said. Nobody has seen them in years. Even if they would have stuck around afterwards, it's for sure they ran away when the Russians showed up."

"So, I'm supposed to accept it? Eda, I want revenge! For my father, my mother, my sisters, friends, neighbors, the whole village. I must have my revenge!"

"Arthur, how many Nazis did you kill out on the Steppes? You yourself told me the corpses were uncountable. I'm not saying a thousand of those worms are the equal of one of your sisters, but you can rest easy that you did take a lot of revenge. They killed two thousand here, but you killed more than that in just one battle at a train depot. You told me so. And, for all we know, some of those krauts from that ambush were among those that killed your family. It's very possible, Arthur. Did you ever think about that?"

"All that's well and good, but I still want to get my hands on Konstantin Jonjac."

"Are you willing to risks our lives to do it? Because, right now you're the next victim in their sights. Arthur, those bastards lost. Right now the Russians and the Americans and the British are wiping them out for good. For good!"

As Eda talked to me I imagined how I might react if I actually found them. Previously, I turned in volksdeutsche to the military police. It was their responsibility to hang them. But in this case my emotional connection went so much deeper. If I found them I'd probably see to their hanging myself, or to be more expedient, shoot them with my sidearm. I might even bludgeon them to death. It was not my manner to be so bloodthirsty and advocate such mayhem, but everything was different now. All bets were off. Eventually, Eda's common sense prevailed, and we decided not to stay another day. If the land where the Vistula flowed didn't want Jews in it, we'd leave them and their twisted sense of purity.

"Okay, but some day I'm coming back here and find that scum!"

Our vague plan included following the advancing Red army west. We'd stay for a few days or weeks wherever we could, exploit my authority as much as possible, and eventually get ourselves out of Poland for good. But remaining in my consciousness was the desire to return and find the man who betrayed Sieniawa. One day I'd come back and complete the mission. When I found Konstantin Jonjac I'd deal with him and do the needful. For now discretion was the better part of valor.

Eda and I loaded up a few basic family heirlooms that had been in my house since before my birth, and we headed for Jaroslaw. Once there we explained the situation to our family and friends and exchanged all possible forwarding addresses. While we were there we heard the good news that Warsaw had been liberated, and Krakow just the following day. This encouraged us that our plan was the right choice, so I went to military headquarters, which was now civilian Soviet headquarters, and affected a transfer of duty to Krakow where I would also have great authority to continue arresting volksdeutsche. I reported the activities of the AKA, specifically the disappearance of the eleven, and left it in their hands.

Having secured my appointment to Krakow, a good hundred and twenty five miles from Jaroslaw, I made arrangements to be taken there in a military transport, making sure to get the most comfortable truck possible in order to insure that my foot and new bride would be as snug as possible. By now I was at ease with my cane and I didn't have to change bandages any more either. I still limped, but I hardly needed any help. We climbed into the truck and I discovered that it was to be only the second trip in a motorized vehicle for Eda, the first being her ride to Jaroslaw from Lubaczow. By comparison I was an old hand, though I knew exactly how she felt. She sat next to me, nestled into my side, and I put my arm around her. It was a relatively smooth road, and we watched the Polish countryside glide by. It was blissful to sit with my young wife and we didn't see a hint of the war to spoil the happiness we felt. For five years this land had been ravaged by the most savage on-slaught any country had ever suffered, but we couldn't see any proof of it from our perch in the truck cab. No burnt out tanks, airplanes wrecks or dead bodies blemished the gently undulating farmland. Pristine green was all we saw. But in our silence it was impossible for either of us not to carry in our hearts some part of that violent conflagration. Although we had never met prior to Jaroslaw we understood each other perfectly. It wasn't really because we shared a faith, because neither of us was what you would call religious. We were just cut from the same cloth. Finally, it was because we were Jews, fellow victims of persecution. Nobody but those who had gone through that horror could understand it, and those that did, like us, could cling to each other as we so desperately did now. We dare not disturb the solemn silence by voicing it, and our mutual respect for our grief was sacred. It was all unspeakable, so why try? Instead we looked to the future. Our future. When I did shatter the silence it was only to speak of the most positive things.

"So my darling, what kind of house do you want? They say I

can take anything. You want a one story, a two story? How about a castle?"

"A castle would be nice Arthur," she said giggling. "You go find us a castle."

We laughed, but deep inside I actually considered that possibility.

The truck pulled into Krakow, and I was surprised to see that the city was mostly in one piece. At Baku we had gotten complete updates of the war and I knew that the allies had been bombing Germany and their occupied countries without let up. But somehow Krakow was missed, or not considered strategic enough to bomb. However, we didn't stay around to speculate about such things. We had gone there with a purpose, and we wasted no time. I had the truck drop us off at the government office. I presented my papers and got right down to brass tacks in perfect Russian.

"Comrades, I have been assigned to Krakow to further the cause of seeking out and persecuting those elements of Polish society still sympathetic to the fascist cause. I am here with my wife and we will require the use of adequate lodgings."

My compatriot was all congratulations and celebration. He kissed me on both cheeks and called for an aide.

"Comrade Sandinsky, drive Commissar Vonovitch down to Karmalitskanaya Street and help him find suitable quarters for a wounded hero of the Battle of Stalingrad and his bride. Nothing too bourgeoisie. Just slightly palatial. Welcome to Krakow, comrade!"

As I exited everyone was applauding.

Our driver, Comrade Sandinsky, was chatty, though I felt bad that Esther couldn't understand Russian. It really didn't matter, because she was thrilled to ride in such a decent automobile and take in the sights of a city she had always heard about while growing up. The town was in amazingly good shape. Most of the cities I had been through since leaving Baku were either totally in shambles or at least partially so. But this place was totally different. You would hardly think that a war had been fought within a hundred miles of it. No buildings were falling down, the trolleys were running, and there were no dead horses in the street. They had been most fortunate. Driving through the streets was practically like a tourist excursion, and I glanced over at Eda who was all smiles. I enjoyed observing her glee, and I confess that I couldn't resist feeling a little proud to already be providing for her so well. She turned her smile my way and squeezed my hand. Then she raised it up to her lips and kissed it. Then she leaned over and gave me a big kiss. This seemed to delight comrade Sandinsky, who was chuckling like a madman over the romantic newlyweds.

Karmalitskanaya Street turned out to be the best address in town. I selected an enormous apartment with no less than five full bedrooms. It had electric lights, indoor plumbing, brocade curtains, crushed velvet wallpaper, oriental carpets and chandeliers. Even counting the fine dachas I used to find for General Bogaevsky, this was the most opulent residence I'd ever beheld. It came completely furnished and was so ornate it reminded me of the salon in the Kremlin where I got my medal. The inhabitants of three shtetls could've lived there. My old wide eyes returned, but I had no reason to hide them. Eda was no less agog. When she came out of the kitchen she was slack jawed. I looked at Eda and said, "Well, you said to get us a castle!" Laughing, she ran across the carpet and threw her arms around me.

Our new stately home was on the second floor, and there was a grand balcony with a breathtaking view of the city. For over a thousand years this town had been the center of Polish culture, and its architecture and wide boulevards were impressive. More than that it appeared to be a blessed city. The Nazis, classic sore losers who routinely demolished cities they had to evacuate, had simply disappeared. Even from our elevated vantage point we couldn't see any wreckage or smoldering ruins, not even in the distance. In my memory no other city during the war went unscathed. I hadn't seen any place else that looked so good. I'd been through Stalingrad, Moscow, Kiev, Lvov and Jaroslaw, and they were all bombed, some totally, but all to a noticeable degree. Many of the hundreds of small towns I'd been through also showed evidence of Russian aerial bombing. The countryside wasn't spared either, with sections of rails targeted by the allies to inhibit the Nazi retreat. But around Krakow I noticed that their rails were still in tact. That was extraordinary. The Russian high command was constantly sending coordinates to the Americans so they could find rail junctures and bomb them. Apparently the Allies didn't think this area was of any strategic value. It struck me odd that they bypassed a major city like this one while the Nazis pinpointed a hamlet in the woods with fewer inhabitants than lived on a single block on Karmalitskanaya Street.

After settling into our palatial accommodations it became clear that we had ten times as much room as we actually needed. This observation was not the result of communist indoctrination, making us feel guilty over having more living space than required. Quite the opposite, it was a completely capitalistic realization. A single bedroom was more than adequate for our personal living space while the ample salon and foyer would make an ideal dining room for a restaurant. The kitchen was large enough and sufficiently well equipped to cook for hundreds, so I found an out of work chef and made arrangements to bring in more tables and chairs. The chef knew where to buy everything and within days we had ourselves a regular establishment, Arthur's Restaurant. Not being on the first floor, exposed to pedestrian traffic, we depended solely on word of mouth, and as I wasn't hiding my real identity any more, we ended up with a mostly Jewish clientele. It wasn't strictly kosher, but our people felt comfortable eating there. Also, by then the concentration camps had been liberated, and I let it be known that recently returned survivors could get a meal there. The concentration camp near Krakow, called Plaszkow, had been dismantled by the Germans in an attempt to hide their crime, but the Russians found enough evidence to know what had happened there. A few of the survivors of the ghetto made their way to our restaurant. They were human skeletons and it broke our hearts to see them. When the camps were first discovered the Russians did what they could to feed the prisoners, and the inmates put some meat on their bones before returning home. Some people though were so anxious to get out they left in their weakened state. On one occasion two such survivors came in. They were so emaciated it was amazing they had the strength to climb the stairs. We fed them, but tragically their bodies were unaccustomed to eating rich food, and they succumbed to the stress it put on their fragile digestive systems. We felt terrible about this, practically responsible for their deaths. The fighting and killing were over, but not the dying. It reminded us of the eleven in Sieniawa and we were encouraged more than ever to stick to our plan to go west as soon as possible.

Thinking about immigration meant, among other things, considering finances. The path from Poland to Palestine was a long one, and would require funding. I was no longer a kid, looked after by my parents. Nor was I a Soviet citizen, ward of the state. At nineteen I was a tough ex-con, battle weary war veteran, and married man, but my experience with monetary matters was so meager it could be summarized with two slim entries in a profit and loss ledger: twenty rubles compensation upon release from jail and a handful of commissions for petty smuggling between Jaroslaw and Lvov. That was all. Now, for the first time in my life, I was going to have to go out on my own and do battle with the world to earn a living. But thanks to the lessons taught by my jail house mentor, and my battles on the steppes, I was no more intimidated by it than any of the other challenges that had thus far come my way. And so far, my first involvement with it was painless. After just a month in the business trenches, Arthur's Restaurant was doing alright, and I was able to sock away some funds toward our eventual flight as refugees. Of course, the restaurant had a lot of overhead, so I could only take a slight commission, but added to my Soviet administrator's salary, rent free status and complimentary meals, our nest egg was off to a decent start.

Feeling unthreatened by personal obligation, and with our exodus from Europe on the table, my natural curiosity, coupled with my need to give my leg therapy, compelled me to explore Krakow. Anyway, as a government agent I should familiarize myself with my beat, at least to be able to discuss it intelligently with my cronies should the need arise. Actually, in all my travels there had never been much opportunity to broaden my cosmopolitan horizons. Except for a few evening hours in Stalingrad and an afternoon in Moscow, my whole life had been a decidedly rural experience. It was high time to take a stroll around an actual city before departing the continent, and one of the oldest in all of Europe was a good place to start.

Besides being in one piece Krakow was truly picturesque. I couldn't help but be charmed by the cobblestone streets and quaint shops. It was somewhat like Lvov, but much more expansive and developed. And being further from the Russian border, it was that much more Polish in nature. Shops offered kielbasa, clothes, toys, books, clothes, kitchenware and luggage, the last of which left a mental note in my mind. Tying things up in bundles would no longer due for our pending sojourn, so I took notice of a luggage shop. I also passed some cinemas, and made another mental note to invite Eda to see one. For years I had heard about them from fellow inmates and comrades in arms, and I was eager to see one. Neither Eda nor I had ever had a chance to see one. We were a real pair of hicks.

As I strolled around I politely greeted the citizens. My uniform put most folks off, but whenever I nodded or tipped my hat the courtesy was returned. The local kids fascinated me, because they reminded me of home. Children are universally identical, always playing and making a racket, and the boys and girls of Krakow were no different. Watching them also made me think of how one day I would be a father. Spoiling my stroll though was the thought that Konstantin Jonjac could be hiding among the citizens.

After a half hour's constitutional my foot started to throb, and thinking it best not to overdue my therapy, I turned for home. My brief hike had given me an appetite, so when I arrived I ordered some warming soup. Then I sat down at a window side table to enjoy the view. As I was eating I heard Eda give a yell, and I jumped to my feet. Though my foot ached I bolted toward the sound of her voice and came upon her on her knees crying, causing me great consternation.

"Eda! What's wrong?"

Now I saw that she had her arms around a boy of about twelve and he was crying too. My jaw hung open, and I was utterly perplexed. She was kissing the boy all over his face. She was rapid fire kissing his cheeks and eyes and nose and ears and forehead with wet sloppy kisses mixed with her tears. Choked with emotion she fought back her tears and squeaked out some words.

"Oh Nathan, thank God you're alive! My little brother. My dear baby brother."

She kissed him some more and smiled and laughed like a mad woman. When she finally composed herself she stood and introduced us. By then I had figured out this was her little brother Nathan who she constantly talked about. He had fled into the woods with Eda, Regina and their mother when the Nazis came to

Krasnik, and she hadn't seen him since the partisans dropped him off at the farm years before. When word of fighting ceased he made his way to Jaroslaw and gravitated to landtsmen who sent him to Joe Glicksman's restaurant. There he reunited with Regina who had just now sent him here. The emotion enveloped all of us and it was joyous. All of my own family had perished, but now, being married to Esther, I gained a new one, and it seemed to be expanding regularly. My blood family was gone, but now I had brothers-in-law, a sister-in-law, and even a mother–in-law. Nathan reported that she was well and back in Krasnik. He also brought letters from her mother and Regina, which Eda poured over fifty times. For all the happiness she felt at being reunited with Nathan there was always the unavoidable sadness for Jews at such events. For every survivor there was always at least one who was missing. In this case it was Eda's father and her other brother Isaac. I knew how she felt. It was a joy to see her brother reappear, but it was impossible to avoid reflecting on the joy her father would have felt to know it too. The wounds were still too fresh to forget. But at least the man's line would not die. Nathan was alive. He was already twelve, and soon he would be a man. Isaac was a year older, but who knew anything about him? Mother Russia in all her incomprehensible vastness had swallowed him up.

So many dire fates awaited humanity in Russia. Now that the Germans had been defeated Papa Joe no longer had any use for heroes. He imprisoned intelligent patriotic officers returning from Germany in remote prison camps and the infamous salt mines. The commies were not as methodical as the fascists. The Third Reich loved to keep records, count the corpses, and weigh their bones. Stalin seemed to favor the much less complicated vanishing act. Now you see them, now you don't. Siberia absorbed more souls than heaven, never to be heard from again.

Nathan stayed with us for a week before going back to Jaroslaw, and I became fond of him. All my siblings had been female, and it was a distinct pleasure to have a brother. Technically he was just my brother-in-law, but I accepted Eda's family as my own kin. My immediate family was wiped out, and as long as they were willing to accept me, I made the same emotional commitment to embrace them as my blood. So, I delighted in helping Eda stuff some pounds back on Nathan's slender frame. We sent him back to Jaroslaw twenty pounds heavier. He was going to take care of his mother in Krasnik and I admired his nobility. Though young, he was imbued with maturity and responsibility. It was the same for all of the survivors in Europe. Without that temperament they wouldn't have made it in the first place. It was a generation robbed of their childhood.

I was tired of military life, but my uniform was our ticket for the time being, so I continued to go through the motions of Soviet overseer. I was no more a fan of totalitarian communism than any other Pole, and it was a great irony to have something in common with people who were indifferent to our torment. Of course, the biggest irony of all was running a successful for-profit business based on our communist presence. But I still had to pretend to act like a commissar, and that meant hunting for Nazi collaborators. The restaurant did not require my presence so I was able to dedicate some time to keeping up the image of a Soviet occupier. I made the usual inquiries among locals as to who were former volksdeutsche, and the usual stool pigeon types came forward to rat out their friends and neighbors. Of course, I was content to find and punish fascists, but I had long since committed myself to abandoning this continent of hate. Meanwhile I persisted in my duty. Arrests were made and suspects turned over to the local police to await interrogation by Soviet authorities. On one particular occasion I arrested a suspected collaborator, and while I was bringing him in we happened to pass Karmalitskanaya Street where Eda was coincidentally enjoying a moment on the balcony. It was a relatively mild February, brisk yet clear, and she was relishing the warm side of the building where the sun always shone down on our balcony. She saw me and my prisoner, but from her vantage point and mind set it was unclear who was in charge, and she became terrified that I had been arrested. For the last five years her experience had always been to observe the Jew as the victim in arrests, so she reacted with the same fear as always. Fortunately I spied her and, perhaps to impress my wife with my authority, I pushed my prisoner forward, brandishing my pistol and bravado. For good measure I loudly threatened my prey, also for the benefit of my wife, and she finally got the message that the shoe was on the other foot, even if it did lack a few toes.

Arthur's Restaurant was doing alright, but we kept our ear to the radio to track the progress of the Russian army. One of the benefits of our new status was the acquisition of that radio, and being in possession of such technology reflected how our lives had progressed. If the Nazis would have found one here they would have shot everyone in the apartment. Of course, the Soviets now controlled the airwaves, so whatever emanated from it had to be taken with a grain of salt. Actually, thanks to one totalitarian or the other, there hadn't been a believable broadcast since 1939. The Germans used it to disseminate Nazi propaganda, before confiscating them all. Now the Russians were using it to spread their own brand of political propaganda, though they were kind enough to put on some music to ease our nerves once in a while. It was mostly Russian classical composers, but it was most welcome. Anyway, whatever information about the war that came over the airwaves was easy to confirm because of my connection to the Soviet military. The briefings at headquarters were far more reliable, and the word was that our troops were in Germany.

Besides moping up the Nazis we considered the Red army to be our vanguard, opening our path before us. And as soon as we heard that it was on German soil we made plans to follow behind. Regardless of the success of Arthur's Restaurant we knew that Poland would never be our home. In the evenings we discussed our alternatives. Czechoslovakia's Carpathian Mountains were only forty miles from Krakow, so it seemed like a quick escape. However we didn't know the political situation there or anything else about it, like the language. It was not an attractive alternative. Berlin was ten times as far away and we knew the Russians were headed there, so that was a possibility. We also knew that the mystical Americans had liberated France, even it was over six hundred miles away. Everything seemed so far away. Was it realistic for two Jewish kids like us to contemplate traversing Europe and a good part of the globe as well? Even with the Nazi threat, Eda had never been more than a few miles from the town of her birth. Of course, after a journey that took me to the Caspian Sea and back, I felt that anything was possible. It was like my combat experience. Even with all that noise and violence I never thought I'd get killed. Likewise, I felt Eda and I could make it anywhere. We shared the same will and were an unstoppable team. The coming trek was nothing insurmountable, and unless you put a bullet through my head I was prepared to kick your teeth in if you got in our way.

OUR OWN EXODUS

XVIII

The strength of will, along with four million Russian soldiers, smashed into Germany and by the first week in May the war in Europe was over. Everyone was celebrating, Eda and I included. We gave thanks to God, cried for our dead, and resolved to leave Poland for Paris, stopping off in Germany for some required travel documents. Through my association with the USSR, now the un-contested, officially recognized government for much of Eastern Europe, including Poland, I got the lowdown on what would be required for us to immigrate. After planning our itinerary, and shar-ing it with Regina and Abe, who would meet us in Paris as part of their own personal Exodus. We packed the luggage I had picked up at a shop in Krakow. I took off my uniform for the last time and put on my first suit, transforming myself from soldier to civilian. Bolstered by the money we had earned at the restaurant, along with my last bit of salary from the Soviet occupational forces, we set off for the train depot. On the way I quietly vowed to myself to return someday and find Konstantin Jonjac.

No more hitch-hiking or horse drawn wagons. From now on our journey would be courtesy of trains, automobiles and ships. Travel by rail was once again available to the civilian population, and we joined the great river of refugees flowing west by that means. At every train stop we voraciously consumed every scrap of news, eager to find out the best routes. When we left Krakow all we knew was that Poland was no place for Jews, and that Soviet territory, now clamping down on the populations it wanted to control, was to be avoided. With Berlin in the hands of the Reds we decided to keep south. Two days slow going from Krakow, stopping constantly to pick up fellow émigrés, we crossed into Germany without any form of documentation. Six months earlier this would have been suicide, but now it was the most normal of circumstances, and most people had Germany to blame or thank for that. Another huge change was being Jewish. Six months earlier our religion would have condemned us to arrest and probable death, and the only train travel we would have known was inside a cattle car. Now being Jewish was actually a benefit of sorts. The whole world was aware of what had happened to us, as well as their complicit guilt in it, and we were finally the target of sympathy instead of hate. And nobody was quicker to demonstrate that new found empathy toward us than the krauts. As they were to blame for our current dilemma they bent over backwards to facilitate the flood of Jewry that was criss-crossing Europe in their attempt to immigrate and resettle. Taking advantage of that situation, we assumed that identity. I had no intention of using my Russian identity, we were Jewish refugees, holocaust survivors like so many others. Russian language and identification papers were useless to us, so when we got to Munich we went straight to the Joint Distribution Committee, a Jewish refugee organization that had just set up offices all over Europe. There, we applied for our first post-war identity papers. We observed a man in the line ahead of us who was asked for some previous form of identification and he practically bit their heads off.

"You bastards kicked in my door and dragged me off to a death camp, took everything away, killed my family, tried to work me death and then starve me to death, and you have the nerve to ask me for some ID? You want to see some ID asshole? Here, look!"

He rolled up his sleeve to show the infamous number tattoo that all camp victims were given. The German official fell all over himself apologizing and one of his own bosses came over to berate him even further. He was reduced to tears and nobody else was asked to show any papers. From then on whatever story was given to the authorities was the official version. It was the second time in my life I was allowed to reinvent myself. After the jail in Kiev was bombed I had that opportunity, and here I was, being given a second chance to chart my own course. In Kiev I made up a name and ignored everything else. This time I could undo a lie and put myself on any path I wanted. Thousands, perhaps millions of people all over Europe were doing the same thing. The war had destroyed the lives of a continent and now we had to get back to some sort of normal state. And the first step was to arrange for some kind of legitimate documentation of who we were. Before qualifying for passports, visas, carnets, or any other kind of citizenship or immigration papers, we had to get some form of basic identification that would be accepted by the world's civilized nations. But like so many before us we had no birth certificates or any other proof of our nationality or religion. Except for our gender we couldn't prove anything. In any case, the opportunity to establish a new identity was a blessing not to be abused. It was clearly a chance to start a new life. Whatever we told them would be accepted, whatever had gone before would be erased, and whatever we aspired to be could be made manifest. We were not criminals in need of disguising our true names, but we decided to westernize them a little just the same. So, Ovram became a memory and I took Arthur as my legal name. As far as Eda was concerned she was married to me for life and was pleased to remain Esther Feder. We told them the truth about our birthplaces and dates, but eliminated any mention of Cossacks. Instead I became another soul, hidden in the forest by the partisans. We were displaced persons, just like a quarter of a million other Jews in Europe. And we were pleased to note that our new ID papers were bereft of any reference to religion. Apparently, in the new post war world such things were blessedly private. But one final step in the process was required. Civilized people get legally married, and there were no exceptions to that rule. We had no argument with that. We loved each other so much it was a pleasure to keep going through weddings. We had been wed to satisfy the Polish authorities, the Soviet authorities, and the heavenly authority. Hopefully though, this time it would last. We wanted the whole world, free of hate and war, to bless our union.

The legalization process took a few days during which time we were provided free room and board at the Red Crossplatz, a special facility reserved for refugees and other displaced persons. It was a cozy one bedroom apartment. We were only in Germany a short time before moving on to France, and it was a strange feeling to be guests of a government that was so eager to murder us all just a few months earlier.

While we were there we took strolls. It had been a long time since needing even the support of a cane, but I had to keep exercising my foot to lose my limp. On one of our walks we finally got a glimpse of an American. It was a special event for us. We had been hearing about them throughout the war and we carried images of them in our minds that made them supermen. The event was doubly interesting because it was also our first sighting of a black man. Growing up in Europe we never saw a person of color except in books, and we were fascinated. Our horizons were broadening. We were only notified of their nationality by the whispers of those around us. Soon we saw white Americans too. Their uniforms seemed so much more casual than Germans or Russians, and none of them carried weapons. No rifles or even pistols. They spoke softly and were all smiles. And none of them bothered anyone for ID papers or anything else. Besides that they were handing out cigarettes and chewing gum and putting little children on their knees. They were the very opposite of any soldiers we had ever encountered. The Soviet occupiers had been kindly compared to Nazis, but these Americans were absolute angels. Their behavior drove home the message that this horrible war was really over.

We had accomplished what we needed to in Germany, so we continued on our trek to France. Every moment west was another step away from the land of our birth, but we felt no regret. Eda had lost a father and many uncles, aunts and cousins, and I had lost my entire family. We couldn't help but feel sad, but it only reinforced the excitement we felt to be moving forward in our lives. We were headed for France, Palestine, and beyond.

It was a beautiful clear day when our train pulled into France, and the border crossing was as uneventful as the others. They had to change locomotives, and it gave us a chance to stretch our legs. It was still two hundred and fifty miles until Paris, but just feeling French dirt below our feet was an adventure.

We napped on the train, and the sun came up just as were approaching the famed capital. After our first taste of French food –some delicious croissants and café au lait for breakfast- some of the people in the car excitedly called out that the Eiffel Tower was in the distance. We got out of our seats and crossed the aisle so we could see the famous landmark. It loomed over the city and filled everyone on board with emotion, us included. Eda seemed especially thrilled, so I squeezed her hand to show her we were on the same wave length. Her eyes filled with tears and she gave me a delicate sweet kiss. Back in Poland she had almost always been a case of nerves. Now she was happy without reservation.

Once in the station we schlepped our luggage outside and took a look around. We could still see the noted tower, but we were lost. We had absolutely no idea where we were or where to go. But we weren't in a panic. We were free and it was beautiful day. So, we took interest in watching all the people and automobiles. There were many sidewalk cafés across the street and we couldn't resist trying out more of the famous French cuisine. With no common language at our command, some sign language let the waiter know we were hungry, and he brought us a nice lunch which lived up to its international reputation. We especially liked the wine. After we finished we looked around for some hint of where we should go and what we should do. It was a beautiful day and the meal had satisfied us, so we weren't in any anxiety. After all, the world was at peace, and nobody was hunting us. Our goal was a refugee camp where we could start the process of immigration to Palestine, but we had no idea how to take the first step. Then we recognized some people from the train with whom we had discussed our plans, and they signaled us to go back inside the station. There we discovered the good old Joint Distribution Committee had some tables with signs in various languages, one of which was Yiddish. This organization had the answer to all our dreams. They knew every governmental requirement in the world and had every official form to match. We told them we wanted to go to Palestine and they were able to handle that as well. But first they explained that one of their services was to reconnect families, and they invited us to inquire if any of our family might be in Paris. We asked about Regina and Abe Kestenbaum, and we were delighted to learn that we could stay with them for a few days before starting our kibbutz training, a basic requirement for immigration to Israel.

Abe and Regina lived on the Rue de Rossier in a Jewish neighborhood in Paris. Eda was especially delighted to see her sister again, and they chatted like magpies. Meanwhile I caught up Abe on what I had learned in Sieniawa, that apparently he and I truly were the only survivors. To avoid getting depressed about it all over again we joked how we were bonvivants in Paris and how earlier we would have thought it the height of sophistication to catch the weekly bus to Lwow. Not that we ever did. To further lighten our spirits we learned that Nathan had been taking good care of his mother. She was well settled and he planned to leave Poland as soon as he could. Unfortunately that opened up the topic of brother Isaac who had gone off with the Russians in 1939, and was by now considered dead.

Once we caught up on the past and present we focused on the future. Eda and I held forth on Palestine while Regina and Abe only had eyes for America.

"Abe, Zionism is the best thing for us. Sure, things look good over there now. But you know how things go. Five years from now they'll be kicking Jews out of New York too!"

"You're mushuginah! Jews have been living there for hundreds of years and nobody's kicked them out! Anyway, I'm too old to be a pioneer. It's America for us!"

It's true that Abe was older than us. I remember being a kid in Sieniawa and visiting his butcher shop. He was perhaps a bit old for Regina too, but she felt protected by him, and they seemed happy. Besides, he had already established himself as a butcher in Paris and was doing a good job of supporting them both. He had found a cousin here in the same trade and had been working since their arrival. Besides, Regina was pregnant and expecting soon. In short, we were not persuasive Zionists. They were determined to stay in Paris for the time being, and later immigrate to New York.

After a month in Paris Eda and I were assigned to a kibbutz south of Paris where we would learn all about our new home and get a head start on Hebrew. Before making that commitment Eda and I took in some Parisian sights.

The activities of the last two months were sufficient to convince anyone that anything is possible. Not ten weeks ago I was hobbling around in a Russian uniform with no clear cut idea of what lay ahead, and now my bride and I were strolling around the most famous city on Earth without a care. It's good to be strong willed, but a little break from all that determination once in a while is good for the soul too. And in that respect one could do worse than do it in Paris, the City of Lights.

We visited museums and art galleries and ate our fill of rich French cooking. It was pure escapism. But while enjoying our escape into tourism we had a momentary fright that the war was still on. There were flurries of shots and then we saw a group of American GIs. Oh my God! The German are making a counter attack! My foot started to throb, and Eda froze solid. To add to the terror the soldiers were laughing. Were GIs like Cossacks, taking delight in battle? To make matters worse they were shouting some English phrase over and over again that seemed to have the word Jew in it. Would the madness never end? Then we saw the source of the barrages, and felt a little sheepish over our panic. The GIs were lighting tiny firecrackers and tossing them on the street. One GI saw our bewilderment and tried to explain to us in extremely loud English the cause of their celebration. He kept saying that word with Jew in it, and then some number. He even held up four fingers. It made Eda nervous, but I was convinced we misunderstood and that these men were harmless. They were so good natured it was a wonder to me that they were able to defeat the Germans, though I was glad they did.

We resume dour tour with visits to some museums and galleries, and it was probably the most agreeable day we'd ever had in our lives, firecrackers included. We had another rich meal and spent the night in a hotel which, truth be told, was eloquent, but not as plush as our flat back on Karmalitskanaya Street.

Having totally relaxed we caught a bus to the Joint Distribution

Committee's kibbutz, south of Paris. When we got there we were warmly greeted and fed, and then interviewed. They were extremely interested in knowing what special experience or training we had.

"Don't worry Arthur. Your past is your past. Everybody invents stories when they get their new ID papers. But here we need to know what you can offer. The British Balfour Declaration in Palestine provides for the possibility of a separate Jewish state. That means we'll need people to build a new nation. So, if you have any unique education or experience to help your new country please don't hold back."

Years of Russian bureaucracy would make anyone shy of government, but I decided I had to trust my landtsmen, and gave them my full resume. When they heard it they knew that I was valuable, for not only did I know the ways of warfare but I was no stranger to administration either. At once they offered to put me in charge of kibbutz security. I was shocked, but they explained to me that they had to go elsewhere to initiate a similar project and had been searching for someone with exactly my qualifications to assume control there. Basically, everything that had to be done was all written down on an agenda, and I just had to make sure that each individual kept to his or her routine. If I did that the kibbutz would run itself. Having killed Nazis on the battlefield I had everyone's respect, so my mandate was never questioned.

The kibbutz was a melting pot of about three hundred Jews from every country in Europe. While it was nice to have something in common with everyone it also created barriers due to the lack of a common language. Basically, we had two kinds of landtsmen present. There were those like Eda who were provincial and spoke either their native tongue or Yiddish. And there were the urbane big city Jews who spoke several European languages, but not Yiddish. To overcome this dilemma we were all supposed to learn Hebrew, the language of our future home. After all we were Jews, returning to our ancestral home. There was a word for this, and we all learned it. It was called Aliyah. It was like a pilgrimage, but permanent. We were returning to the land from which we sprung. It had been a long time, two thousand years, but we were on Aliyah, the return.

The best part though was nighttime. Each evening, after a hot August day of practicing to be farmers and linguists, we ate and then relaxed outside in the sweet breeze. No group of people ever had so much in common, and we shared a great camaraderie. The feeling of love and acceptance revived the muses of many of us, and violins, accordions, clarinets and guitars came out of their cases. My own musical career died when I returned that comb to its rightful owner back at Collective Farm number eight hundred and thirty one, so I sat with Eda and enjoyed the impromptu concerts, sipping a little French wine. Photos of the Promised Land were passed around and we marveled to see orange trees and picturesque looking schools. Most striking were the smiling faces of the pioneers. They were all suntanned and robust and made us eager to join them. In general it was a happy time. No more thoughts of uniforms. No more military. No more war. My foot was almost perfect, and I had a little money in my pocket. Eda's mother and brother were safe back in Krasnik, and Regina was content living with Abe Kestenbaum in Paris. We were confident about our decision to go to Palestine and we even had family there, even if they were just distant cousins. More than anything else though, we were happy just being in love. From the moment Esther and I met we both knew our common destiny, and we made a fearless couple. As long as we were together there was nothing that scared us. Wherever it was that we had been headed before we met, once our paths crossed, we had reached our mutual destination. Everything else was of secondary consideration. I have a very strong independent spirit and I don't deny it. A year in jail, two on the battlefield, and another in the hospital, were only possible because of that self sufficiency. Without it survival would be jeopardized. Getting together with Eda did not compromise that. Rather, she was its perfect compliment. And whatever it was that she needed she also found in me. But who can analyze such things. I'm no poet, so I just thank my lucky stars that some stranger on a train steered me to that restaurant in Jaroslaw. And Jaroslaw to Paris was quite a leap for us. What's more, it was a romantic leap. There's something in the air of France that inspires amorous sentiment, and I can't tell you that we were immune to it.

The kibbutz gave us all a chance at trying our hands at being farmers. Many of us did indeed come from agricultural backgrounds, but some of us had never had the honor. So calluses were a common occurrence for many as we refined our techniques with shovels, hoes and picks. After a lifetime in the sticks Eda and I were disinclined to farm work. Although we were getting a taste of kibbutz life, a formality that all future Israelis had to try, we were far more interested in living in the city.

Besides learning practical disciplines, the kibbutz atmosphere fostered a great kinship among us. We were encouraged to think of ourselves as a people, a nation, a tribe, as opposed to a collection of rugged individualists. This also reinforced our resolve to rise above the horror of the last six years. Together we would prevail. But ever present, below the surface of our night time frivolity, was an underlying current of melancholy. Though it wasn't spoken one couldn't help but notice the far away stares of those lost in bitter remembrance of loved ones lost in the great madness. One moment we might be enjoying a group sing-along, and the next a lyric reminds someone of those six years, and a voice drops out of our chorus and its owner becomes a zombie, looking at nothing in particular in the endless French night. This mood crept in almost nightly and put our merriment into grim perspective.

Being at the Kibbutz we were not out of communication with the outside, like I was at the collective farm. We constantly communicated with Regina and Abe, and we were thrilled when Regina and Abe had a healthy baby girl. Many little girls died in Sieniawa, so it was a blessing to have one born to one its few survivors. Our best revenge against the Nazis was just surviving, and we were already starting to replenish the blood line.

After just a couple of weeks of practicing to be enthusiastic kibbutzniks, we got word that our ship was ready. Three hundred of us were going to catch a train to Marseilles, our point of departure, over four hundred miles away on the south coast of France. From there it was a four day sail over eighteen hundred miles on the Mediterranean Sea to the port of Haifa in the Holy Land, our new home. Although being uprooted had become a fearsome, tedious and numbing experience for most of us, we couldn't help but feel excited over the prospect of leaving behind forever a continent that had given us nothing but misery. This trip was different from recent ones. We had more than a few minutes to select and pack our lives, and there was no armed guard standing over us, exhorting us to *schnel*. We packed at our leisure, and enjoyed it, knowing that it was our choice to do so. In one sense we were forced to do this, because of the situation created by the goyim, but now there was a myriad of alternatives from which to choose. At least we had that freedom. With the luxury of time at our bidding we prepared carefully, cooking and packing lunches to take along. Spartan treks were behind us, so we brought along some fine French wine as well. Chartered buses took our entourage to the train station, and we settled in cozily in a series of coaches reserved especially for us. Train trips themselves had become traumatic reminders of our wartime suffering, so great care was taken to make our accommodations as comfortable as economy allowed. We reveled in our freedom and exercised our hard won right without shame. By now we all knew each other and we merrily chatted, sang songs, and made toasts. If you have three hundred Jews together in one place there has to be at least a couple of comedians, and we were no different. They made hilarious observations about the sights flying past our windows, and Eda was one of the best kibitzers. All in all, the four hundred mile trip was a blur of conversation, noshing, and entertainment. We were in Marseilles before we knew it.

The port was humid, probably more so than any place I'd ever been. And it was a real international hodgepodge. There were ships and men under the flags of Algeria, Libya, Egypt, Italy, Greece, Turkey, Spain, Portugal, America and Russia. As we walked along the docks we heard one foreign tongue after the other. It was like the kibbutz times ten. A guide from the Joint Distribution Committee met our incoming train and was sweating to keep us all together. He also had under his charge several other groups, totaling another four or five hundred souls. When we were finally all together he had to take a roll call. All our names were on his clipboard, and he constantly referred to it.

It was agreed before our train left that I would continue in my position of authority, even assuming the role of maritime policeman once we were all on board. I herded our contingency into one spot and we all responded to the roll call with the boisterous enthusiasm of school children on a field trip. The other groups did likewise and soon we were led down a long pier to our grand dame of the sea, the Matarua.

Out ship was neither a beautiful ocean liner nor a rusty bucket of bolts. It was just a substantial looking commercial vessel, and no one feared for their life. What matter if this wasn't the Queen Mary? This was not a tourist cruise. Only our destination mattered, and as long as we didn't think we'd sink half way there, we were thrilled to be on board. Our goal was the Holy Land and our lives as free Jews. Most people were so excited they were trembling with emotion. Even to people like us, who had been through so much, this was special. We could take anything in our stride, but this was extraordinary. And on that August day in 1945, when the Matarua finally slipped away from its berth, many of us went up on deck and repeated a ritual that Russian Jews had been doing for a century. We spit toward Europe and turned around to face our new destiny, and dared not turn back, lest we suffer the fate of Lot's wife. What lay ahead absolutely had to be better, and all seven hundred and forty five of us prayed aloud for it to be so.

PALESTINE

XIX

It was a quiet voyage. The seas were calm, but we were rapt with thoughts of the war and so many loved ones who could not join us, now or ever. Although the weather was mild we were enveloped in a somber atmosphere that persisted for the entire trip. People stood at the railing, their salty tears falling and mingling with the brine below. It was as if we were finally free to mourn our lost families. Even the comics and musicians were reserved and melancholy.

Being at sea is like being in a time warp. There are no responsibilities and there is unlimited time for reflection. It's easy to get lost in your thoughts and nobody interrupts your meditation. The only variety in the day was meal time, but we had long since become adjusted to eating again, so there was no great rush for that either. Some people even missed meals, so deep was their reflection. Having shared similar experiences there was universal respect for this quiet. Besides, we all knew what was going through their minds. There was never a boatload of people as alike as ours. I stood at the rail, staring into the sea, Konstantin Jonjac staring back. I left Sieniawa, departed Poland, and now I was leaving all of Europe behind. But, someday. Someday. Perhaps I was not the only one to make such a pledge. Who knew what the others had gone through?

By the fourth day most of us were a bundle of nerves. Europe had been our home for centuries, and regardless of the war, starting out in a new continent was for some an intimidating prospect. The Matarua steamed forward and the Port of Haifa edged closer. Beyond it we could see the hills of Carmel and we were all struck by the land and how different it looked. Europe was green, like one big farm. Its hills, valleys and river banks were all verdant, but this place was yellow. We already knew this of course. How many photos had we been shown by eager Zionists? We knew it, but actually seeing it first hand was something else. Palestine was a long way from Sieniawa and Krasnik.

There was no welcoming committee or brass band to greet us. Swarthy skinned people were scurrying around the old wooden pier, securing lines and shouting. We couldn't understand a word they shouted, and they hardly paid us any mind at all. Our liaison from the Joint Distribution Committee had his clipboard back in hand and saw to it that we disembarked in an orderly fashion. A British flag fluttered over the dock, and our first destination was a low building at the end of the pier where we had to do some paperwork. Eda and I walked down the unsteady gangplank, each of us carrying one of the valises I had purchased in Krakow. I would've carried both, but I was still limping a little bit. Eda didn't mind though. As long as she was with me she seemed content. She was by now very attached to me and looked to me for security and protection. For my part, I did not let her down. The war and post war occupation had transformed me into a confident being, so I faced this new challenge with determination.

A bevy of British officers interviewed our group and they seemed satisfied with our documentation. They were polite though blasé throughout the process. In any case, it was an affair of several hours, during which time we sampled some Palestinian food. There were Arab vendors around the dock, so we had our first taste of humus and pita bread. Most of our group was indifferent toward the local delicacies, but I didn't mind it. I had eaten Russian prison food and Cossack cuisine, so I could stomach anything. Beyond the food the biggest dramatic difference of our first moments in Palestine was the utterly different atmosphere. None of us had ever known such heat and dryness. Furthermore, there seemed to be a thin layer of dust everywhere. It was actually sand as fine as talcum powder. All told, it made us feel like we were in another universe.

The air, the land, the people, the dress. It's as if we stepped into one of the pictures from my old geography book. To complete the incomprehensible exotica of the place we were dependent on interpreters for everything. None of us spoke Hebrew yet, and even if we had it seemed like everyone around there spoke either Arabic or English. This tended to make us clannish and disinclined to mingle. It was our first day though, so we held out hope that things would improve. As long as we were together we felt at home.

After the paper work we were shepherded onto some buses and driven to a camp to undergo some introductory orientation. Landtsmen from Europe had a lot to learn about their homeland before living in it. We were Ashkenazi and quite different from the native Jews, the Sephardim, who seemed more like Arabs to us. Anyway, we were determined to give it a try, so we moved into the tent city.

By now the comedians were back in fine form, as were the musicians, and we had a pleasant evening under the stars. Besides whatever racket we produced, there was only the wind and the distant sound of sea birds, all of which revived a bit of the residual mood of the voyage. We were momentarily trapped between European nostalgia and the exciting challenge of a new country and culture. There was much to think about, and some of our party felt a little intimidated. As for myself, I was eager to get to Tel Aviv and find a job. We had been in limbo for too long and I looked forward to the routine of family life. During this period of orientation we observed some kibbutzniks tilling the land, and it confirmed my decision to opt for city life.

In France we practiced planting things like proper pioneers, but it really didn't prepare us for anything. France, like most of Europe, is by and large composed of black, fertile soil. The Holy Land had nothing in common with that. Perhaps being holy was the secret, because it looked to me like it would take a miracle to grow anything in that sand.

On the morning of our third day some buses came and collected those of us bound for Tel Aviv. The sixty mile southbound trip was encouraging, because the road was nicely paved by the British and we could relax and enjoy our first good look at our ancient tribal land. But it was just more sand and rocks, and it could easily make you wonder why the Lord gave such barren real estate to the people whom he had chosen, and why our ancestors fought so hard for it. Back where we came from you couldn't sell land like this for a penny an acre. It was barren and dry and didn't look as if you could raise anything except lizards and scorpions. Be that as it may, this was the original *Eretz Yisroel*, the land of the Torah and our forefathers. Many in the bus, trying to supplant the depressing images of endless desert with something more inspirational, commented about the Biblical prophets and judges who had walked these ancient hills. This brought to mind my father and how he used to always discuss these sacred topics. Doubtless he'd be enthused to be here and not be put off by the lackluster terrain. He probably would have gotten down on his hands and knees and kissed it upon arriving. Compared to him this whole experience was lost on me. After all, this trip was not a pilgrimage. Our main motivation for coming was to be free and materially progress. Of course that was part of the pragmatism of Zionism. How could we progress back in

Europe if every other generation got disenfranchised? It only made practical sense to make long range plans if you could count on being allowed to stay put someplace. For some, being able to freely practice one's faith was just a bonus. The unfettered success of the Final Solution had bred within many of us indifference toward spiritual practices, and now our main religion was the preservation of us as a people. Once our security was established we'd consider the luxury of worshipping God.

By now I was resigned to my family's death, and it was as if they had died long ago of natural causes. It was fortunate that I had not witnessed their suffering. All remembrance of them was as living, breathing, content beings, so all my thoughts of them were filled with warm nostalgia. In my mind's eye father was alive. That's the only way I had ever seen them. Regrettably, there were thousands of us who had been forced into hiding and had actually observed the suffering of our loved ones. But all my reminiscences are scenes of noble proud individuals, untainted by those final moments of horrific humiliation and violent death. Of course, part of me still wanted revenge, but I had to put it on a back burner for now. Rather, it was vital for my consciousness to stay positive about their memory. And being in Palestine is something that I knew would have greatly pleased both my parents, and it filled me with pride for having undertaken Aliyah. After this, they probably would have been inspired to make Aliyah of their own.

Regardless of our reminiscences and idealistic adoration of historic religious leaders, it was hard to ignore what we observed, which was mostly uninviting terrain. What's more, the arrival itself was anticlimactic. While Tel Aviv was bigger than Haifa it was hardly more impressive. We had just lived in Krakow and Paris, so it suffered greatly by comparison. All in all, Palestine was pretty rough. Even the most provincial European is more cosmopolitan than his Middle Eastern cousin, so the general impression was that it was a backwards place. Why couldn't God have given Paris to his chosen people?

We were chaperoned from the bus station to the Jewish Refugee Agency where we were provided simple lodgings. These were only temporary, and we were expected to find jobs and get on our feet as soon as possible.

After we unpacked we got together with our cousins. Eda had been looking forward to this since departing Krakow. Family means a lot to her, and she felt that having some in Palestine was a blessing. We got a warm reception from all our kin, and we shared stories, though much of the news was pretty depressing for them. News of the holocaust had long since reached Palestine, but now they were learning first hand of the suffering of their relatives. Apart from the family reunion I observed that they were poor and in no condition to help us. This worried me. Here were people who had been in this land for years, yet they were financially worse off than kinsmen back home. Did a similar fate await us? I decided that my dear relatives just weren't very ambitious, and that we would do better. Maybe the sun made people here lethargic, and it would take a sharp European to shake things up?

My first job in Palestine took me to the beach. This might sound glamorous, but it had nothing to do with sunbathing or being a lifeguard. One of Eda's cousin, Sruley, had a small construction business, and he needed sand to make cement. So, he gave me a shovel and one lira per day. It made the work at the Soviet collectives seem like camp. I *schvitzed* like an ox and all my muscles ached. I tried to encourage myself by feeling as if I was building a new homeland for Jews, but it was a far cry from the romantic images conjured up by the Zionists who passed through our shtetls years before. Also, our efforts in France to expand our family had born fruit. So, one lira per day meant that the three of us would be starving pioneers. Uninspired by shoveling sand, I walked around after work looking for something better. I wasn't the only one. Clearly, Palestine was going to be an uphill battle all the way. But I told myself that it was too early to tell. And as always, my old jail house mentor materialized and asked me, "Do you want to live or do you want to die?"

An important aspect of life in Palestine that was underplayed by the Zionists was the position of the British Empire. They were the victors in WWI, and this place was part of their spoils. They were definitely in charge, and they ruled with a strong hand. Compared to the Nazis they were cream puffs, but they were not out to do us any big favors either. The Arabs in the region were the majority by quite a long shot, and the British were more inclined to appease them than us. But they had signed the Balfour Declaration at the end of the Great War, and there now was a lot of pressure on them to finally act on it. That piece of paper made it clear that there should be a Jewish Homeland here, and Zionist organizations were leaning on England to make good on that promise. However, there was still a war in the Pacific to be won, and all their energies were invested in that. Until that conflict was resolved the trickle of Zionist pioneers into Palestine, vexing to the Arab community, was a minor headache. Meanwhile I kept shoveling sand in the heat.

Toward the end of the first week in August we heard some incredible news. A radio newscast that said the United States had dropped a gigantic bomb on Japan. This super weapon was invented by a German born landtsman named Albert Einstein, and was more terrible than anything that had ever existed. Everyone was of the same opinion. First we were sure that the Japanese would now surrender. Secondly, we all thought it was a real shame they hadn't dropped it on the krauts. Of course, the Germans had already surrendered, but we still thought it would have been a good idea, just for good measure. Next day the newspapers and radio were filled with news about this horrific new weapon, and our conversations were dominated by it. They said that Hitler himself tried to come up with it first, and we all gave thanks that he didn't. The whole idea of such a weapon was overwhelming to me. Fighting the Nazis in a unit that used swords and horses made this new weapon seem especially inconceivable. Though I hadn't thought about my old Cossack comrades in a long time it was impossible not to imagine what those old fashioned warriors would think about all this. I knew they'd lament how the good old days of cleaving a man in half were through. Ultimately it would probably take a good while just to convince their unsophisticated minds that it was even real. A few of us expressed some small degree of pity for the Japanese victims, just like we used to feel sorry for the Nazis we ravaged. We didn't really know anything about the Japanese at all, but if they were allies with Hitler then I figured they deserved to have the atomic bomb dropped on them. The next thing we heard was that it happened all over again. It was September second and I was shoveling sand into Sruley's pride and joy, his truck, when I heard the fireworks. But this wasn't like Paris. I definitely heard real rifle reports and a bona fide air raid siren. Were we being invaded? If so, by whom? When we first came to Palestine they had told us about past incidents when Arabs attacked Jews. If that was happening we were in serious trouble. I knew of no weapons, and I imagined that we depended on the British for protection. If the Arabs attacked we'd be so outnumbered it'd be a desperate situation. And if it wasn't the Arabs who could it be? Were the British defending themselves from an attack by some errant German unit, unaware of their surrender? Were they attacking or defending? What was going on? We were in a panic. But there were no columns of smoke anywhere or airplanes coming our way. Rifle and pistol shots echoed off the hills and buildings, and it was impossible to guess the direction of the invasion. Someone was shouting my name, and I turned to see. One of the men I knew from the Jewish Refugee Agency was waving at me. "Arty, the war's over. It's ov…"

His voice cracked in mid-word, his chest heaved, and his eyes glazed over. What he and everyone had wished for the last six years was finally at an end. All that shooting and noise was the start of a huge celebration. British soldiers were shooting into the air. Vehicles of every description were racing through the streets honking and everyone was embracing. We were no different. The Germans had already been defeated, but the Japs were fiercely defiant. Those atomic bombs did the trick, and now the world was truly at peace. Eda and I embraced and kissed and we couldn't help but cry. Our tears mixed with those of every continent as the worst calamity that had ever befallen mankind was finally put to rest. No more killing, torture, hiding, starvation or fear. Germany was in ruins, Hitler was dead, and Japan had suffered assaults so unspeakable that further thought of war was unthinkable. Over and over again people bellowed out, "The war is over!" It was good to say it. "The war is over! Thank God, it's over!" We were shouting and crying and laughing. People were literally dancing in the streets. "Yahoo! The war is over! Yippee!" Strangers hugged and normally serious people drank straight from the bottle. Children who didn't even understand the significance caught the infectious gaiety of the event and were spinning around and shouting. Even the most reserved British officers had their hair mussed. By nightfall the British organized a parade complete with brass bands. Entrepreneurs set up food kiosks and a festive atmosphere invaded the usually quiet night. People who heretofore had second thoughts about bringing children into a world at war, now inspired by the irresistible mix of glee, hope, drink and lust, endeavored to make up for lost time and repopulate the planet. The party lasted until dawn.

In the morning a more somber tone engulfed the revelers as they observed the passing of fifty million souls sacrificed to senseless, ranting megalomania. Eda and I were prime examples of those celebrants. We were festive all night, and then grave the next day. But the war was over. It was really over. Thank God!

But there was one battle of that war still undecided. There was no truce over the quest for Konstantin Jonjac. Doubtless, there were a thousand Konstantin Jonjacs. So many volksdeutsche informed on their neighbors it was an impossible task to track them all down. Anyway, there were usually just two kinds of witnesses of their betrayal, their victims and the Germans. The former couldn't talk and the latter, while harboring no respect for them at all, were just as unlikely to talk. Yet, my soul could never be completely at peace without bringing some closure to that episode. Maybe he as alive somewhere, and maybe someday I'd find him.

THE LIVES OF PIONEERS

XX

War or peacetime, I didn't like shoveling sand. It wasn't that I was lazy, but it just didn't give me enough income. So I continued to look for a better job. The truth was that my lack of training and experience didn't qualify me for too much. I had an eighth grade education, and most of my previous work was performed almost exclusively in uniform. Arthur's Restaurant didn't count, because I had free rent and all the other perks a local commissar gets in a Soviet state. The only thing free at my disposal now was free enterprise. So, I looked and looked, and after a couple of weeks I came across a candy store that needed some help. It paid better than shoveling sand, and it was a lot easier on the back. Not that I mind hard work. Anyone who knows me knows that I'm a workaholic. But if I'm being paid less to dig in the sun than stand in the shade in a store, than I see no reason to prove my manliness with a shovel. Anyway, I didn't leave Sruley in the lurch. He replaced me in one minute flat.

The candy store paid me triple what Sruley did, but three lira a day was still not what I had vowed to myself back in Poland. Then it dawned on me that the candy company that sold their goods to this store probably sold a lot more of their goods across the city, so I came up with the idea of delivering their goods to all the stores in town. To do this of course I needed transportation. Cars were very hard to come by in Palestine, not that I could have afforded one, but there were motorcycles all over. It was the most popular mode of independent mobility there. Town or country they were everywhere. One could almost imagine Moses riding one in the wilderness. Anyway, a cousin knew someone selling an old motorcycle, a Czech Yaba, and I was able to convince him to let me have it for payments. Of course, owning it and actually being able to drive it were quite different. During the war I observed truck drivers a hundred times, but I never saw a motorcycle in action close up. The seller gave me a few lessons, but I had to use my bad foot to change the gears. The motor must have died on me a hundred times before I finally got it under my control. Once I learned it though, it became second nature to me. Most of the year a motorcycle is the ideal mode of transportation for Tel Aviv. It's extremely economical, getting by on just a couple of gallons a week. But the winter can get chilly and rainy, making those months pretty uncomfortable. Once I became master of the motorcycle I got myself some large cans and rigged the bike to hold one on either side like saddlebags. Next, I approached the two most popular purveyors of sweets, Eliat and Tamar, and convinced them to let me deliver their products. Furthermore, I negotiated the value of having their names of the sides of those cans as advertising, and they paid me a little extra just for that. My business plan was simple. Back then entire businesses were dedicated to selling nothing but sweets, selling them by weight. They were popular with children and teens, and even adults stopped in for sodas. The owners of those stores appreciated the convenience of having someone deliver their good to them, so they didn't mind paying a few extras cents, which is where my profit lay. Then I turned salesman and convinced restaurants and other kinds of businesses to sell candy where they previously had not, and exact an even higher price. It was not a large city at that time, but everyone likes candy. And, thanks to my ingenuity and hard work, I was able to earn twenty times what Sruley paid me. What's more, I learned every street, alley and pathway in Tel Aviv. Nobody ever knew it better. I had the freedom of being my own boss, and could expand my enterprise to any part of Tel Aviv. I made my deliveries five days a week, collected on one, and took a day off. I was doing okay, but we were still stuck in the lower economic quagmire that was the Holy Land of that era.

To escape our financial doldrums, as well as the heat and humidity of the coast, we often went inland where it was elevated. There the milder climate allowed us to commune with nature in a low budget holiday. We brought a picnic lunch and spent quiet times together. Sometimes we took a bus all the way to Jerusalem, about thirty five miles southeast. It's incredibly picturesque and full of tourists. It's also like a place of pilgrimage for people like my father. They stand before this sixty foot high wall, the western wall of King Solomon's temple, and dovit. Observing them made me miss my father more than ever. How he would have relished praying there! So many of the men resembled him, with the beards and the talus, it almost broke my heart. Hearing their heartfelt chanting evoked his spirit and I felt his presence. Eda was quiet and calm before it too, reflecting on her own father. Besides orthodox Jews, everywhere we went we saw British soldiers. We all knew that there were clandestine forces at work here, hell bent on establishing a Jewish state, and they saw England as their enemy. There were no more Germans left to fight. The new fascists were the British. Maybe they weren't really followers of fascism, but they might as well have been, because they were limiting many Jews from settling in Palestine. We came to learn that ships were no longer leaving from Marseilles. The Matarua was one of the last ships to make port here without incident.

The British didn't want any more trouble, but the world situation gave them nothing but. Everyday in the newspaper we read about more trouble for them. It wasn't just the Jews that wanted their own country. We heard that Hindus and Moslems were revolting in India too. England was weakened after six years of fighting Germany and Japan and was not prepared to go to war again. Ironically, it was England we had to thank for defeating Hitler. After all, she fought on for almost two years alone until Russia was dragged into it. But now the English bulldog was a policeman, keeping Jews from immigrating here. We had been lucky. The year we came here only one other ship from Marseilles was allowed to land. Tensions were coming to a head with daily arrests of Jewish rabble rousers. I was torn. By nature I'm not a political animal, but there was no doubt in my mind but that we deserved a homeland. And with my wartime experience I might have been of some good to the military arm of the movement for a Jewish State. On the other hand I had already had my fill of that kind of life. What's more, we were expecting a child, and what good would it do to leave a widow and orphaned son behind?

Eda and I were both ecstatic to be expecting a child and we discussed possible names. Naturally we were going to honor our parents who had died in the Holocaust. Of course, back then you had to wait for the birth of your child to know its gender, so we planned some names for either eventuality. If it was a boy we would name him after my father, a girl after my mother. Eda would wait for a second child to name it after one of her own parents. Meanwhile I continued to ride around Tel Aviv delivering candy. Who knows how much chocolate passed through my fingers before I grew weary of changing gears on that old motorcycle? One thing was for certain. After schlepping candy for so long nobody knew that city better than me. Not even a Sabra. I knew the streets, the neighborhoods, the businesses, and even the alleys.

After nine months of buzzing around town on the motorcycle, and saving every lira possible, it was time for my beloved wife and me to become parents. A motorcycle is not the recommended vehicle for a lady in labor, so I hailed a cab and took Eda to Hadassah Hospital on Albany Street. It was June 24, 1946.

How quickly moves the hand of time. Just five years before Hitler was planning Operation Barbarosa, and I was languishing in a jail in Kiev, longing to be reunited with my family. So much had gone down. And here I was, the sole representative of that family, reestablishing it after a period of depressive dormancy. We were down, but not out. All the big Nazi bosses were dead, but Ovram was alive and kicking, albeit with just three toes, and carrying on his cherished father's legacy. No man has the right to say any birth is easy, but by God's mercy it was an uneventful delivery. Just as mercifully, the Lord saw fit to grant us a son as the first addition to our family. A son! How my father celebrated when I was born. My parents had expanded the Feder clan with four females before my appearance, but we produced a male heir first time out. Perhaps it was to make up for so much loss to our family. Half a decade after the murder of the family patriarch his line was assured. We named our boy Irving in honor of Yisroel, my father. When he was born I looked down and saw my father minus the beard. He had his eyes and that same beatific countenance, and it made me very emotional. How he would have loved to have known his grandchild. But the nachis skipped a generation, and we had to feel happy for all generations. Despite bittersweet memories and meager financial conditions, Irving's birth was a bona fide celebration. When a Jew is native born in Palestine, and later in Israel, he's called a Sabra, and it gives him a prominent status within the community. Even being the parents of a Sabra carries with it some prestige. Social clout aside, Irving's birth was the fruition of our dreams and the justification of our survival. Eda held the tiny being to her bosom and wept for joy. While I saw my papa's kind eyes she saw traces of her own dear father as well, and was swept way on a warm surge of blissful sentiment. Her consciousness was not unlike a state of holy trance, elevated to a transcendent realm of tranquility so long absent from our lives and those of our people. We had been despised and considered unworthy to live. Now, we would not only live, but thrive. And our little Irving was proof of that determination and vindication. I beheld my Madonna with child, reposing on the plain white sheets of the hospital, and wept my own tears of happiness. Wrapping my arms around my family a prayer of thanks escaped my lips plus a vow to always protect and provide for them.

My parental duty did not frighten me. Rather, I was reminded of my old ultimatum. We would all live. Live, and be well. Our cousins came to the hospital and they felt the same affirmation for life that I did. After losing such a large percentage of our people it was always a celebration when a baby was born. It was a day like no other, and lives still in my memory.

The candy route expanded, but I still wasn't satisfied. And while I lurched over Tel Aviv's bumpy streets I kept my eye peeled for an opening, but those investigations into other fields of employment yielded nothing. Besides, I was far from the only Jewish immigrant in the job market. Competition was fierce in Tel Aviv. Its streets were teeming with landtsmen looking to make a buck. Many of them were highly educated men of letters and captains of finance while all I had was an eighth grade education. Now was anybody looking for comb and paper troubadours, Black Market mules, Commissars or Cossack pimps. Prospects were dim, so I continued to wear away the stone paths of Tel Aviv with my two tires and two cans, bringing candy to the sugar loving dwellers of the Holy Land.

After two years of delivering candy discouragement started to rear its ugly head. It seemed as if no opportunity at all awaited me in the Promised Land, and thoughts of leaving invaded my consciousness. Then political news gripped us all, and we forget about our humdrum lives. For some time there had been agitation for the British to make good on its old promise to establish a homeland for Jews and quit Palestine. There were even Jewish organizations that were openly violent against the British. They felt that the time was finally perfect to take action. Encouraged by the success of India's independence movement, we felt confident of our chances for self determination. Most importantly, we felt we had nothing to lose. So, British installations, military and otherwise, were routinely bombed. Groups like Lechu, Etzl, Shomeer, and the Stern Gang were committed to independence or death. And outside the Middle East world opinion, greatly swayed by repeated images of the holocaust, were favorable toward the establishment of a homeland for Jews. This theme dominated our every conversation, and the newspapers and radios spoke of little else. Even nonpolitical minds like mine were caught up in the fervor of independence. It had been just ten years since listening to the Zionists visiting Sieniawa, and now it seemed like that distant dream could actually materialize. Every day we spoke about it, and at night Eda and I stayed glued to the radio as reported progress gladdened our hearts. Then, when Irving was just a year and a half years old, the radio came alive with the tensest moment in our time there. United Nations resolution number one hundred and eighty one, the partition of Palestine between Jews and Arabs, came up for a vote before the fifty six members of that fledgling organization. With each country called we held our breath.

If you were brought up as a European Jew in the first half of the Twentieth Century you were heir to two millennia of anti-Semitism. You learned to live with pogroms, disenfranchisement, male children ripped from their families and pressed into military service for decades at a time. You had no protection under the law, and more things were denied you than permitted. Quite simply, you lived at the whim of your Gentile overseers, and just as often died. Finally, the holocaust befell us all and hope was lost. But from the ashes of that conflagration Zionism arose and screamed to be heard. And now the unthinkable dream was actually a possibility. We really didn't think the world would vote in our favor, but it might come close, and then there might be another vote in a few years and we'd get even closer. So, maybe our grandchildren would see liberty and independence. We dared not dream that it would happen on November 29, 1947 with baby Irving sitting on Eda's lap. That would be impossible, and to dream it too fervently would be too much of a heartache and disappointment if it did not come to pass. After all, the Arab countries would vote against it. And Russia and China were no friends either. So, there we sat, heads inclined toward the faint glow of the radio, hoping to get at least a few votes and not feel so reviled as we had been for so long.

The kind Scandinavians favored us as they always had. They were among the few we considered true Christians anyway. And America, though they hadn't done much to allow us to immigrate and escape the Final Solution, came through. And a few western European countries, guilty over their participation in our worst persecution, had the guts to vote for us too. We kept tally. An abstention. Then another. A vote against. A few in favor. Another abstention. Was it possible? Were the reports accurate? Were the yeas outnumbering the nays? Did we hear right? Could it be? Would we win? Would the world take pity on us and grant us this tiny plot of sand? Another yea. Another abstention. We were so on edge it was unbearable. Was that light at the end of the tunnel suddenly bright? Little by little it dawned on us that it could actually pass. We looked down on the score sheet we were keeping. Thirty three in favor, thirteen against, ten abstentions. But before we could confirm the math a symphony of beeping car horns echoed its conclusion through the city, and a celebration two thousand years on hold erupted across the country. Our country. The dream had inexplicably come true. Israel was born.

We wept in thanks and praised God. We weren't religious, but it was such a momentous event it seemed somehow trivial to show gratitude toward anything less than an almighty power. People everywhere were falling on their knees, on their faces, and kissing the ground. It was no longer just another British protectorate. Now our crumby little apartment was located in Eretz Israel, the land of Solomon, the sages and prophets.

Incomprehensible. That's what it was. Thirty three to thirteen. It was practically a landslide. Did the world finally love us? We weren't prepared to feel anything, because there was no point of reference. If any European Jews in the last few centuries would've been informed of this development they probably would have gaped in disbelief, oblivious to its significance. Likewise, we were overwhelmed with emotion, but also simultaneously numb. Were our tears of joy enough? Was our laughter sufficient? How happy should we be? Truth be told, people were crying and laughing at the same time like madmen. We didn't know how to behave, and it was tough to stay sane. Eda placed little Irving's tiny feet on her knees and bounced him up and down. It made him hysterical with delight, and he seemed to be dancing in ecstasy over hearing the unprecedented news. Thirty three to thirteen. The yeas almost tripled the nays! Unbelievable! If the rest of mankind didn't love us at least they seemed to feel sorry for us. Or maybe it was guilt. Who cared? As long as it passed. And it did. It did.

The party went on all night. We all chatted and drank tea. In thousands of apartments we drank more potent toasts to our infant nation, but also lamented those who couldn't live to see this day. But as we did there came alive the stunning realization that it was their deaths that made this possible. Six million cold blooded landtsmen murders was the price for this piece of real estate, so we damn well better enjoy it. It's true. The shooting, gassing, strangling, starving, burning, bludgeoning, poisoning, torturing and experiments resulted in the birth of a homeland for the survivors. The miracle of United Nations resolution one hundred and eighty one justified all those brutal deaths. Thanks to this day they did not die in vain. It elevated them from victims to martyrs. They were the front line soldiers who sacrificed themselves in order for Israel to be born anew. Had the holocaust not taken place world opinion would not have urged the British to act, and the United Nations might have put it on a back burner for another hundred years. My father was now a fallen hero. So were my mother and sisters. The fall of Sieniawa and a thousand other shtetls were no longer senseless acts of mayhem. They were one-sided battles, fought and lost to bring about this day. We lost every battle, but won the war. The Third Reich was buried, but we lived in a country all our own. It was a wonderful irony. Back in the war the krauts had early on declared their intention to claim *Lebensraum*. Now their country was sliced in half, and the Jews got their own *living space*. It was truly inconceivable. But as difficult to comprehend as it was, we all knew it was worth celebrating. The bodies of the Gestapo were festering in the earth, being consumed by worms, while we danced the hora and drank schnapps to usher in the world's acceptance of a free Jewish state.

The first night of Israeli independence was a nonstop party, but nobody had the liberty of sleeping off their hangover. Within less than twenty four hours of the announcement of the UN vote, armies from five Arab nations invaded, boasting that they'd drive us into the sea and annihilate us. It was like a fleet of unwelcome wagons from Egypt, Syria, Lebanon, Jordan and Iraq. They sent their forces against us just as Pharaoh had done long before. Saying that it looked grim was an understatement. With so many European

Jewish immigrants Israel had more than their fair share of mathematicians, and all these learned men had their doomsday facts and figures at their fingertips.

"Do you realize the territory those armies represent?"

"Why, easily over three hundred thousand square miles!"

"We have barely eighty-five hundred!"

"They're not just twice as big as us."

"Or even ten times our size!"

"They're not less than thirty seven times greater!"

The math was so one-sided. It was David versus Goliath all over again. We were free, but now we were going to have to all be Davids to hold on to it. But, so what if we were tiny? Germany was small compared to all the territory it conquered. And after its conquest of Western Europe and Northern Africa it set its sights on the gargantuan land mass of the Soviet Union. If those bastards had such chutzpah why not us? And what about Japan? It's a speck on the edge of Asia but it was able to conquer half of that continent and the islands of the Pacific. And before that it beat Russia which was literally a thousand times its size. And don't forget England. It was another small island dwarfed by Fascist Fortress Europe and it still managed to take on the wermachte, the Luftwaffe and withstand relentless rocket attacks, all without missing tea time. We were small too, but we had to win. They were larger, but not greater! There was absolutely no choice or even discussion of defeat.

"Sure, we're outnumbered, but this time we got guns."

"And God's on our side!"

"Who?"

"Why wasn't he on our side in the last war?"

"That's what the Arabs say, that Allah's on their side."

"So what? Praise the Lord and pass the ammunition."

None of us waited for the call for help to go out. Every able bodied man and woman was needed to preserve our nation, and we knew it without having to be told. Naturally, with my vast military experience, I went down and signed up. The groups that had previously been considered gangs of terrorists were now merged into the Israeli Defense Force. Twenty four hours ago the company I joined had been a radical political party, run by a fellow named Menachem Begin, and now it was a rank and file military unit. Begin and all the other committed Zionists had been stockpiling arms for years in preparation for this day, as well as training our citizens several days a month. They had smuggled in rifles, pistols, hand grenades, mortars, machine guns and ammunition from Czechoslovakia along with surplus from other countries. Our new national arsenal was a hodge-podge collection of guns from all over, though mostly British and German. An Israeli soldier might carry a rifle from one country loaded with bullets from another, stuffed into magazines from a third. Uniforms were practically nonexistent, but most of us were issued berets. And the humiliating Star of David that we were forced to wear in World War Two, was now our proud national symbol, and it graced those berets, as well as our flag. Even without uniforms we could identify each other. Most of us looked European while the Arabs were mostly swarthy.

I went down to where they were organizing defensive barricades and presented myself and my wartime resume, and they were excited to have me. I was made a corporal again, and assigned to train our volunteers in the operation of weapons, especially automatic. I hadn't touched a gun in five years but it all came back. We had less than two hundred machine guns, so it was vital to use them to their fullest advantage. I trained both men and women, and I concentrated as much on sighting the weapon as its loading and maintenance. We had to make every shot count. We also had thousands of submachine guns, so I gave instruction in that as well.

The invasion by the Arab forces had long been anticipated, so we were well prepared. We even had a small air force of vintage planes, ironically of mostly German design, also purchased from Czechoslovakia. We quickly achieved air superiority, because the Arabs stupidly attacked a British airbase, prompting their outrage and overwhelming response. The RAF struck back as if they were our allies. Along the way we also acquired some artillery, and we continually captured armaments from retreating Arab forces. I felt echoes of my hitch with the Cossacks, though the climate was far milder.

From the start we repelled the Arabs. We were organized and determined while they argued among themselves as to how they would divide the soon to be conquered territory. Having so much more land and population than us they assumed their victory would be speedy and complete. They boasted that they would slaughter us all and repeat the Arab success of the Crusades. They must have been thinking that we'd be easy victims like we had been in Europe. This time things were different. We had guns for one thing, and with those guns we were prepared to fight to the death to keep our homeland. Philosophically, our fighters were split into two basic camps. There were those who believed that it was our divine right to live on this land. The Torah said God gave it to us. Then there were the non-pious, whose one and only religion was the Jewish people as a nation. After WWII many Jews stepped back from religious orthodoxy. They felt they'd been betrayed and abandoned by the Almighty. However, they could not escape being Jews as a people, so they were committed to defending Israel. In other words, both philosophies ended up at the same point, the determined defense of Israel. So, it actually might've been possible to find atheists in our foxholes. The Arabs, on the other hand, just didn't have our kind of commitment. Any of the soldiers of those five invading nations could have gone home and been none the worse for wear. As they saw it, nobody was taking an inch of their own land. They asked themselves, "What did a Palestinian ever do for me?" Their politics were based on ancient tribal allegiance, and they lacked solidarity. Ask any Arab and he'll lay it out for you. "It's me against my brother, my brother and me against our cousin, the three of us against our neighbor, and all of us against the stranger." As long as we weren't directly invading them they didn't really care all that much.

From our point of view we saw all the Arabs, whatever country they were from, as selfish bastards. They had millions of square miles of land, from the western edge of Africa, through all of Asia Minor, and the Middle East. They couldn't spare a hundred and fifty mile stretch of sand for their cousins after they had gone through such hell? Our backs were to the Wailing Wall, and just like Stalin's directive 227 our credo was 'not a step backwards.'

Basically, our Arab foes were long on threats and short on determination. They couldn't even field a large army. Although the population of the Arab world was in the high millions the countries that participated in the invasion could only muster an invading force that numbered twenty three thousand. On the other hand, tiny Israel put that number plus another fifteen thousand under arms, including men and women. It's pretty impressive that we were able to raise an army of thirty eight thousand, and it would have been nice to have a weapon for each one. But at the start of our war for independence we had less than thirty thousand hand held weapons. We had three million bullets however, which was convenient as we had far more submachine guns than rifles, and that means we went through ammo fast. And we sent a lot of men and women into battle with just hand grenades, which numbered around a hundred and fifty thousand at the start. In addition to that, we had nine hundred light and medium machine guns and eight hundred mortars. Reciting all these numbers reminded me of the tally of the captured German weapons that General Bogaevsky read out to us during our campaign on the Steppes. Of course the number and size of the armaments in WWII were far greater than this conflict, and almost any single military engagement with the Nazis involved more men and munitions than the entire Israeli War of Independence. But the stakes in this fight were higher to us. And because of that, it wouldn't have mattered if we'd only had sticks. We were prepared to fight to the death, no matter what. We had already seen what happens when you don't stand up for yourself. After the Holocaust we Jews were not about to let ourselves be bullied again. If we're going down again then we're taking as many of the bullies down with us as we can. Besides, all those countries voted for us, and we couldn't let them down. Feeling that dire necessity, even our women were better fighters than our foe. Our level of esprit de corps was unmatchable and the Arabs rarely put up a good fight. The only sector where the Arab forces were successful for even a little while was Jerusalem. Being inland it was removed from our main centers of population and hard to keep supplied. The Arabs had long been entrenched there, and the fighting was especially fierce. Some Jewish outposts were manned by less than two hundred defenders and were totally overrun by superior numbers. But our troops there fought to the last. Surrender was never an option. Our soldiers were so precious to us that when an officer of ours was captured we intentionally spared two dozen Arab fighters, capturing them instead of killing them, just to trade them to get our man back. But the Jerusalem campaign was costly. As it was not part of the original UN partition we wanted to capture it, and by war's end it was a treasured spoil of victory.

After about a month of hostilities the United Nations brokered a truce. But we didn't trust the Arabs, so we stayed at our posts. Our routine jobs would have to wait, and we kept training during the lull. It gave me great satisfaction to put to such good use what I had learned in the Red Army. Of course, by nature I'm not a violent person. I wouldn't hurt a fly. Nor do I believe that war is a reasonable way to resolve our differences. But history stands with me when I say that whatever violence we used against the minions of Adolph Hitler, it was utterly justified. Utter mayhem was the only way to deal with them. They were not prone to negotiations. With them it was kill or be killed. It's just too bad that we didn't know that before they invaded. It wasn't just their blitzkrieg tactics that took everyone by surprise, but the level of their savagery. They waged total war on civilians. They shot babies in cold blood at point blank range and laughed about it. And what we did to them in the train station of Slav'ansk and on other fields of battle was fair and gentlemanly compared to their own conduct. But the Arabs sympathized with Hitler. We learned that they even sent a hundred thousand volunteers to join the dreaded Waffen SS to help round up Jews in Poland and other countries. For us that made this fight an extension of the last, and equally justified. Only now it was actually a fight. Those hundred thousand Arab SS officers gleefully murdered unarmed children, but this time they were squared off against armed adults who meant business. We discussed this during the truce and it emboldened us further. We were so determined there we even felt a glimmer of sympathy for them as we did back on the Steppes. But we knew they'd look for a chance to attack us when we least expected it, and that truce was the perfect opportunity to employ their favorite tactic, which was surprise aggression under a white flag. But it wouldn't work, because we were ready for any dirty trick. And we weren't above street tactics either. Simply put, coming after us was a suicide mission. And if they weren't prepared to fight to the death then they had best clear out of Dodge. So, I continued to train my landsmen in the use of machine and sub-machine guns, and we stood ready. Sure enough, they violated the UN agreement and the fighting renewed.

By now I had to give up the training and take up active combat. I manned both the medium caliber machine gun, and took to the street with a sub-machine gun as well. On the stone roads of Tel Aviv I was finally shooting at an enemy I could actually see. Back on the Steppes the Germans were usually too far away from me to determine if my bullets really hit their mark or not. I fired in their direction, but could never conclusively ascertain if my bullets hit home. Even when I fired at point blank range at the Slav'ansk train depot ambush, and was reasonably certain of my bullets hitting home through the wooden sides of the coaches, I didn't confirm it conclusively. This time though there was no doubt about it. I was firing a surplus British Sten submachine gun, and the Arabs were closer to me and less protected than my previous adversaries in WWII. I shot at them when they were a couple of streets away, advancing on our position. We were in the middle of the street, though not in an intersection, entrenched behind a barricade of sandbags. The sand that I had shoveled in my initial employment was now our protection. We had plenty of it and it was free. Bullets cannot penetrate sacks filed with sand, so from behind this solid protection I drew a bead on my targets that were out in the open. I squeezed that trigger for a second or two, letting lose a blast of five or ten rounds. Instantly my human targets stopped, dropped their guns, and fell. The force of my nine millimeter slugs was not powerful enough to throw them back, and they usually froze for a second before falling to their knees. After another instant they slid to the ground and lay in motionless heaps. When I saw this I often recalled what General Bogaevsky had said after the terrible ambush in Slav'ansk train depot, 'They should have stayed home.' Certainly, they should have stayed back in Egypt, Jordan, Lebanon and Iran. We wouldn't have pursued them back to their homes. They should have stayed with their families and tended their flocks and crops and businesses. What business of it was theirs that we had returned after all these years? It wasn't their country anyhow. All we wanted was peace, and we offered it to them as well. Like I said, I am not a violent person. But, just like I learned in my first day in that cell in Lvov, you can't let the bullies take over.

The kick from the Sten was not so bad. The larger caliber rifle in use back on the Steppes gave a far more serious kick, but these sub-machine guns fired smaller pistol ammo. The Americans used the deadly Thompson which fired forty-five caliber ammunition, and gave a murderous kick. Our Stens though used smaller nine milli-meter bullets and were easier to hold steady and aim. Just the same, when you're hit with a blast of lead, five to ten at a time, regardless of the size of the bullet, you become a casualty of war. And let me tell you, Arab blood is just as red as German. The white streets of Tel Aviv and Haifa and many other ancient towns gave proof of that. It struck me how the blood stood out from the bleached hues of Israel just as it did from the snows of the Steppes.

I did most of my fighting on the streets of Tel Aviv, but we also had to defend the port of Haifa. We drove down there on a bus that went so fast I think the tires left the ground. Regardless of where I was fighting though I never felt the same tension as when I fought the Nazis. We all hated the Nazis of course, but we had to give those devils their due as combatants. After two years of trading shots with them I knew they were tough cookies. We respected their ability as soldiers so much that our main tactic was to engage them for only short sorties, lest they counter attack. The Arabs on the other hand lacked the mettle of real soldiers. We'd lay down a line of fire and they'd retreat. They hated us as part of an ancient tribal envy full of antagonism toward all tribes, other Arabs included, but that knee jerk attitude didn't fill them with the resolve to go all the way with us. They retreated from nearly every battle. I remember hearing their rifle fire, but rarely hearing their bullets buzz past us as the truer aimed German rounds did. It seemed clear that once the Arabs realized that they were not going to drive anyone into the sea so easily, they did not stand their ground. We stood ours because we truly believed it to be ours. Besides, our backs were to the wall, and nobody fights harder than a cornered beast. In plainer terms I'd have to say that they were afraid of us. They knew we had nothing to lose and were not going to give up. This attitude allowed us to forget the imbalance of the size of our countries, and it filled us bravado. As a matter of fact, our indomitable morale was a concern for our leaders. So, to keep us from feeling overly confident David Ben Gurion announced that we had only a fifty/fifty chance of winning. Apart from the military aspect of this conflict, he also knew that diplomacy was still a powerful weapon in our arsenal. As the fighting raged he continued negotiations with all factions. As it turned out the Arabs were splintered, with some of them actually in favor of the partition. The Lebanese, for example, were hardly committed to driving us into the sea, and sent a half hearted force of barely a thousand men as a token of solidarity with their Arab brethren. Jordan was no less apathetic, and the Jewish Agency met with their King who privately shared that he was not opposed to the partition.

Whenever there was a lull in the fighting I visited wife and child. Eda was always relieved to see me, though she was confident we'd win. At first, she was frightened. After all, her previous experience with enemy soldiers was utterly terrifying. But after a few weeks, with constant news of our military successes pouring in, she became like a cheerleader for the Israeli Defense Forces. No longer afraid, she wanted to know every detail of the fighting, as she had on the night we first met. Another encouraging part of my visits home was seeing Irving. Every visit he was bigger and happier to see me.

A second cease-fire decided little, but by July 20, 1949 the Arabs were too disheartened to continue. They retreated, and we were left with a country. To make it official, the State of Israel was admitted as a full fledged member of the United Nations.

It had been just under ten years since Germany invaded Poland,

and the world was a different place. Who could have foreseen a decade earlier the events we were now celebrating in Tel Aviv. Israel was a unified nation while our previous tormentor, Germany, was chopped into pieces. We had armed forces to protect ourselves while they were prohibited from doing so and were policed by the foreign occupying forces of several nations. Their country was literally in ruins. The tasted the bitterness of defeat and were shamed before the world. Their former leaders were all dead from suicide, execution, or were on trial as criminals. Israel was admired by most of the planet's inhabitants who wished them well. The Germans and their allies were in misery. We were in heaven.

With peace established, or as much peace as Israel could expect, I went back to delivering candy. Although we still knew poverty, the exhilaration we felt over recent events gave us the confidence to persevere in our struggle for day to day survival. So, from morning to evening I puttered around Tel Aviv, satisfying independent sweet teeth.

Around that time we got a nice surprise. Nathan Apthekar, Eda's brother immigrated to Israel. He came as a pioneer, and settled on a kibbutz in Rehovot, around twelve miles southeast of Tel Aviv. Eda was thrilled to have her brother so near, and I was becoming close to him as well. Back in Poland he was just a kid, but he was now a young man, and we had more in common. He had positive reports about his mother, but no word about Isaac, the long lost brother.

After six months of patriotic fervor it was becoming clear to me that it would take Israel a good long while to achieve any measure of economic stability. Of course, we were ecstatic over being Israelis, and proud of our Sabra son, but I was aching to find my niche in this world. I longed for it so strongly I had to consider that my place in this world might actually be in some other place in it. And soon I got a message from abroad that seemed to mystically confirm my suspicions. Rose Reich, Eda's Aunt from America, was coming for a visit. Now that Israel was a real country Jewish and Christian tourists started turning up everywhere with their Kodak Brownies. One evening after a simple dinner, one that probably tasted even simpler to Eda's Aunt, we fell deep into conversation. As in all conversations topics arose and we all expressed our viewpoints. But there was something in my manner that prompted her to make a pronouncement.

"Arthur, why are you piddling around with candy and these Yiddisher red necks? You're no pioneer! I can tell that you're a *tummler*, a real businessman. Come to America. It'll fit you like a glove! Gesheft! That's for you, Feder!"

If you met a Jewish refugee between 1945 and 1955 and they told you that they weren't interested in immigrating to America they were liars. While it's true their government didn't do much to help us escape Hitler before the war, it was now our Promised Land. Landtsmen were moving there and flourishing like weeds, and nobody was shooting at them. Eda and I were no different. We felt we should give Palestine a try, and we did. I even fought for its independence. So, guilt did not tarnish our new dream which was to go west. So, one night I sat Eda down and had a little chat.

"Eda. Are you happy here?"

"Yes. Why?"

"I don't mean if you're happy to be in Israel. I want to know if you're content with our condition, our situation."

"I'm happy to be with you, Arthur."

"So, if we're somewhere else you're happy as long as we're together?"

"Of course, Arthur. Don't you feel that way?"

"Of course Esther, you know I do. You and Irving are my whole world. But I'm unhappy about not being able to provide better for you. We need to go where there is more opportunity."

"You want to go to Jerusalem?"

"No."

"Haifa?"

"Eda, I think we should go to America. I hear nothing but success stories of people who go there. It's the Promised Land. Your own sister says so!"

"If that's what you want, then it's what I want too. Let's go."

With that resolved we made a pact to be frugal in the extreme and save every cent. After all, there would be great expenses involved in immigrating there, and we didn't really believe that the streets there were paved in gold. What we did believe was that America was still the land of opportunity, despite their apathy toward our plight a decade earlier. It seemed the whole world had changed in that interim. Not just economies and the balance of power had adjusted. It seemed as if human attitudes had been transformed as well. It took fifty million human deaths and inestimable destruction to shake the planet from its old fashioned values. Whole nations were faced with the need for introspection and soul searching. Humility had to replace arrogance or mankind would perish. The Americans demonstrated that conclusively, and even set a good example. Who could imagine the horror had the Nazis developed an atomic bomb first? It would have been the end of mankind. They couldn't resist using new weapons and they felt no remorse over any of their heinous crimes, justifying every cruel act of violence. They killed defenseless civilians, including their own kind. By war's end they were shooting Berliners, old and young alike, just for failing to be braver and better soldiers. With atomic bombs in their arsenals they would have whimsically sent a nuclear Luftwaffe over the face of the Earth to destroy every city they deemed unworthy to live. Thank God it was noble America that got the bomb. Their intent was to end war once and for all, and their tactic was to ultimately save more lives on both sides. They could have used it against Stalin, but they didn't. Had Papa Joe gotten his hands on such a bomb he wouldn't have been much better than Hitler. But Uncle Sam didn't use it to play aggressor. He was a gentleman and played by a higher moral code. Americans were just kinder, fairer people. And Eda and I wanted to be part of such an idealistic country. Thus, we decided to immigrate to the United States and become Yankees. And, who knows? Perhaps we'd make our fortune there.

Eda, Irving, and me on my old Czech motorcycle in Tel Aviv.

Irving at five years of age in Israel.

Eda and Irving, on vacation outside of Jerusalem.

Eda and me, recently arrived in New York.

GOING WEST

XXI

We saved every nonessential lira, and when we finally got the fare together I booked passage to Italy. From there I'd go by train to Munich. In Germany they were still dealing with Jewish refugees from all over Europe, and I would be yet another. My tactic was simple. I'd present myself as a displaced person, a survivor of the camps, without bothering to mention Cossacks or Israel. So, leaving Eda and Irving with enough funds to see them through a couple of months in Tel Aviv, I made my way back across the Mediterranean.

The famous tourist sites of Italy held no attraction for me, and with single minded purpose I pressed on towards Germany. I was in a quiet mood on the trip so I spent most of my time looking out the window of the coach. After years in the desert it was quite a comforting sight to see the fertile green landscape of Europe again. It made me wonder. Here it was green, and Israel was pale yellow. What color was America?

Aware of the sky high prices for food on the train I didn't eat much on the trip. So, as soon as I got off the train in Munich I looked around for a café to get a bite. As I searched for something appealing I was amazed to discover a small Jewish café right there in the station. It was certainly a welcome change to see a Jewish establishment free to operate in Germany, so I sat down. While I was eating I noticed an extraordinarily large fellow at one of the tables. As there was nobody else in the place he smiled and greeted me in Yiddish. He was as friendly as he was big and he asked me where I was from. When he heard that it was Israel he took a special interest in me. He moved over to my table and he wanted to know all about the Holy Land. We chatted for a while and he shared with me that he was the owner of the restaurant, but was also into professional wrestling. I had no idea what that was, and he explained it to me. One thing led to another and in short order he offered me the position of being his manager. This convinced me that I had done the right thing in leaving Israel. It had only been a week since leaving and already I had found a better job.

My client's name was Shimon Rudy, and he seemed to know everything about the pro wrestling game in West Germany. So, during the day I did the paperwork to immigrate to America, and at night I learned the ropes of the wrestling scene. Actually, Shimon had to teach me everything. He was as expert as I was clueless, and I wondered why he even bothered with me. It just seemed to him that a wrestler was supposed to have a manager, and I was elected. Also, Shimon trusted me because I was from Israel.

We became a team, and we drove to his matches in his Mercedes. He had to do the actual driving as I had yet to learn to drive a car which was quite a different animal than a motorcycle. Anyway, the fact that he owned such a car meant that he was apparently a big success. Professional wrestling, like the boxing game, had contacts in organized crime, and before I knew it, I was making extra money dealing with the Black Market. It had pretty much disappeared from Western Europe, but Eastern Europeans were governed by Soviets who didn't offer certain goods to its people that they were long since accustomed to having. Munich was on the Black Market route going east, and our Mercedes served as a short link in that chain. Meanwhile, the immigration office provided me with lodgings in something called a Bunker Hotel. They were built during the war to withstand allied bombing, and were sturdy and clean, if a bit Spartan.

For the next month I split my days fabricating lives in the immigration offices, and watching Shimon pummel his adversaries by night. He was a great brute and never lost. Sometimes I wondered if there was some hidden agenda in those matches. Maybe he took extra delight in beating up goyim while the Gentiles themselves felt guilty over possibly hurting another Jew. In any case, he was a bona fide winner and became the regional Champion. And as it was Shimon who was really earning the money, as his manager I made sure he kept most of it. I took just enough to eat. Mostly it was gratifying to have something to fill my time while waiting for Eda and Irving. They left a month after me, and I had all our papers arranged by the time they got there. All she had to do was go down to the immigration office and repeat the story we rehearsed. We kept our same names, but had to get new papers. After all, we couldn't very well show our papers from France. We were supposed to be camp survivors wandering around, looking for surviving family members. The whole process was actually easy. After all, they dared not ask for any corroborating evidence or identification. We simply stated that the Nazis took our papers, along with everything else, when they dragged us off to the camps. Certainly, there were millions with this exact same story, but we didn't feel that we were doing anything in questionable taste. Most of both of our families were real victims of the Nazis, whether it was in a camp or the woods, and that made us victims. So, we signed the affidavits, posed for pictures, and were issued visas and tickets to America. You hear of people kissing the ground when they get off the boat in

America, but I couldn't wait. When they handed me those tickets I gave them a big smooch, and really meant it.

Our train ride north to Hamburg was relaxing and Irving loved looking out the window. He had a million questions about Europe and the war, and we told him as best we thought a five year old could comprehend. Once in Hamburg we had a day to kill so we saw a few sights. The city had been bombed by the allies, and I don't deny that we took a secret satisfaction in seeing the rubble. After all, as far as we were concerned, the whole damn country could sink into hell.

People often ask me the dates of certain events in my life, but my lackadaisical memory usually obliges me to be vague. But the date we departed for America is one I'll never forget. On March 3, 1951 we set sail for the west.

Unlike our voyage to Palestine, full of introspective sulking, Eda and I were as excited as kids. Irving had heard about America too, but being on a boat was such an exciting adventure in itself, he could pay little attention to anything else.

Upon arriving in the Port of New York we went through the entire immigrant experience. We gaped at the Statue of Liberty, craned our necks looking at the tall buildings, and marveled at the elevated trains and masses of people in the street. It dwarfed any metropolis we had ever known, and I almost felt as if I had just arrived from Sieniawa. The Joint Distribution Committee had arranged for an apartment for us in Brooklyn, and, with Regina and Abe already settled there since 1948, we felt right at home. And to distract us from feeling like newcomers we became overwhelmed by another arrival. On the very day we arrived Regina gave birth to a son. She appointed me its godfather and a few days later I held him in my lap for his bris. It was a strange land, but we were not strangers. Family made us feel welcome and normal.

After the thrill of discovering America wore off I had to get down to brass tacks and earn a living. America was the end of the line for my dream of getting rich. Europe didn't do it for us, or the Middle East. I absolutely had to make it here. Of course, I still suffered from the same lack of formal education and worthwhile experience. Delivering candy didn't seem in the cards, but after going door to door asking for work in Brooklyn, a man hired me to deliver bagels. It wasn't much, but it was a start. Just like Tel Aviv, I got up early and drove around on two wheels. Only this time I was delivering something as round as the wheels, bagels. And the wheels were not part of a motorcycle, but rather a regular foot propelled bicycle. The pay was meager, but I had plenty of free bagels to take home after work. After a month or two of getting fat from bagels Eda made contact with a cousin in Manhattan named David Sherak who owned a purse company. He manufactured women's' pocketbooks of a very peculiar design that was popular at that time. They were made on a frame of light, thin wood and covered with leather. David needed a framer and I was his man. This was perfect timing, because the Joint Distribution Committee only provided apartments for a fixed period of time, assuming that landtsmen can provide for themselves relatively quickly. So, we all moved to the Hinsdale section of Brooklyn, and I learned how to commute on the subway to Manhattan to work for cousin David as a framer.

A pocketbook framer is someone who puts on the finishing touches such as buckles and handles. It's a lot of busy work, constantly fitting little pieces of metal adornments and straps to purses, but it was relatively easy. To make me appreciate this job more I constantly compared it to delivering candy in Tel Aviv. After sitting on the barely padded seat of that noisy, motorized contraption back in Tel Aviv for years, framing was a dream. My *tuchis* thanked me for letting it sit in one place without constantly vibrating, and I didn't have to chase after my clients to pay up. The best part was that David paid me weekly, and I didn't have to waste any more of my income on gas and maintenance. It was practically like a vacation. I was grateful to cousin David, and the best way to show my appreciation was for me to do the best job for him that I could. But I wasn't kidding myself. One notch above delivery boy was not my goal either. Framing purses would suffice only until something really worthwhile came along. In one sense the pocketbook factory was a drawback, because the candy delivery route had me out and about the city, exposed to every opportunity. It's true that my countless treks across Tel Aviv had not revealed that lucrative mystery job, but at least there was always that possibility. Now, being cooped up in the purse plant, that option was eliminated. For the time being however, I was happy to have a steady job in my new adopted country. Whatever it was that was out there waiting for me would have to keep. But I didn't feel poor. My wife and baby were my fortune and we weren't starving. That complacency was the attitude of many of our immigrant friends. We all recalled what the war years were like, so anything after that was like a walk in the park. Still, I wanted to give my family more. Though I had no profession or expertise there was something inside me dying to get out and strut its stuff.

We enrolled Irving in public school, and within four months he was speaking English perfectly without an accent. He made a million friends and he never even asked about Israel. Our mastery of the language did not rival Irving's, but we were learning. After all, if I could learn Ukrainian, Russian, and Hebrew I could learn English. But regardless of linguistic progress we loved to stroll through the Big Apple. It was cheap entertainment too, and every week we discovered something new and interesting.

In 1952 the Korean Conflict embroiled our new homeland, and David's number one framer was drafted. Wasting no time I insisted on filling his position. I knew exactly what he did and could fill his shoes. Likewise, David knew I was more qualified than anyone else, but he tried to take advantage of the situation by offering me just five bucks a week extra to assume the post. I would have none of that. I knew exactly what the financial arrangement was between David and the exframer, and demanded the same. Instead of getting paid by the week I would now be paid by the piece. This meant the harder I worked the more I'd earn. It was the American capitalistic ideal. Almost from the start I was earning in the neighborhood of eighty dollars a week. At the time of this writing such a sum does not sound like much, but it was still enough at that time to live the middle class American dream. It was a step up, but bigger visions fueled my dreams.

On exploratory strolls through different parts of Brooklyn I came upon a dilapidated candy store near Rockaway, and considered it an opportunity not to be missed. Perhaps I could repeat the success of Arthur's Restaurant in Krakow? By that time I had saved up two grand, so I borrowed another from Abe and made a down payment on it. We fixed it up like new and stocked every kind of candy and ice cream you ever heard off. And I became an expert soda jerk, creating frozen delicacies that drove the local kids crazy. I made unique sundaes, ice cream sodas and banana splits. I put sprinkles on top of huge ice cream cones and smiles on everyone's faces. Arthur's Candy Emporium was a hit.

My English vocabulary was dominated by ice cream flavors, and Eda studied at home with her principal English professor, Irving. Hebrew was of almost no use, though Yiddish came in handy with a lot of our neighbors. It improved her social life, but of course it slowed her adaptation to English. Meanwhile, candy and ice cream were making us even more money that our restaurant back in Krakow. Summer was the season for ice cream and I did so well I was able to send Eda and Irving up to the Jewish Alps, the Catskills, to holiday in the Bungalow Colony. It filled my heart with joy to see my wife and boys romping so carefree. It made me feel like a millionaire, and I saw it as justification for having made the move to America. Such things as vacations were unknown luxuries back in Sieniawa. The notion that my father or mother might abandon their routines for even a day seemed absurd, and such bizarre behavior on their part would have proven incomprehensible. That I might even join my family for a brief respite from my usual duties was itself reason to reflect on how unique America was. But I was becoming a USA, and Americans as I learned, were not obliged to work more than a forty hour work week. They all deserved the right to a vacation. So, I hired some employees to free me for a few days of idle bliss in the cool mountain air. The woods there were not unlike Europe, and it reminded me of Poland and Russia and all their accompanying visions. Those visions crept into the ice cream parlor too. Sometimes when my hands were thrust into the depths of the freezers, digging out the three and a half ounces of frozen delight that went into one of our cones, the extreme temperature brought to mind my life out on the Steppes. What would a mahorka puffing, vodka guzzling, saber rattling kazak think of seeing a member of the General's staff dishing out whipped cream and chocolate sprinkles to children? They would know without question that I was indeed a counterfeit Cossack. And the truth is, I would have gladly agreed with them. Actually, they would have observed that I was not only a phony Cossack, but a phony Russian to boot. I wasn't much of a Pole either. We aspired to be nothing but Americans. We liked American movies, cars, magazines, music, radio and clothes. We marveled that there had never been a pogrom in this country.

"Not one? Not a long time ago? Not even at the hands of the Indians?"

Actually, we found out that the Indians themselves suffered pogroms. You might even say they endured their own holocaust. Regardless of America's flaws we loved the place, and would've kissed the ground were it asked of us. We were working toward becoming citizens and we were more than eager to forsake all foreign potentates. My old Cossack comrades might have also observed something else about me. It was something I was starting to see in myself as well. The reason I was good at framing pocket books was the same reason I was a successful soda jerk, and that was because I focused myself on whatever I did. That's why I learned to ride a horse so handily. That's how I learned to shoot so straight. Whatever I tried always had my full concentration. So, for now I was focused on ice cream. But someday I'd find my business niche and focus on that.

About a million scoops of ice cream later, in 1953, our second son was born. We named him Larry after Eddy's father. Just like in Israel, we were again the parents of a native son. It helped deepen our ties with our new home, and with the extra responsibility of an expanding family, I felt more pressure than ever to find a more lucrative trade. And, as part of my need to improve our lives, I was growing tired of New York winters. Actually, as far back as 1941 I had sought out warmer climates. After all, that's what prompted me to head for Stalingrad. It was further south than Kiev and theoretically warmer. As it turned out, I had been as wrong about that place's climate as the invading Nazis, but this time I had the Florida climate confirmed. Every Jew in New York was talking nonstop about someplace called Miami Beach. It was in Florida and it was supposed to be heaven on Earth. It sounded great, and I became convinced that I would find my fortune there. So, I sold the ice cream parlor.

Europeans heard so many stories about the USA they sounded almost like myths. There was talk of the freedoms of speech and religion, and that everyone was rich. Some of it made sense to me and some of it seemed unlikely, but the main message that all that propaganda broadcast loud and clear to me was that a guy like me would find greater independence there than any other place on Earth.

Independence. It suited me to a tee. I had lived by someone else's rules my whole life and I ached for independence. Israel was a democracy, but I couldn't earn ten cents over there. I wanted wealth, and I saw freedom as an integral part of achieving it. Part of that freedom was mobility, and I lusted after an automobile. Even though the Russians claimed that they were responsible for the invention of the car it was clearly an American product. I never heard of Comrade Fordsky. If I had a car at my command I'd feel one step closer to my goal. Maybe it was purely psychological, but independence equaled success to me. With a car you could go where you wanted and do what you wanted. You didn't have to rely on any municipal train or bus schedules. You were blissfully self reliant. So, we shopped around for a decent used one and took the plunge. My first status symbol was an old Plymouth. Now, we were real Americans. I must admit that my first automobile was not a great beauty, but it made me feel like Aladdin all the same. A got a friend to teach me how to control the beast, and in no time I got a license and was on my way. Or at least I thought. Once I became committed to driving to Florida I made a more realistic appraisal of the route, and it was decided that a cheap old jalopy like mine was not the most reliable way to travel nearly two thousand mile. So, I convinced Abe Kestenbaum to take a little drive with me, but in his own far superior car. Back in Europe everyone took trains between cities. And in Israel a bus would've been the only choice for someone in my financial condition. But seeing the USA in Abe's Chevrolet was the only way to go. I filled his head with visions of tropical opulence and he was as excited as me to head south.

Driving from New York to Miami is pretty commonplace, but for an emigrant in 1953 it was as big an adventure as Sinbad searching for lost treasure. I didn't need a Genie however, because a map clearly showed me that nobody could wind up in the wrong state as long as they headed south and stopped at the ocean. So, I kissed Eda and the boys, and headed down to sunny South Florida, certain of success.

Abe's deluxe car had a radio, and on that trip I got exposed to more American music than ever before. Radio signals got strong and loud driving through the cities, and then weaker out in the country, and every fifty miles we picked up a new station. Most of the music was new to me, as was the food. Every time we stopped for gas we discovered some interesting local dish. What a land of variety! If some of the music or food wasn't to our liking there was always a common sandwich that could be found anywhere. But one sandwich I would never try, despite each region's boasting of having the best one, was a hamburger. Early on in America I had the not so enviable privilege of observing a restaurant prepare the meat for this ubiquitous delicacy. Once I had learned the disgusting things that went into it I vowed never to eat one, and to this day I never have. I'm no vegetarian, but after counting the extraneous ingredients in a hamburger I was permanently turned off to that most popular of American treats. I've never eaten in a McDonalds or a Burger King or any other such place. On that trip though, I did experiment the bill of fare at one of the first big food chains in America. Every decent sized population center had one of these establishments with the oddly shaped roofs painted unusual shades of orange and green. They all boasted unbeatable ice cream and cheap menus. I tried a cone, but didn't find it to be any tastier than the ice cream I served up. Mr. Johnson would just have to do without my steady personal patronage. Of course, I couldn't help but observe in subsequent road trips that Howard became quite popular despite my infrequent patronage. Besides, he had a lot of competition. All along the roadside there were endless varieties of local delicacies to taste. And a few times we were even treated to an impromptu concert by a local musician or two, strumming and singing for pleasure, as well as for free. The great American network of highways had not been built yet, so we passed through countless small towns. Some were so tiny they reminded us of shtetls. Such thoughts took me back to Sieniawa. What delicacies would we in that tiny shtetl have offered to the great parade of travelers in their autos passing through? Would my mother have cooked up some of my father's fish to sell at a roadside stand? It reminded me of the candy I stole from my mother's store and a great wave of nostalgia overtook me. Thoughts of a less frivolous nature often gripped me when remembering our first home. I didn't share my vendetta vow with Abe, and I stewed in silence. But I couldn't help but recall and renew my pledge to one day return there and find out what I could about their betrayer.

Besides food, the roadside was an endless art exhibit of commercial signs. They invited us to sleep here, eat there, and visit everywhere. But our meager finances prevented us from trying anything beyond the most humble lodge and diner cuisine. But that really didn't matter. From the moment we left New York we were someplace new and exciting. We were automatically tourists, seeing for the first time almost two thousand miles of America.

As the states rolled by I was fascinated to see all the different looking people and changing scenery. But although we had passed enough territory to have equaled Europe itself, the people here were still the same, Americans. They varied in many aspects, but they were all from the same place, that big melting pot known as the United States. The climate though was varying, just as we had hoped. It was far warmer and more humid, and after five days of highway adventure, we rolled past an inviting sign proclaiming Welcome to Miami. And with some last minute directions from a friendly gas station attendant, we made it to our final destination, Miami Beach. We didn't know anyone there, but someone had given us the name of a cheap, comfortable motel. Without delay I went around to all the drug stores to see if they needed an experienced soda jerk. There was nothing available, but one pharmacy owner suggested I look for work at a restaurant. "A good waiter can make a lot in tips."

Tips. Such an approach to making money never occurred to me. At my restaurant in Krakow we certainly would have gone out of business had we relied on tips. Of course, that was an unusual restaurant and circumstance, but I don't recall anyone every leaving behind any money on the table. That was something I learned about after leaving Poland. In my whole life I had hardly ever eaten in a restaurant, but in America it was pretty common. Here, I learned about the quaint custom of tipping. The idea of getting remunerated based solely on the value of one's service interested me, and I meditated on the whole concept. Ice cream customers back in New York rarely tipped, because the orders were too small. Ice cream cones were a nickel, and a sundae or soda went for a quarter. I made a mean banana split, but how much would a tip be on such a small order anyway? But here a family might spend ten dollars for lunch or dinner, and that meant I could easily wind up with a whole buck just for serving them. If need be I figured that nobody could provide better service than yours truly, so I went looking for a likely restaurant. There were no lack of them on the Beach, but nobody was hiring. Then I found a Jewish restaurant called Hoffener's on Collins Avenue and Second Street that needed a busboy. But after just a couple of days I convinced the owner to make me a waiter. At first she told me that she couldn't afford to hire another waiter. My immediate response was, "Don't worry! You don't have to pay me. I'll work solely for tips." She thought it over and said, "Okay. It's your funeral."

From the start it worked. People were happy with my excellent service, and I made the owner happy, because I convinced the people to order more things.

"You haven't tried the cheese cake? You don't know what you're missing!"

"The salmon is fresh today! It's to die for!"

I did well, but I couldn't help but notice that their bill of fare was modestly priced. A family of five could eat for under ten dollars. Fifteen percent of nine dollars was a fat dollar, but I figured that a higher bill would reward me with a greater gratuity for the same amount of time and energy. So, I searched for a restaurant that had slightly higher prices. I found it across the street from the City Hall on Washington Avenue. It was run by a man named Isaac Gellis. I convinced him with the same tactic, working solely for tips, and he hired me. I greeted my customers as warmly as possible and then told them in my heavily accented and broken English, "Don't tip me if I'm bad, but don't tell my boss either." The people found this funny and charming, and they usually left me a generous gratuity. But it wasn't out of pity, I tell you. I treated my customers like visiting royalty. I was friendly and made economic suggestions from the menu. They got their food as fast as the cook rang the bell, and their water glasses and bread baskets were kept full. I even lit their cigarettes. But I was always quiet and subtle. Some of the other waiters had the habit of constantly bothering their customers by asking, "Is everything alright?" They'd ask it a dozen times during the meal, and I could see the customers were annoyed by it. It was obvious that those anxious waiters were campaigning for a big tip. I just told my customers at the start to call me if they needed anything, and stayed nearby without making a pest of myself. The folks must have loved this kind of attention because parties started requesting to be seated in my section. Tips were good and I was able to send Eda money the second week.

It was so interesting to discover this side of America. It reaffirmed my feeling that Americans were naturally generous and inspired me to be even kinder to them. It also reminded me of seeing the kind GIs in Europe. My feeling about them then was only reconfirmed by living in the USA. Some cultures don't tip at all, but somehow the habit became ingrained in American restaurants. And it's an utter mystery how the percentage of fifteen became the minimum standard. My customers used to study the bill and do the math, sometimes even with a pencil, and always leave me at least the minimum of that mystical figure of fifteen percent. Of course, there were the cheapskate exceptions, and I ultimately discouraged such people from sitting in my station. On the other hand, there were the extravagant exceptions and I welcomed these ratites with warmth. The final benefit of working for Gellis were the free meals. Every employee could eat either lunch or dinner on the house once a day. No fancy wines, but a substantial meal at any rate.

I stayed at the same motel until I could afford to move to a tiny room, and before long I opened a savings account. Isaac Ellis closed for shabbos, otherwise I never took time off. Anyway, I was there to support my wife and boys, not socialize. If they needed someone to work a double shift, both lunch and dinner, I did it. Meanwhile, Eda wrote that Nathan and her mother had both immigrated to America using the same plan as we did, and were living in New York. This was very comforting to her, as they had always been very close. Basically the last survivors of Sieniawa and Krasnik were now residents of the Big Apple. They lived in the largest city in the USA, where a single apartment building housed more people than the combined populations of both our shtetls.

After a few months I heard of an opening for a fountain man at the Saxony Hotel, one of the ritziest places on the Beach. I figured with my experience in Brooklyn, I could be a big success in Miami Beach. The Saxony had a combination snack shop and ice cream parlor in the lower level of the hotel, and I dug right in, figuratively and literally. I made sundaes and sodas like they never saw, and the whole town used to come over. Such was my fame that the local newspapers even wrote articles about me and my banana splits. But I learned that there's a difference between rich and famous; they don't always go together. And having my choice, I'll take rich over famous any day of the week. Missing the gratuities I asked for a job as a waiter in their formal dining room, where the food was pricy. I charmed my way in, and the tips were better than ever. After a few months I saved up enough to rent an apartment with two bedrooms, one for Eda and me, and the other for the boys. They came down on a bus, and it was blissful to be together again. The kids loved playing on the beach, and they were fascinated by doing so in January. It seemed like such a long way from Baku where I used to lay in the hospital bed and dream about my future. Now I walked perfectly fine and was living a life I had never imagined.

My reputation grew among the dining out set, and some of my contented customers even recommended me to their friends. People from New York and Chicago would show up and ask for me. One of my regulars was the Miller family from New York. They were good tippers and proudly told me that their son was the noted playwright, Arthur Miller. It seemed as if I was supposed to recognize the name and who he was, so I pretended to know what they were talking about. Actually, I was ignorant of the theater and the arts, but after that I made it a point to find out a little. It was quite impressive to learn that my customers' kid wrote such famous plays, and that they were even made into movies. His most acclaimed work was called Death of a Salesman, and I found a copy of it in the library. Fortunately, I can read English a lot better than I can write it, although it would've been a great boon to find a copy in Polish. Anyway, I felt it best to become a little familiar with his stuff in case the topic came up. Also, I had an ulterior motive to know something about it in case I ever had an opportunity to talk to him. And then one day that became a possibility. An intellectual looking fellow with glasses walked in and asked to be seated in my station. When I went over to get his order he spoke to me.

"Hello Arthur. My name's Arthur too, and my family told me not to let anyone but you take care of me."

I gave him the usual treatment, but I hadn't put two and two together. Then another waiter pulled me aside.

"Do you know who you're waiting on? That's Arthur Miller, the most famous playwright in America! Not only that, he's married to Marilyn Monroe!"

Marilyn Monroe! Now that's someone I heard of! I might have been an immigrant from a shtetl in Poland, and maybe I never saw a movie until after I was already married, and perhaps I was ignorant about most of the artistic culture of the world, but I absolutely knew who the biggest sex symbol on the planet was. It was this guy's wife! Actually, at that time there were probably more people impressed by that piece of information than the fact that he was such an important writer. But I wasn't one of them. My main interest was firmly rooted in the arts. Ever since his parents had told me about their big shot son I had gotten into my mind that this great man of letters might find my wartime adventures interesting and maybe consider writing about them. I felt that if I could just talk to him in private he might go for it. But it was quite a challenge to find such an opportunity without bothering him or making a scene. After all, he was a big *macher* in the theater and Hollywood. People probably *nudgied* him all the time for his autograph or something. Our hotel offered refuge to such people. Many celebrities stayed there, and they had every right to expect to be left to dine in peace and quiet without being harassed by the star struck masses. To further complicate things, speaking to him about a personal matter, as was indeed my intention, could very well jeopardize my job. So far he behaved like a total gentleman and a regular fellow, but so far nobody had interacted with him beyond refilling his coffee cup. A lot of people look nice until you bother them. Perhaps he would consider the overture of any topic besides food to be an effrontery to his good will, and an unforgivable invasion of his privacy. Imagine the scandal if I handed him his check, along with an unexpected plea to hear my biography, and he exploded. I had to consider the possibility of losing an established customer. Not just him, but his whole family. And what if, upon hearing of my ill timed chutzpah, they recommended to all their friends not to seek me out at all, but instead to avoid me at all cost, and maybe the hotel as well. Cadres of northern tourists might picket the Saxony, carrying placards proclaiming its rudeness. I'd be fired, and then the word would spread all over the Beach and I'd be washed up for good. Should I cross the customer/waiter line? Dare I address the illustrious bard like a regular human being? I was more anxious over talking to this guy than I was on the eve of my first battle on the Steppes. Well, more lay in the balance. What would have been the consequence had I died while in Cossack uniform? My entire family was already dead, so who would have mourned me or suffered over it? General Bogaevsky might've regretted my demise for about a minute, and then selected a new adjutant. I would've been replaced in five minutes. And one soldier more or less in that campaign would not have changed the tide of battle. But now I had a wife and kids who depended on me. Out on the steppes Corporal Arkadi was not responsible for bringing home the bacon. But it was incumbent upon Arthur Feder to feed three hungry mouths. Catching a Nazi slug would not have doomed Operation Uranus, but losing my waiter position would be a minor catastrophe by comparison. Then fate stepped in and made it possible to speak to the great man. I got moved to room service. Besides opening the way to speak Arthur Miller, it was a blessing all around. We took orders over the phone, so I didn't even have to stand at a table with a pad. I just wheeled a tray up to a room and entered the room with great flair. The more flair I displayed the better the tip. The only down side was having to wait longer for those tips, because credit cards had become popular and the customers usually added the gratuity onto their bill. But it was usually worth the wait. And practically the first day I was assigned to room service Mr. Miller, the author of All My Sons, asked for me. This was perfect, I thought. We'll be alone in his room, greatly diminishing the chances of creating an incident. He'd be relaxed, and I could casually approach the subject. Full of confidence and hope I headed for his suite with the cart laden with a large lunch, easily enough for two. As I wheeled it into his room I discovered why there so much food. He was not alone. Sitting at the table with him was a pretty blond woman. She was engrossed in a book and didn't look up when I entered. But Arthur was cordial.

"Would you mind putting the food on the table, Arthur?"

Sometimes guests ate right off of the cart. There were leaves to rise, allowing chairs to slip underneath. But just as often I had to transfer everything off the cart and set the table as if we were in a restaurant. Such was the case now.

"A pleasure," I graciously though automatically replied. Arthur spoke to the woman.

"You don't mind, do you Marilyn?"

"Sure. Go right ahead."

The blond woman had a very sweet voice, like a little girl. It seemed to me as if I had heard that voice before. Then it hit me. This was Arthur Miller's wife, the world famous movie star, Marilyn Monroe. Miller spoke to her again.

"Marilyn, say hello to another Arthur."

She got up from the table and looked straight at me, purring, "Hello, Arthur."

I don't think she meant to sound alluring. It was just the natural timbre of her voice.

It a happened so fast I didn't have time to get nervous or tongue tied.

"Hello," escaped my lips, and I busied myself with my job, clearing the table and setting it with their lunch. I was taking everything off, but the man of words stopped me when I went to heft his electric typewriter.

"Please leave that where it is, Arthur. Thanks."

I tacitly did as he requested. Being quiet was a hallmark of my service, and one of the reasons people asked for me. Out of the corner of my eye I noticed that Marilyn was dressed in a robe. Arthur asked her how she was enjoying the book, and it seemed as if it was one he had recommended she read. He talked to her almost as if she were a little girl, which was not totally surprising as he struck me as being a bit older than her. Before entering I had planned to talk to him personally, but now my comfort factor was gone. Maybe they were on their honeymoon and wanted to be left in peace. Anyway, I wasn't prepared to talk about myself or anything else in front of Marilyn Monroe. It's not like I got up that morning and said to Eda, "S'long honey. I gotta go now and chat with the silver screen's biggest sex symbol." But I did want to make sure I'd have another chance to speak with him. After all, how often was I going to come in contact with a big *macher* from Hollywood? Once I found out about movies, which didn't happen until I was an adult, I always felt my story could be turned into one. But what did I know about all that? Even if you gave me a million dollars I wouldn't know how to go about it. My only hope was to meet someone in that field who was friendly to me. And the odds of that were impossible to calculate. It might never happen in my lifetime. But here was that opportunity, and I couldn't blow it. But I had to pave the way. It wouldn't be proper to open up on my first trip up here, so I tested the waters.

"So nice to have you back at the Saxony, Mr. Miller. I hope we have the pleasure of your company for a while." Then I quickly added, "And Mrs. Miller too."

I hoped that it didn't sound obvious that I had momentarily omitted his wife, whether or not she was a movie star. I don't know if he caught my slip, but he thanked me, and added "Hope you're around for dinner, Arthur. See you later."

Marilyn chimed in, "Buh-bye," sounding as friendly and child-like as she had before.

I left full of confidence and resolve to open up the matter on his next order. After all, didn't he say he'd call me for supper? Even though I was on the day shift, from breakfast through the shank of the afternoon, I requested a double shirt so I'd be there to bring them their dinner and engage him in that conversation. Of course, I had to dedicate a great portion of my time that afternoon describing Marilyn to the other workers in the kitchen. They demanded a complete account of her physical attributes. I had to detail the color of her hair and lips, the shape of her bosom, and the curves of her hips and legs. They insisted I imitate the sound of her voice, but I had to hold onto a shred of my dignity and deny them that spectacle.

After a dreary afternoon of bringing tourists their iced teas Arthur Miller finally called back with his dinner order. I wasted no time hightailing up there, determined to finally bend his ear.

I wheeled the dinner cart into his room, asking him if he wanted it on the table again.

"That's okay Arthur. Looks like I'm dining alone right now. I took this to mean that Marilyn was absent, but I spied her form in bed. Judging from his demeanor, as well as his wife's state of dress, I discerned that she had been that way all day and that he was less than happy about it. But I had already seen plenty while on room service. I had seen people in every state of dress and undress, drunk and sober, in the middle of arguments, and even engaged in sex under the covers. Actually, the more embarrassing the situation the bigger the tip. But a tip was not what I was after right now. Marilyn was clearly asleep, or at least unconscious, so I opened up.

"Mr. Miller, forgive me, but I was wondering if you had a minute. I'd like to tell you a little about my life, because I think you'd find it interesting subject matter. You know, it could be a play or a movie or something."

"Well Arthur, I have no dinner partner as you can see, so go ahead. Now's as good a time as any."

What a gracious man! A big shot on Broadway and he agrees to talk with me just like that! So, I didn't waste any time. He heard me out with great patience, and he showed great empathy for what happened in Sieniawa. He also seemed fascinated by my jail experiences and time with the Cossacks. He was particularly impressed that Stalin had personally cited me. He seemed slightly embarrassed to be eating while I spoke, but I insisted on it, and finally completed my tale as he did his dessert. And when he finally spoke he seemed quite sincere.

"You know Arthur, this is definitely a story worth telling. As for me, I've got writing commitments that'll keep me occupied for quite some time. But if you can get someone to write this for you, and you bring it to me, I assure you that I'll put it before someone important in Hollywood."

Wow! I had a contact in Hollywood! What generosity! I believed him, but I really had no idea how to go about finding a writer. My time for thinking about this was immediately cut short when he asked me for a favor of his own.

"Actually Arthur, there is something that you can do for me."

I was eager to hear what he wanted from me, and felt especially gratified to be let into his exclusive circle by this intimacy.

"Arthur, I have to spend the next few weekends up New York for meetings, but Marilyn's not looking forward to getting back to the cold weather. So she's going to stay here. You know, she's like a kid sometimes, and doesn't take good care of herself. So, I'm asking you to take care of her for me while I'm away. See that she eats okay. A good breakfast and a healthy lunch and dinner. Could you see to that for me please? You know, as one Arthur to another?"

What an honor! Everyone assured me that he was the top writer in the world, and here he was, asking me to take of his wife, the most glamorous movie star in America. Actually, he could've been an insurance salesman and it would have been the same thrill. I was being asked to baby sit Marilyn Monroe. How could I refuse? How could anyone?

"Look Arthur," he continued. "I'm leaving her a wake-up call for eight thirty, so she doesn't oversleep. Try and see she gets her breakfast by nine. Okay?"

"Sure thing, Mr. Miller, as one Arthur to another. Don't worry about a thing."

I felt terribly guilty that I didn't mention this to Eda. I had always been true to my darling wife, and had no plans to ever do otherwise. But maybe she wouldn't understand that I was going to be in the boudoir of America's major sex symbol and be alone with her. Women are a jealous sort. American, Polish, Russian, Jewish, Gentile, it doesn't matter. Why look for trouble? And the fact that I'd be on double shift for a day was no reason for concern. I did it all the time.

The next day I got to work by six and started filling orders. I noticed that by eight thirty Marilyn hadn't called down yet, so at nine o'clock I took it upon myself to order for her. After all, my Hollywood contact was counting on me. As he treated her like a child I seriously considered getting her some oatmeal. It's not an insult. Plenty of adults order it for breakfast. It's nutritious and filling, and not fattening. But then I considered that she was a glamorous celebrity, and probably accustomed to eating fancier things. So I ordered eggs Benedict, croissant and café au lait. But to make sure she ate healthy I added a big glass of orange juice and a fruit salad.

After enduring all manner of kidding, including countless wolf whistles, I loaded up her cart, including a single rose in a small crystal vase, and embarked on the short trip up to her suite. One short elevator ride later, and a walk down the hallway to the ocean side rooms, and I was knocking on her door. It's funny. It was no longer Arthur Miller's suite. Now, it was Marilyn's. At once that soft, sweet voice answered from within. I wasn't really sure what she said specifically, but it sounded musical and inviting, so I dared to test the door knob. It was unlocked and I inched forward, the cart before me. Then I was unsure what to call her. Marilyn? Miss Monroe? Mrs. Miller? I suddenly became aware that I was a bundle of nerves.

"Uh. Your breakfast is here."

That voice chimed again, "It's okay, Arthur. Come on in."

I was relieved she was awake, and proud that she remembered my name.

"Couldja bring it over here?"

That breathy voice. It was real. Now I was aware that she was still in bed in a night gown. Marilyn Monroe was talking to me, and she wanted her breakfast in bed. No surprise there. Lots of people did. But lots of people aren't sexy, blond, glamorous Marilyn Monroe. She wasn't wearing make-up, and for some reason that made her look earthier and sexier. People in the kitchen had informed me that she about thirty by now, and even inferred that by Hollywood standards she was a has-been. For days the kitchen staff had been analyzing all her films, the titles of which I mostly didn't recognize. I liked going to the movies as much as anyone else, but I was no maven. They told me she had been briefly married to Joe DiMaggio of the New York Yankees baseball team, and they filled my head with endless trivia about her. The more they told me about her the more nervous they made me.

"Watch out Arthur, I hear she's a nymphomaniac."

"Remember Feder, you're a married man!"

"Don't do anything I wouldn't do."

If I had been shaky about talking with a middle aged writer with glasses I was now trembling to be alone in a bedroom with this gorgeous creature with the birdlike voice. I was so startled I almost forgot my usual gracious service. I managed to squeak out, "How are you this morning Mrs. Miller?"

I think she liked that I called her that, instead of the other names I had considered, but she was friendly and insisted I call her Marilyn. After I put everything on the tray and laid it across her I turned to go saying, "Enjoy your breakfast Mrs, er, Marilyn."

But she stopped me, and addressed me in that singular breathy tone.

"Oh, I hate to eat alone. Please stay with me a while."

She patted the bed, and invited me to sit down near her. This caught me totally by surprise. Marilyn Monroe was asking me to occupy the same bed as her. The dream girl of every man in the world was suggesting we share a mattress. I froze. Every molecule in my being was ready to obey her, but one hold out brain cell forced me to consider the situation from every viewpoint. I mean, what could be the harm? I was fully dressed, and she was in her nightgown with the blankets drawn up tight around her. There was a tray full of food between us. It was broad daylight. Anyway, what would the most desirable woman on Earth want with me? Certainly, just company. Didn't she say she hated to eat alone? Every conceivable scenario flew through my mind. These Hollywood types were infamous for illicit affairs. But I wasn't a matinee idol. She could go to bed with Cary Grant, Gregory Peck, Gary Cooper or John Wayne. Or maybe she was tired of movie stars and wanted a regular fella, a man of the people. After all, those guys just pretended to be fighting men. I was a bona fide veteran of two shooting wars. Perhaps her husband had related to her a little of what I had told him, and she was full of lust for the counterfeit Cossack. I wasn't handsome like a matinee idol, but I wasn't exactly chopped liver either. In addition to that she was a recent convert to Judaism, and her husband might have filled her head with the glories of Israel, and here I was, its valiant defender, standing right before her. My mind was filled with a million crazy notions. After all, I was a married man, and had never been unfaithful. Of course, I had never been alone in a room with Marilyn Monroe. I was only human. I'm sure Eda would understand. Wouldn't I understand if Clark Gable seduced her? Wouldn't I? No! I was getting crazier by the second, and I had to snap out of it. It's just Marilyn Monroe inviting me to get into bed with her. No! Not into, but onto. That's completely different. She didn't mean anything. She was hungry for food, not sex. My friend, Arthur Miller the playwright, had entrusted his young bride to my care, and I was not about to betray that confidence. What's more we were landtsmen. She was safe with me. But it's Marilyn Monroe, and according to the cook a nymphomaniac, in desperate need of constant sex or she'd go crazy. Maybe that's what landtsman Arthur Miller really meant when he said, "Take care of her." No! That's madness! I'm Arthur Feder, married man, friend to the writer, and what's more, to his wife. What did it matter if she was horny? All that bounced around inside my head at the speed of mind, and after those two seconds of inner conflict I dragged a chair over next to the bed of Marilyn Monroe, international sex symbol, and sat down to keep her platonic company. She giggled when I did it, as if she was privy to the silent battle within me.

She turned out to be sweet and friendly. Well aware that I knew all about her, having probably seen every detail of her life in the press for years, she took the focus off herself and asked about me. I told her a synopsis of my war experiences, and she seemed sincerely interested. Of course she had visited countless American GIs at the front, and had probably heard it all a hundred times. Furthermore, she was an actress, and could probably pretend to care about my life without much effort. While holding forth on the life of the counterfeit Cossack I was delighted to see her eating her breakfast like a good girl, and looked forward to reporting to Miller that she had made all gone. As I talked I did my best to suppress any desire to ogle her breasts which I had previously seen blown up a hundred times on the big screen. After all, she was Marilyn Monroe and I was a man. And just looking was hardly infidelity. So, I visually appreciated her cleavage, pouting lips and bedroom eyes, but that was all. Just because any red-blooded male on Earth would have given his mortal soul to be where I was didn't mean a thing to me. She heard my tale, and then I cleared off the dirty dishes. Eda had nothing to worry over, and I hadn't done anything to be ashamed of. I don't kid myself either. It's not like I could've *shtupped* a movie star, but didn't. Except for a nanosecond of fantasy lust within my mind, my association with Marilyn Monroe was as wholesome as the new driven snow on the Steppes. Not even a meaningful look passed between us. Arthur Miller returned from New York to his faithful wife, and gave me a huge tip. I continued babysitting Marilyn Monroe for the next two weekends, and that was the sum and substance of my relationship with the great star. But it was not sexual frustration that I felt, but rather that I was thwarted by my utter ignorance as to how to go about finding a writer for my biography. After all, if I could just do that much Marilyn's husband would do the rest. But where to even begin was so out of my league it was futile to consider. Thus, my dream of committing my life to the written page would have to wait for a long, long time.

Though things were fine at the Saxony I decided to try for something even bigger, the best place to be a waiter on Miami Beach, the Fontainebleau Hotel. Just looking at the enormous size of the place I figured that tips had to be the best there, so I wheedled an interview with the restaurant manager. It's all well and good to spot an opportunity when it comes along, but it's no sin to nudge that opportunity in the first place. Also on my mind was my dream of discovering my mystery career. Making big tips seemed big compared to shoveling sand in Palestine, but I was still convinced that my calling was out there calling to me, even if I couldn't hear it yet. Rose Reich's voice echoed in my mind, "You're a tummler. Come to America!" To make a long story short, for a change, I impressed the Maitre' d at the Fontainebleau and got into the room service operation there where the tips were even bigger. More tips meant more savings.

By then Eda had earned a certificate as a beautician and was also bringing income to the family. We moved into an apartment on Ocean Drive and Ninth Street, and the owners were retirees who missed their own kids so much they loved to baby sit for Irving and Larry for free.

Everything seemed to be going well, but we had a lesson to learn. Tourism in Miami Beach was seasonal. Europeans didn't visit Miami Beach at that time, nor did people from South America or the Orient. Not too many Arabs either. It was just a certain crowd called Snow Birds. They migrated south when it got cold up north, and returned once the ice melted back home. So, to keep the income rolling in, we had to do the same. When things got dried up in Miami we went up north to the Catskills where I waited tables, and Eda did hair. The tips were excellent there as well, and with the close of summer we returned to Miami. We did this routine for two years, until we had enough to get our own place in Miami. We found a small four unit apartment building on

Biscayne Island in Miami Beach. We rented out three of the units, which covered the mortgage payments, and we moved into the fourth one, allowing us to live rent free. The counterfeit Cossack was now into real estate, and it felt right. Very, very right.

'Ye Noshery' At Saxony Hotel Exciting Spot For Rendezvous

three people are kept busy night and day just making the frothy sodas and sundaes, that are the "sweet talk of the town."

Among the ice cream favorites at Ye Noshery are: "Skyscraper," a super sundae featuring your favorite ice cream, strawberries, whipped cream and garnished with sugar wafers, crushed nuts and cherries; "Georgia peach," a large scoop of French ice cream served over Elberta peach on a sponge square and topped with melba sauce and whipped cream; and the "double scoop," an overstuffed soda topped with whipped cream and fresh fruit. All ice cream specialties are served in large size dishes and glasses with whipped cream or topping heaped on in generous portions.

The Noshery is open from 8 a.m. to 3 a.m. daily. In addition to dinners, sandwiches and ice cream concoctions they also serve salad platters and fruit specialties for diet diners.

JUST FOR YOU—Arthur Feder and Liz Greenwood, makers of the Noshery Soda and Sundae concoctions, shown with the "Double Scoop."

Everybody about 2,000 people step into Miami Beach's snack tempting treats offered to the after hour diner.

My ice cream creations made the Saxony Hotel's Noshery famous.

As I looked when we lived in Laurelton, New York.

THE PROMISED LAND

XXII

After a couple of years of waiting tables and doing hair in Miami Beach we saved up about forty thousand dollars. It was quite a respectable amount of money at that time, and we could have easily built ourselves a home with a swimming pool. We could have added a new car to that opulence as well had we wanted to, but lurking in the back of my mind was what Aunt Rose had told me back in Israel, that the title of businessman was destined to be on my resume. Being a waiter brought me great tips, but I still felt I was meant for something bigger. Sadly though, nothing bigger seemed to be looming on the Florida horizon at that time. So in 1959 we returned to New York. My days as a waiter were over. However, that apartment building on Biscayne Island was nurturing vague ideas of real estate in the back of my mind.

We moved out to the town of Laurelton where the homes were bigger, and the rents were lower. Regina and Abe also moved to Laurelton, not far from us. Nathan did so as well, as did Eda's mother. Eda felt wonderful having so much family there, and it struck me as inconceivable that so many occupants of shtetls could transplants themselves to the greatest country on Earth and thrive.

As a kid I was so provincial Lvov seemed like an unattainable quest, and here I was, living the American Dream. And It was a pleasure to watch my boys grow and enjoy the benefits of this magnificent society.

Having a few bucks in my pocket I decided to take my time to see what interesting business opportunities awaited me. And while looking for that special thing a warm friendship between Nathan and me blossomed. He was just a kid when I knew him back in Poland, but now he was fully grown and scanning that same business horizon as me. It was very nurturing for me to have a family. When I married Esther I not only got a great girl, she came with a ready made family in the bargain. Now we had a family of our own, and Regina and Abe did too. Nathan married soon after and started his own as well. Within a decade of barely surviving Hitler's onslaught we were blossoming. Another generation of Feders and Apthekars was assured. We celebrated Pesach, Purim and the High Holy Days together, as well as adapting the American habit of making a big deal over Hanukah. Life in America was good.

We were living off my savings and I was getting frustrated that my mystery career had not yet materialized. Then one day Nathan and I passed an empty lot that had a for-sale sign on it. The piece of property was up against a hillside and the thought occurred to me that I might become a real estate tycoon, and that this might be a good place to start. So, even though I had no idea what to do with it, I bought it. Around that time I met someone in the real estate trade who thought I had the makings of a first class salesman. He offered me fifty dollars a week just to learn all about it, and the thought crossed my mind that, as I had already acquired a piece of property, and now a real estate business was making me an offer, perhaps this was what I was looking for. After all, we had a steady stream of income from our Biscayne Island property already. Maybe this indeed was what I had been looking for all this time. After my first month of selling real estate I was convinced of it. Just as I did with fighting on the Steppes, and dishing up ice cream treats in Brooklyn, I focused myself one hundred percent on real estate and it worked.

Money started pouring in almost at once, and when Irving's Bar Mitzvah rolled around we were able to give him a typical American middle class party. He invited all his friends, and we invited every living relative, no matter how distant, plus my business associates. Although Israel and America offered us the freedom to become as devout as my father we led lives more similar to the congregants of Sieniawa's big brick shul. Also, like most other American emigrants of our generation, we wanted to give our kids everything. Subsequent generations would condemn us for spoiling our kids, but we couldn't help ourselves. We came from impoverished backgrounds and we were determined to make up for it by denying this new generation nothing.

After about six months of selling properties I had learned enough to know that being the agent of real estate transactions was not the top level of this land game. Improving a lot and selling it was where I wanted to be. So, I went back to that hillside property and built a house on it. I had not handled tools since my stint as handyman at Collective Farm Number eight hundred and thirty one. Clearly, this was not something I could do myself. Anyway, as I real estate agent I learned that a builder had to be legally qualified. So, we hired a licensed contractor. Basically, it turned out awful, but we were able hide the imperfections with plaster and paint. Even so, we managed to sell it for a tidy ten thousand dollar profit. Ten thousand dollars, and I didn't have a boss, and I didn't have to apologize for the steak being overcooked. This was it. This is what I had been waiting for me since leaving Europe. Building was the Promised Land! The counterfeit

Cossack was meant to be a consummate contractor!

I took Nathan on as a partner and we learned the construction trade. To do so we hired some experienced builders and watched them like hawks. We didn't watch them so much as to prevent being cheated, but to learn how to do it ourselves. They ended up overcharging us, but it was a worthwhile experience because of what we learned. We stayed next to them every step of the way and studied the right way to do things. I was a good student and felt better prepared to carry on alone. I became a licensed contractor and did the things the kosher way. My father back in Sieniawa could build his daughter and son-in-law a house without government interference, but in America you had to do things one way and one way only. So, we hired only licensed carpenters and plumbers, and our next house was far better. And the next after that was better yet. But I left nothing to chance. If I could get up at dawn to deliver candy I could do at least that much when bigger things were at stake. I got up at four in the morning to plan my days, and kept an eagle eye on my workers, staying after they left to double check everything against the plans and our stock of building materials. My past had taught me to be careful. But our hard work and strict business practices were paying off. Every night when my eyes closed a sense of accomplishment and satisfaction lay on my pillow with me. My dreams were finally being fulfilled. This is what I was meant to be doing. I had found my calling. Throughout all those candy and bagel deliveries, banana splits and baskets of bread, this dream never died. As far back as Sieniawa and during the endless lonely nights in Kiev I had this vision, although not well focused. Even when the fierce fighting on the steppes abated, thoughts of my future invaded my mind. Fifteen years later my time had come. Success was mine at last, and as you can imagine, my darling Eda was thrilled. Not only were we flourishing in America, but we were working together as a family. We survived the Nazis and their threat of annihilation. Then we tolerated the Soviets who didn't believe in free enterprise. And our hard work in Israel was too early for such a poor country. Now we were free to do more than dream. We lived in a country that nurtured those dreams and set the stage for our success. For me America was heaven, because you could keep what you made. If I would have tried this back in Poland it'd have been run by the government, and instead of earning the money I would've been awarded a Hero's Worker Medal. And no doubt it would have been presented with a speech congratulating my glorious endeavors. I preferred the financial reward. It was far more glorious.

After building so many single family homes we expanded into the metropolitan New York area with Majestic Gardens, an apartment complex. We applied the same work methods and business model as always and it worked just as well. And, as it was no longer vital for us to scrimp, we went on vacations whenever possible. We took motor trips and flew. Eda dressed like a queen and we were enjoying our lives to the fullest. We also delighted in seeing our sons grow strong and healthy. Nathan's own family and Regina's as well expanded our clan even more. We now had handsome nephews and lovely nieces. With such success, and no more babies to dote on, Eda suggested that it'd be nice to have a daughter, so we went back into the baby making business almost ten years after Larry's birth. Of course, nothing guaranteed us that daughter, but we decided to take the gamble anyway. And on the last day of August, 1963 our daughter Hedy was born, named for my mother, Hadassah. The following year we moved to Cedarhurst, and two years after that we threw Larry a truly gala Bar Mitzvah. It seemed like America was heaven. We enjoyed wealth and health and nobody bothered us. Then, during one especially cold winter day in New York, Nathan said to me, "It's too cold here Arthur. Let's take a trip to Puerto Rico. It's beautiful there." Years before we had visited Cuba, and we enjoyed that tropical vacation. So I replied, "Let's pack!"

We stopped off in Miami on the way and stayed in the Saxony Hotel where years before I had waited tables and chatted with Marilyn Monroe. That was behind me of course. Ahead lay a whole new life.

PUERTO RICO AND BEYOND

XXIII

We touched down in San Juan airport and took a cab to the Sheraton Hotel which is walking distance to the old part of the city called Old San Juan. It's a preserved Spanish colonial style village, nestled between a beautiful wide bay and the immense centuries old Morro Castle. It's a tourist delight with narrow cobblestone streets and picturesque shops. Nathan and I strolled around, snapped a few pictures, and got a bite to eat. The climate was very relaxing and a welcome change from the New York winter. After a night's rest we rented a car and went out to explore the island. Even though Puerto Rico is a tropical island it's still an American possession. That means they have McDonald's and decent roads. We passed through long stretches of greenery and suddenly, without warning, we'd come upon a small collection of houses along the road. Just as abruptly, we'd be plunged back into nature, and it went that way continually.

"This is like Poland," I said.

"Poland? This beautiful tropical paradise with palm trees and papayas is like Poland? You're *meshuga!*"

"Well, Poland's green too, at least in the summer. It's like a giant forest, and once in a while you come to a little piece of civilization, like your Krasnik or my Sieniawa."

Nathan couldn't deny the comparison, and agreed, "Oh, I see what you mean."

That casual observation triggered old memories, and for the first time in a long, long while I was transported back to a shtetl in the East European forest. And to myself I once again vowed to return there and get to the bottom of my family's disappearance.

It the evening Nathan and I went back to our hotel for dinner. When we got to the lobby we noticed that by the most incredible of coincidences there was a convention for builders going on in one of the ballrooms. We strolled in and looked around. There were displays with architectural plans and some models, and we heard a mixture of Spanish and English. Nathan and I added to the language mix by chatting with each other in Polish, with a few words of Yiddish thrown in. Even though we both spoke accented English, his less than mine, we often lapsed into Polish or Yiddish as a comfort device. Our Slavic/Semitic conversation attracted the ear of one of the exhibitors and he stopped us dead in our tracks by greeting us in a combination of the very same languages we were just practicing. Hearing someone else speak these tongues in New York wouldn't have surprised us a bit, but after listening to a romance language for two days it was utterly startling.

"Allow me to introduce myself gentlemen. My name is Morris Demel, and I couldn't help but notice you were speaking in my native languages. Are you builders?"

We introduced ourselves and admitted to having in common with him all of the things he suspected. It turned out that Morris was a Polish Jew whose family had fled to Cuba just before things got bad in Europe. He jokingly referred to himself as a Juban and explained how they had to flee again when Castro took over. So, we had that in common too. We had both fled the two big totalitarian regimes, fascism and communism.

"This might be fate, landtsmen. May I tell you about my project?"

I didn't admit it, but I felt in my bones that this might be fate indeed.

"Right now I'm working for this company, overseeing construction of a small apartment building. Everyone here thinks small. Anyway, I'm gonna build them a first class structure and they'll make a huge profit. And all I'm getting is a measly hundred and a half a week. But I have a plan that can make us all rich."

Whenever people say they're going to make you rich I think you should be very careful. The first thing I wonder is why don't they do it themselves if it's such a good idea. Morris then explained to me why he couldn't and why he thought fate had brought us together.

"Do you know why I'm sure that my bosses are going to make a killing on the project I'm building for them? Because Puerto Rico suffers from a terrible lack of decent housing. And on top of that thousands of young Puerto Ricans can easily qualify for the GI Bill and afford to move right in. I'm telling you, they're literally standing in line to move in before anything is even built here. My idea is to build large apartment complexes. Not just one building, but ten or twenty in one place. Big buildings! I'm talking hundreds, maybe thousands of units. Make nice gardens around them, and provide lovely common areas. And not just in San Juan, but in other areas that the government wants to develop. And that same government will cooperate in any way they can to see that it happens. I have the plans. All I need is a backer with some chutzpah."

I had never heard such a glorious idea in my entire life. I looked over at Nathan who was already turning toward me. We were both hooked, even though we were not about to let him reel us in just yet. We were weary, because when something sounds too good to be true it usually is. Morris was one astute landtsmen and he wasn't about to let us off that easy.

"There's a town called Manati about thirty miles from San Juan on the road to Arecibo. I got my eye on a lovely little five acre plot there that's ideal for a series of high rises. Right now most of the homes there have two families living in them. And they're dilapidated. The humidity here is a killer, so we're gonna build everything out of poured concrete. They'll outlast the Roman Coliseum. We can get local labor, *obreros*, for six bits an hour and they'll be happy for the steady employment. Plus, the Puerto Rican government will facilitate permits and materials importation. Señores, whadda ya say?"

He made perfect sense. Nathan and I looked at each other with big wide eyes and simultaneously smiled. Right there on the spot we shook hands with our new partner. The counterfeit Cossack and Morris the Juban were going to take Puerto Rico by storm.

Nathan and I cut our vacation short and returned to New York to arrange financing. Morris was right. There was more than enough land to build anything you could imagine and people needed and wanted modern housing. In addition to that the government was eager to have audacious companies like ours to modernize the island. And, just as Morris said, the GI bill would finance most of our prospective customers. The timing was perfect. Morris was the goose that laid the golden egg. As quickly as I ever recognized anything in my life I saw this as not just a golden egg, but a golden opportunity. Nor am I prouder of anything else in my life than having had the good sense to recognize it and then act on it without hesitation. Realizing something without acting on it is useless. My evolved and honed senses served me as well as any of my ancestors.

From the very beginning April Industries, which is what we ended up calling the company, took off. Our apartment developments, or *urbanizaciones*, as they're called in Spanish, were an unprecedented success. The government was proud to have such fashionable and affordable housing, and the people who lived there felt that their lives were greatly improved. We sold the first units for only thirteen thousand dollars apiece with a three hundred dollar deposit. Puerto Rico had never seen anything like it. Even the governor came out for the inauguration. We commissioned a popular artist to paint giant murals on the sides of a series of four story apartment complexes in Manatí, and Governor Ferre attended the opening ceremonies. He wasn't just coming out because we had built a pretty building. April hired practically the entire town of Manati. And they continued to work for us. With a thousand locals on our payroll April was the biggest single employer in Puerto Rico, and I was its general. If I was focused making banana splits imagine how intensely focused I was there! On the Steppes I had worn the uniform of a general, but here I was truly like Napoleon. He was all over the battlefield, and I was all over the construction site. Instead of artillery, cavalry and infantry deployment I was involved in every detail of building, from the plans to mixing cement. I was up at four in the morning, driving from San Juan to the site. I made sure every brick and nail went in straight. After a month I was more like Caesar than Napoleon, because I knew the names of my troops. "Juan, the concrete needs more sand. *Mas arena!* Miguel, get a hammer with a longer handle or you'll waste your energy. *Un martillo mas largo!* Pablo, you're using too much rebar in that wall! *Demasiado!*" And besides employing them I was concerned for their welfare. When one worker came to me crying that he wasn't making enough to feed and clothe all his kids properly I gave him a thirty percent raise. He actually kissed my hand. But I told him firmly, "Roberto, five kids is plenty. Enough is enough! *Ya basta!*" On top of all that I was commuting back and forth between the island and New York. I couldn't convince Eda to make the move so I became a jumping bean bouncing from weekdays in Puerto Rico to weekends in New York. I had a fixed first class reservation on Eastern Airlines every Thursday afternoon The stewardess held seat number A-1 open for me for three years. Monday morning I was back on the return flight in the same seat. But I was spending most of my time on the island. It was necessary, but I was also attracted to some activities that were so much more accessible here than in New York, such as horseback riding. In the war I was a first rate equestrian, and now a renewed passion for it urged me to saddle up whenever the rare free hour presented itself.

We gave our projects beautiful names like Bella Vista Gardens, Sierra Linda, Jardines de Manatí and Villa Evangeline. They sold out as soon as they were built and everyone was content. We had over a thousand employees making April a healthy contributor to the local economy. We trained all our people ourselves to do things our way and gave administrative positions to locals. This made them feel more like they were part of what was happening and not just some exploited laborers of gringo imperialists. We also gave generous bonuses for jobs well done. All of this led to very little pilferage so we too were content. Of course, I added Spanish to my list of languages, so I actually felt *contento*. We built a dozen complexes on the northeast part of the island, and we were so far ranging we had our own radio network just to communicate with foremen on the sites.

After my first year down there Eda finally decided to give Puerto Rico a try. She found it too humid and had an awful time trying to learn Spanish. She lasted just one month before moving back. Not long after she insisted that I do so as well, so I had to figure out how to wind down my activities there. Wall Street had the solution. April Industries was so successful it became the first construction company to go public. In 1972 it went on the stock exchange. I sold out my interest and moved back to New York.

When I returned to New York it seemed as if I had a wonderful dream about a tropical isle. It all happened so fast it really did seem like an illusion. Our adventures in paradise only lasted three years, but we had become wealthy beyond any dreams we might have had in Sieniawa, Kiev, the Steppes, Baku, or anywhere else. Then, what happened next put even that into perspective. Eda got a letter from Russia that made her swoon. Her brother Isaac was alive and well and heading for America with his wife and daughter. Thirty four years had transpired since the communists had taken little Itzhak away from Krasnik to be reeducated as a cog in the Soviet machine. Eda and Regina and Nathan had long since given him up for dead, and I haven't got the words to describe their emotional reunion at Kennedy airport. He was of course a grown man by now with a wife and grown daughter. It's impossible for me to imagine a tighter bond than the one I've observed between Eda and her mother and her sister and brothers. It was forged in Krasnik and has remained steadfast through separations of time and space. Since Isaac's return they've never been apart.

After years in the tropics my blood was too thin for the Empire State, so like so many *paisanos* before us we moved back to the Sunshine State. We still kept an office in New York and Nathan stayed there to run it. He oversaw a huge two hundred acre project for us in Connecticut and I built more homes in South Florida. Though I wasn't yet fifty I could have easily retired, but I was energetic and enthusiastic, so I kept working, building homes in Florida. I built interesting homes on pilings in Hallandale, and I did a big apartment complex in West Palm Beach with my own whiz-kid daughter Hedy.

Although I had done so much I still had one more big project ahead of me. Nathan moved to Houston and opened a perfume store just to stay busy. It was in a large shopping center on Harwin Street called Harwin Discount Center. He called me and told me to come out and see it, because it was a good investment opportunity.

I went and even brought Hedy along. After studying the whole layout I decided that Nathan was right. By then I also considered Hedy's opinion, because she has a real head for business. Rose Reich would have called her a tummler too. Nathan and I also brought in two other partners. First, there was Ruben Kloda, an old friend who had become the hosiery king of America. Hedy thought it was such a good investment she actually bought the hosiery outlet there. And our other partner there was another old friend from Israel named Jacob Gilboa. As soon as we acquired the shopping center I hired a bright young man to manage the property named Ricky Glaser. He was good looking too and Hedy fell head over heels in love with him. Fortunately, the feeling was mutual and our family expanded again. Eventually they moved back to Florida, and we all live near each other.

After so many years of success Eda and I had more than enough money to last ourselves and our children for the rest of our lives. Not that they needed it. Irving got an MBA and learned the construction trade. He also became an avid scuba diver and invented SCUDA (self-contained underwater drinking apparatus) which allows divers who dive deep and long to hydrate their mouths and bodies, so they can stay healthier. He patented it in 1989 and sold the company shortly thereafter. My other son Larry became a successful attorney with offices in nearby Hollywood. And Hedy is nicely settled with her husband Ricky. She's has a real talent for business and can compete with the best of them. Best of all, the future of our family is guaranteed. Larry and his wife Barbara have two beautiful children named Stephen and Lisa, and Hedy and Ricky have two lovely grandchildren, Rachel and Alex. It's such a blessing to have a big beautiful clan. I was the only survivor of my family. I was it. No ancestors and no descendents. I was literally alone. But Eda changed all that. First I inherited wonderful in-laws. As soon as we were married I gained a sister and brother and a

lovely mother-in-law. Then Eda and I created a whole new generation, and then they begat another. God willing, that generation will
likewise evolve. I was once on my own, but now I need a paper and
pencil to count the whole family. Actually, we have thrived so well
that I probably need a calculator to keep tabs.

Having reestablished our bloodline my heart was at rest. Now
it was time to put my mind to rest. At last, it was time for me to
go back to Poland and learn the true circumstances of my family's
death.

S-2 SAN JUAN STAR SUPPLEMENT — Tuesday, August 22. 1972.

The Landmark Murals Of Manati

The murals of Manati may be seen from Highway 2.

While experts muse over aesthetic considerations in low cost housing, a group in Puerto Rico spontaneously did something about it which apparently has delighted everyone from the Governor to the residents in Manati.

On June 10 this year over 3,000 residents of Manati, a city of approximately 30,000 attended the unveiling ceremony for five massive murals, each measuring 30 feet in width and 42 feet in height, which will be a part of their daily vista for years to come. The ceremony was attended by will demand the same concern for their aesthetic environment. I salute this beginning of what I hope will become a trend.

The murals were painted by five artists from the University of Puerto Rico. Gov. Ferre who attended the ceremony discussed the abstract forms and colors of the murals, and nature uses similar shapes to create the landscapes the people love.

The initiative for the massive murals of Manati, as they are known, came from Morris Demel, executive vice president of April Industries, who started about my "thank you to Manati" in environmental terms.

The murals are a bigger and better approach to public housing aesthetics than anyone here remembers. Many of the islanders have lived in or know public housing projects well. Jose Robles, secretary to the mayor of Manati, and a former New York City welfare worker, is one of these. His work has taken him into many projects. "We all used to discuss the effect of environmental drabness on the morale of the residents. I can tell you from personal experience how im-

April Industries took Puerto Rico by storm!
Governor Ferre visits our Manati complex.

SAN JUAN STAR SUPPLEMENT — Tuesday, August 22. 1972. S-9

Value's April

(Continued From Page S-7)

is led by 46-year old Arthur Feder."

The publication queried, "How is April able to achieve its wide profit margins (32.5) pre-tax last year) in the competitive Puerto Rican homebuilding environment?" "The answer centers", it goes on to say,"...on the company's total construction capabilities: April controls all of its operations, including earthwork, building, personnel, equipment, and the like. As a result, it is able to provide low-cost alternatives to Puerto Rico's varied housing submarkets. At present April employs close to 1,000 workers, most of whom have been trained by the company.

"Labor costs are considerably lower than in the U.S.; bonuses and overtime pay are commonplace. There have not been any strikes and the company's pilferage experience is minimal.

"It helps considerably that top management is on the job site with the workers on a daily basis. Many homebuilders in Puerto Rico are merely subsidiaries of large corporations headquartered in New York, or other large cities. In addition, Puerto Rico's year-round, mild climate, as well as its long hours of daylight aid productivity.

"Another operational innovation is April's extensive use of an ultra high frequency radio-telephone system which interconnects headquarters with

Bella Vista is the name of this April project in Bayamon. The photo shows how it got its name.

April Plans 2,500 More Homes

April Industries, Inc. is now planning, producing and selling over 2,500 homes in Puerto Rico on six separate sites. These projects range from public housing and subsidized housing, to private homes plus a construction and management contract with another large publicly owned, mainland based construction company.

April went public on Feb. 4 of this year, after over seven years of building activity in Puerto Rico. Their history may conservatively be labeled suc-

cessful, in terms of integration into the construction scene of the island and in terms of profits.

Arthur Feder and Morris Demel, the principal officers of the company, attribute their success to a policy of developing self sufficiency in the field. In their projects, the only sub-contract is for kitchen cabinets. They do everything with their own people. "Our most important asset is the people, most of whom we trained, who move the earth and build our houses," says Morris Demel with pride

Demel directs field operations for the company, and has acquired a reputation for quality construction within tight schedules. April roster of field workers numbers over 1,000 and is steadily rising.

This work force is the result of much effort, dating back to the very beginning of this company. "Today it is our basis for accurate estimating and efficiency in utilizing this organization. Schedules are not

predicated on the convenience of sub-contractors."

A rather dramatic result of April's policy of training and upgrading personnel is Rene Hernandez. When Rene arrived here from Miami with his wife and three children, he was an ex-potato farmer and a former war hero. He survived serious wounds in the Bay of pigs, which required heart massage to restore him to life. But Hernandez claims that the earth refused to take him because

(Continued On Page S-18)

RESIDENCIALES

Our project in Bella Vista.

August 22, 1972.

SAN JUAN STAR   TUESDAY AUG. 22, 1975

RECORD SALES

Arthur Feder, president of April Industries, Inc. (OTC), above reported this month record sales and earnings for the six and three months ended June 30, 1972. For the six months, the company reported revenues of $4,025,777 compared with $1,876,959 for the year ealier period, a gain of 114 per cent. Net income increased by 110 per cent of $768,000 from $365,697, as earnings per share rose to $.55 compared with $.29 in the corresponding period last year. In the three months ended June 30, 1972, net income rose by 98.9 per cent to $431,860 from $217,128 for the comparable period last year, as per share earnings increased to $.31 from $.17, a gain 82.3 per cent. Revenues rose to $2,164,527 from $1,231,399 for the earlier period.

In 1972 we went public. I sold my interest in April Industries and joined Eda in New York.

Center is Morris Demel, exec Vice-Prez. Far right is Prez (me).
We're all hiding from that bright Puerto Rican sun in our sunglasses.

Nathan Apthekar, vice president and a director of April, has been named by its board of directors to manage April's new acquisition of 200 acres in Connecticut. Apthekar's headquarters are in April's New York office.

Nathan, my friend and brother-in-law. He went from hiding in a barn to being Vice President of April Industries.

*Eda rushes to embrace Isaac, her long lost brother
who came back from the dead in 1973.*

My sons, Irving and Larry.

My mother-in-law, Helen Apthekar, Larry's wife, Barbara,
and my wife Eda in Florida.

After selling April Industries I could afford a Rolls Royce.

We traveled extensively after I sold April Industries.
We especially enjoyed Switzerland

Since I was back in Israel why not hop back on a motorcycle?

The Counterfeit Cossack rides again!
Mounting up in Turkey.

YOU CAN'T GO HOME AGAIN

In 1990 Eda and I went on a vacation to Europe with the ultimate goal of reaching my birthplace. We stayed a few days in Paris, reminiscing about our brief stay on that kibbutz, and the mysterious Fourth of July celebration that frightened us. But, I wasn't totally free to enjoy it all, because in the back of my mind was my ultimate showdown in Sieniawa. For so many years I had anticipated this confrontation. Every scenario possible had ricocheted inside my mind. For years, when I was still a young man, I envisioned Corporal Arkadi blasting Konstantin Jonjac with a submachine gun. I could feel the cold steel in my hand and its kick. As I became older I started to consider that civilization had long since replaced the Poland I knew, and ignoring the due process of law could only result in more complication for me.

It was easy to enter Poland. Just the year before the Premier of Russia, Mikhail Gorbachev had declared that the USSR would no long interfere in the internal affairs of Eastern European governments. Poland held free elections and the democratic Solidarity Party took control. It was the first time that Eda and I had set foot in the land of our birth in forty five years. We were teenaged newlyweds when we left, penniless refugees. And now we were returning as affluent westerners. It'd be disingenuous of me to try and tell you that I did not want to throw my success in the face of the goyim of Sieniawa. Being back there made me regress a bit, and I was once again young Ovram, bitter over the past. We rented a chauffeured Mercedes and we pulled into Sieniawa in style. Had such an event occurred in my childhood every living soul for miles would have come to gape and stare at the strange automobile. Of course, people will always take a look at a fine car, but we were hardly big news. Sieniawa now had paved streets and people had been driving through here on their way to Jaroslaw or Krakow for decades. The streets had curbs and it was nothing special to park there like any other place. Our arrival was not met with fanfare. Nobody knew who we were or cared. And although I had known every square foot of this shtetl fifty years before, now I was lost. First of all, nobody had referred to Sieniawa as a shtetl in half a century. The Jews were gone and that's all there was to it. But the main reason I was there of course was to investigate that very fact. So, I had the chauffer slowly drive until we found the old house. It took calculations to even convince myself that we had found it. Naturally, it had been transformed. The color, roof, doors and windows had probably been changed countless times. But its proximity to other houses and the road, revealed its location to me. This was where I was born, and where my parents and sisters all lived. I just stood there. It looked too different to make me feel nostalgic. In some strange way I felt cheated.

"Hello, sir. Can we help you? Are you lost?"

I was so lost in my thoughts I didn't notice the owner had come outside, forcing me to compose myself. This was not going to be like after the war, finding Bodek in my house. I was no longer a powerful commissar, nor was anyone concerned that I might have come back to claim my property. Finally, an annoyed Eda spoke up.

"Well, did we come three thousand miles for you to sit there like a *shtick fleisch*?"

That jarred me. But it was the way she spoke that took me far into the past. Dear Eda sounded exactly like my old jail house guru. Her inflection and emphasis were precisely like that long ago challenge, do you want to live or do you want to die? It was delivered with the same brash insistence and immediacy. And in both cases I had to act. I cleared my throat and spoke.

"My name is Arthur Feder and this is my wife Eda."

The man was cordial, but he looked a bit curious. I had to explain.

"You see, I was born in this house."

I had never anticipated this. The last time I came I knew exactly who lived here. I even remembered his name. It was Bodek, an old school mate. But now it was a total stranger. This was the worst shock of all. But a broad smile manifested itself on his lean face and he nodded knowingly. He understood why I had tarried so long before his house, and his positive attitude alleviated some of the anxiety I felt over the whole scene.

"Well, that's interesting! How long have you been gone?"

"Forty five years."

He opened his eyes side and seemed both amazed and amused by that great cipher.

"Well, welcome back old fellow. How can I help you?"

I wondered if I should speak to him, or if I should go to the authorities. After all these years I had no plan. He could see I was flustered and he became more cordial. But I was actually afraid to go in. I didn't know if the emotion would overwhelm me, or if we would be murdered, such was the curse of Sieniawa on my soul. After all this time the place still had me under its frightful spell. I was still afraid of my old home town. So I elected to remain outside and conduct my investigations from there.

"Does the name Konstantin Jonjac mean anything to you?"

He seemed to be sincerely mulling it over in his mind for a while, but came up empty.

"Doesn't sound at all familiar. Was he a neighbor?"

"No. But do you know of any older folk who might have lived here for a long time?"

He seemed to understand what I really meant.

"You mean like back during the war?"

"Well, I don't know them by name, but there are a few old residents around. Sieniawa's not much bigger than it was during the war. Ask around. It'll be easy!"

The fellow thought a bit then seemed to come up with an idea.

"Why don't I tell your driver? He's probably a little more familiar with the roads."

"You've been most kind. Thank you."

While the man explained things to our driver Eda took some photos of me standing in front of the house. I shook hands with the friendly Pole and got back in the Mercedes to head off to what would doubtless be the end my search. The driver drove barely fifty feet before he passed an old couple. He stopped the car and spoke to them, but they seemed reluctant. When asked anything specific they just shrugged their shoulders. The driver turned around.

"Boss, I know these old folks. Give them a few bucks and their mood and memory will both improve. If the man doesn't take it the woman surely will."

I handed the driver some cash I had brought along for just such a purpose. As hoped for it loosened their lips. The man spoke Polish in a cracked voice, but I understood.

"Sir, it's no secret. What happened to them happened all over. It's history. They were marched into the woods where they were forced to dig a huge hole. It was to be their grave. Then the Nazis machine-gunned them all into it. I'm sorry, but that's the truth. It's really common knowledge sir."

Actually, they were really quite reasonable, if perhaps a bit icy. At least they didn't deny the holocaust. Now, I wanted to know where that hole was.

"Where's that hole? Take me there and half the contents of my billfold are yours."

They thought for a moment.

"That's alright, sir. That much would be like blood money. And I don't wish to profit from your misfortune."

Then he addressed the driver, explaining in detail how to recognize the entrance to the old path into the woods. Then they added something that surprised me at first. But after a moment's reflection I appreciated it very much.

"When you get there just park the car. It's more fitting if you walk."

I felt momentarily shamed that he thought of this instead of me, and I admired his willingness to solemnly pay homage to the all but forgotten event.

The driver easily found the spot in the road where we had to get out. We walked silently down the road and turned off onto a dirt path. After nearly half a century I was going down the last mile my family had walked. What terror they must have felt as they broke this trial. They did not know their fate, but certainly presaged nothing good. My poor sisters wept while my mother tried to comfort them. My father remained dignified throughout, showing no fear, his mind and lips focused on prayer. Doubtless, many inquired as to their destination, either not comprehending their dire situation or hopeful of a less fatal end. How long did it take to dig the hole? Who did it? Were my sisters forced to dig or was it just the men? Once the digging began did it become clear to all that it was their grave? Did blind hope sustain them until the inevitable rose up and exploded? Did they die at once or were some only wounded, still breathing as the moist earth was shoveled over them? Nausea gripped me as I considered all of this. Eda was gravely silent and perhaps the most pragmatic of all. She saw no point in any of this. For her it had all ended when I took off my uniform and we left Poland. She was satisfied that Hitler was dead, even if by his own hand, and cared little for personal vengeance. Their country was divided while Israel flourished. Evil had been vanquished and we had won. We should enjoy our victory, our success, and our lives. We walked on quietly, and nobody broke the silence until we were there.

It was a clearing among the tall trees, about a hundred feet across and sixty feet long. If this held the corpses of two thousand people one must remark on the efficient Nazi expertise at killing and burying such a group of people. They knew from experience how much area was needed to commit such an act and successfully hide the evidence. They could factor in the cross section of large adults and small children, fat and thin alike, and select an appropriate location to carry out the uncontested sentence. It was neither too large, nor too small, but rather ideal for the task at hand. It was all in a day's work for professional murderers. And the weapons were chosen with icy calculation to most efficiently kill as well as propel the bodies into the gaping hole. Each blast both killed and pushed its victim toward its final resting place, lessening the number of Nazi manpower hours needed to deposit any corpses unaccounted for. And finally, what were their final seconds like? Once the hole was dug the civilians knew with utter certainty what was about to occur. Crying, begging for mercy, praying, cursing the Germans. The uncontrolled vomiting and loosening of bowels and bladders. The unbearable noise of large caliber iron machine guns destroying the tranquility of the forest, mixed with the piercing screams of the innocent. The animals scurrying off, and the birds taking wing, all scared away by a noise so horrible it knew no reason. The stench of urine, vomit and excrement. Finally, the irony of having the beauty of a lovely summer's day defiled by savage cruelty. All I could do was stare at the ground. But it looked so peaceful! It was overgrown with lush green grass and bushes. Even a few saplings had taken root. It was exactly the façade the Nazis had sought. Let the earth claim them and hide them. The dirt would suck up the blood and other bodily fluids. Soon the worms would eliminate eighty percent of the evidence. Of course, we now know that this form of mass execution only had the appearance of efficiency. Along with the cost factoring of ammunition it was calculated that poison gas was far more cost effective. But Sieniawa was still early in the war. The Final Solution had yet to be honed to perfection. But as crude and inefficient as its methods might have been on that bright summer day everyone in Sieniawa succumbed. And fifty years later here is what was left. Here was my family's grave. I had not been this physically close to them since that cold winter's day when I trudged off late to school in that horse drawn cart through the snow.

Nobody had to tell us this was the spot, because there was evidence that others had been here before us. There weren't individual graves, as the site was unexcavated, but many headstones had been erected by visiting relatives. But there were no stones placed on any of them, indicating that no relatives had been here for a long time. Dozens of the upright markers stood around the edge, and I started to read them. Most of them were in Hebrew, but I had no trouble with that. As I read I came upon a startling discovery. Some distant cousin on my mother's side had been here long before us and had erected a marker where their aunt or uncle had died. While my father had moved to Sieniawa my mother was born there, and had relatives living here. In my youth I remembered an uncle and his family who were doubtless murdered along with everyone else. It's a mystery to me who it was that came here to erect a headstone.

To me it meant someone else had survived to keep Sieniawa alive in their hearts. The Hebrew inscription commemorated all of our family members and it warmed me somehow to know that there were others beside me to remember them. I had Eda take a photograph of me with the grave marker.

Comments were futile, but our driver felt compelled to speak.

"Sir, I am sorry."

Such a comment required no response. Of course, one had to wonder if he meant it. Was I the first one he had brought here? Were there Jewish agencies recording statistics for years? Maybe the Polish government wanted the same data. Did the driver know more than he led on? He seemed greatly affected by being there. After all, wasn't he brought up on tales of Nazi horror as well?

"Sir, can you imagine. All the people in town must have heard the shooting. Such a noise is unmistakable. Even if you never heard it before. It frightened all of them. They probably thought they were all next"

"Why? They weren't Jewish."

"Sir I beg your pardon, but they murdered millions of us too."

I stopped for a moment. It's true. Poland suffered more than any other country. Over five years of Nazi occupation. Unthinkable. The Jews were a special project of Hitler, but he hated Poles too. My head turned toward Eda. She was looking at me tenderly and with great understanding. How long had she been staring at me? How long could this go on? I was at the end of my trail. If I found him I was prepared to kill the betrayer of my family. But he was older than me even when it happened. The odds he was still alive were impossible. I finally realized it was time to put it to rest. I looked around. They were in the forest they loved anyway. I reached into my pocket and pulled out a smooth stone I had collected on the way. I ceremoniously placed it on the headstone. Then we headed back to the road. As we got to the part of the woods that opened up onto the road I was surprised to see the old couple standing there as if they'd been waiting for us.

"There was a young couple that was never discovered. A neighbor of mine named Stanislav Zowistowski hid them. They came out after the war and immigrated to Canada. They came back here about ten years ago. They went to the woods too."

I was astonished, but as soon as I heard this news my heart lightened. I was not alone. Far from it! I was not the last survivor of Sieniawa. Two Canadians were, and apparently hidden by Righteous Gentiles right here in this little shtetl. Not being alone brought to mind my whole family. Eda, Nathan, Regina, Irving, Larry, Hedy, the grandkids, nephews and nieces, the cousins in Israel and their children too. There was so much to be thankful for. Why obsess over Konstantin Jonjac? He was probably killed in the war anyway. So, I thanked the old folks for the information and got back in the car. As we were pulling away I thought I heard the old man say, "Good fortune be yours."

It was about two in the afternoon and we drove out of town. Years of remembrance and obsession and it was all over in a half hour. In some ways I was like that old couple. We all bore the scars of that war, but I finally learned to accept it. Some things cannot be negotiated. You just gotta bear it as best you can. Live in the present. Eda had known that for years. I leaned over and gave her a kiss on the cheek, and she squeezed my hand.

That was our last trip to Europe. After visiting Sieniawa and the site of the Auschwitz concentration camp we needed to raise our spirits. Of course, in our hearts we knew that the Feders had persevered, and that we had successfully overcome the Nazi plan to eradicate us. We had replaced every murdered family member with robust youths, committed to their Jewish heritage, and such awareness helped to balance our mood. Even so, we wanted to distract ourselves from the grim itinerary of recent days. We needed to relax and get back to being plain old tourists again. So we visited all the typical sights of Europe. And once we'd had our fill we returned to the United States, the best place on Earth.

After such an emotional time in the old country we were especially glad to see our family again. I don't know if anyone perceived the therapeutic benefits of our heritage tour, but it was a good feeling all the way around for me. I was glad I went, but glad to be back too. So many things were now resolved, and both my mind and heart were finally at peace. So much so that I was ready to tell my story. In 1997 Steven Spielberg's project, Survivors of the Shoah Visual History Foundation, got in touch with me and I agreed to sit for an interview. Before a video camera I recounted all that you've read in this book. I was glad and proud to be part of this brilliant filmmaker's historical document, and I sincerely hope that future generations will watch it. It's my sincere wish they read this book as well. Whoever does so will learn what our world was like. After all, it's their world too.

Though I don't need to I still dabble in real estate. I have a wonderful friend and partner named Joe Casudo who manages our apartment complex up in West Palm Beach. Hedy is also involved in this project. And I socialize with many of our neighbors in the vast Winston Towers condominium complex where we live. It seems like half of Europe moved here. Hardly anyone speaks without an accent. Some people may observe that everything I touched seems to have turned to gold. And the same can be said of my neighbors. Why this is I cannot say. On the surface it appears to be a mixture of hard work and luck. I can't help but observe that this was true for many others like me as well. Sometimes it looks like there's a certain amount of good and bad things that can happen in your life, and that for my generation all the bad took place during the war.

I lead such a comfortable life now I can hardly imagine my earlier years. It seems like it was someone else who traversed the snow covered Steppes on horseback, hunting Nazis. Who was blasting away with a machine gun on the streets of Tel Aviv? Was it me that fought for a patch of floor in a cell in Kiev? I couldn't have entertained Soviet collective farmers or taught the tango to a Cossack general's daughters. It just seems impossible! And Joseph Stalin personally pinned a medal on me? And Marilyn Monroe invited me onto her bed? Me? And it must have been someone else who turned a Puerto Rican vacation into a Wall Street coup. Who did all that? Who did that happen to? Certainly not that little *pisher* Ovram Feder from the shtetl. It can't be! And now that I finally have the time and means where is legendary writer Arthur Miller to help me like he promised? I guess there are some things that even money can't buy.

We went back to Sieniawa and found the house where I was born.

A lot of it looked remarkably the same, but the old
memories haunted me, and I feared staying the night.

The site where the massacre of Sieniawa took place.
My family and 2,000 other Jews were shot and buried there.
Over the years relatives have erected headstones.

One of the last synagogues in Poland.

The memorial to the Warsaw Ghetto uprising.

Yad Vashem, the Holocaust Memorial
and study center in Jerusalem.

EPILOGUE

I lead such a comfortable life now I can hardly imagine my earlier years. It seems like it was someone else who traversed the snow covered Steppes on horseback, hunting Nazis. Who was blasting away with a machine gun on the streets of Tel Aviv? Was it me that fought for a patch of floor in a cell in Kiev? I couldn't have entertained Soviet collective farmers, or taught the tango to a Cossack general's daughters. Joseph Stalin personally pinned a medal on me? Marilyn Monroe invited me onto her bed? Me? And it must have been someone else who turned a Puerto Rican vacation into a Wall Street coup. Who did all that? Who did that happen to? Certainly not that little *pisher* Ovram Feder from the shtetl. It can't be! And now that I finally have the time and means, where is Arthur Miller to help me? I guess there are some things that even money can't buy.

After a lifetime of extreme adventures and hard work I enjoy the fruits of my labor. And because I really am a born *tummler* I learned just enough computer skills to play the stock market. And though it's been eighty years this old Jew is still under the care of a Polish *shiksah*. When I was four a Gentile Polish woman named Marisha was our housekeeper, cooking for us every day. And now, after the greater part of a century has passed, another Christian woman from Poland, named Helen, comes over every day to see that Eda and I get good old fashioned European food. Some things never change. Regina was a little unlucky regarding husbands, being widowed first by Abe, and then twice more after that. She's married to number four, and they live right across the hall from us. Isaac lives in our condo too. From sunny southeast Poland to sunny southeast Florida, we're still together. It seems like half of Europe moved here and hardly anyone we know speaks without an accent. Though I really don't need to, I still dabble in real estate. I got an apartment complex up in West Palm Beach, looked over by my friend and partner, Joe Casudo. Hedy's involved in it too.

Some people may observe that everything I touched seems to have turned to gold. Why this is I cannot say. On the surface it appears to be a mixture of hard work and luck. I can't help but observe that this was also true for many others like me. Sometimes it looks like there's a certain amount of good and bad things that can happen in your life, and that, for my generation, all the bad took place during one era, the war.

Eda and I have traveled a lot, and we've gone to enough movies, and eaten in enough restaurants, to more than make up for a lack of it during our youth. We still love each other, and we adore our kids and grandkids. When the grandkids were first born I used to look for traits of my father or mother in them, but now I appreciate them for who they are. And I try to teach them what I think is important. First, stay on your toes. You don't have to be hostile, but you can't blindly trust anyone either. It's best to depend on yourself. And, like I always say, you gotta be tough, and be able to take things as they come. Who knows what's gonna happen next? We didn't know a war was going to disrupt our lives, but we dealt with it. Anything can happen, and when it does, no matter how bad you think it's going to be it's unbearable, and you can take it. Anyway, when something rotten comes your way, and I pray it never does, all you have to do is compare it with the adventures of the counterfeit Cossack and you'll see that it could be a whole lot worse. Get a good education and try to find your niche. Of course, the earlier you find it the more fulfilled you'll be, but don't push it. It'll come around on its own. Don't ever abandon your religion or your people. I confess that I lack the great faith that my father had, but I strongly support my temple and observe all holidays. And I stand by Israel. I wasn't a business success there, but I'm proud to have served in the Israeli Defense Forces in her War of Independence. There was a lot of sense in what those Zionists preached back then. Our people have stood tough for millennia, so don't be afraid of anything. We always pull through. That means you will too. I also believe that America is the Promised Land. It offers complete freedom of religion for Jews and for everyone else as well, and it's still a land of unlimited opportunity. You just have to keep your eyes open. Finally, I say this: Keep honest and straight. Make the best life you can the best way you can. Strength? I owe a lot to that guy in the jail in Lwow who asked me, "Do you want to live or die?" He gave me will and foresight. And I want to pass that along. Whenever there is a choice you should go for what is the most positive. Deep down inside your heart will always tell you. So, just listen. And once you hear that voice, don't hesitate. Always grab hold of life. Always!

Arthur Feder
Rosh Hashanah, 2009
Sunny Isles, Florida

Our third child, Hedy, was named for my mother, Haddasah. She's here with her husband Ricky, and their first child, Rachel, named for one of my sisters.

*Four generations of our women: Eda's mother, Helen, Eda,
our daughter Hedy, and her daughter Rachel.*

Hedy's grown children, Rachel and Alexander.

Eda and I enjoy a family dinner with Larry and his wife, Barbara.
Irving sits in the middle.

Lisa and Steve, the grown children of Larry and Barbara.

Lisa and her husband, Mark Youngelson.

Returning to Poland at the end of the war, I discovered that my family had perished. But my darling Eda and I became the matriarch and patriarch of a thriving clan, and we lived to see our generations persevere. We feel eternally grateful.

L-R: Ricky & Hedy Glaser, Barbara, Lisa & Steve, Larry, Eda, the Counterfeit Cossack, Irving.

SURVIVORS OF THE
SⁿHᵡO¹AʷﬡH
VISUAL HISTORY FOUNDATION.

18 June 1997

Arthur Feder
19500 Turnberry Way Apt. 16E
Aventura, FL 33180

Dear Mr. Feder,

In sharing your personal testimony as a survivor of the Holocaust, you have granted future generations the opportunity to experience a personal connection with history.

Your interview will be carefully preserved as an important part of the most comprehensive library of testimonies ever collected. Far into the future, people will be able to see a face, hear a voice, and observe a life, so that they may listen and learn, and always remember.

Thank you for your invaluable contribution, your strength, and your generosity of spirit.

All my best,

Steven Spielberg
Chairman

CPSIA information can be obtained at www.ICGtesting.com
Printed in the USA
LVOW051102070213

319094LV00001B/59/P